WE ARE NOW A NATION:
CROATS BETWEEN 'HOME' AND 'HOMELAND'

ANTHROPOLOGICAL HORIZONS

Editor: Michael Lambek, University of Toronto

This series, begun in 1991, focuses on theoretically informed ethnographic works addressing issues of mind and body, knowledge and power, equality and inequality, the individual and the collective. Interdisciplinary in its perspective, the series makes a unique contribution in several other academic disciplines: women's studies, history, philosophy, psychology, political science, and sociology. For a list of the books published in this series see page 225.

DAPHNE N. WINLAND

# We Are Now a Nation

Croats between 'Home'
and 'Homeland'

UNIVERSITY OF TORONTO PRESS
Toronto Buffalo London

© University of Toronto Press Incorporated 2007
Toronto  Buffalo  London
Printed in Canada

ISBN 978-0-8020-9346-2

∞

Printed on acid-free paper

**Library and Archives Canada Cataloguing in Publication**

Winland, Daphne Naomi, 1957–
We are now a nation : Croats between 'home' and 'homeland' / Daphne N.
Winland.

(Anthropological horizons)
Includes bibliographical references and index.
ISBN 978-0-8020-9346-2

1. Croatian Canadians – Ethnic identity.  2. Croatian Canadians – Politics
and government.  3. Croatian Canadians – Ontario – Toronto.
4. Nationalism – Croatia.  5. Croatia – History – 1990–.
6. Transnationalism – Case studies.  I. Title.  II. Series.

FC3097.9.C93W55 2007      305.89183071      C2007-903347-4

University of Toronto Press acknowledges the financial assistance to its
publishing program of the Canada Council for the Arts and the Ontario
Arts Council.

University of Toronto Press acknowledges the financial support for its
publishing activities of the Government of Canada through the Book
Publishing Industry Development Program (BPIDP).

# Contents

# Figures

# Acknowledgments

This book has been a long time in preparation and as a result, the list of those to whom I am indebted has grown and deepened. The project of writing a book requires the patience and generosity of research participants, the efforts of research assistants, and the mentoring of colleagues and experts in the field. But it involves so much more. The support and encouragement of friends and family has been instrumental in getting through the many projects that, combined, make up this book. Some whom I mention here may be surprised to see that they factored significantly in the process; I owe my gratitude to all.

I was fortunate and privileged in many ways to share with diaspora and homeland Croats 'in the moment.' The years both during and after the war in the former Yugoslavia were extremely trying for Croats everywhere, and even during this time of crisis, they allowed me into their world to witness and to learn. On many occasions, my time with Croats involved sharing tears of joy and of pain, seeing the remarkable albeit frenetic energy of diaspora Croats mobilizing their communities for medicine, food, and fundraising and the hopes, anxieties, and frustrations of people who wanted peace, stability, and, most importantly, certainty. Gratitude in written form does not do justice to the debt I feel towards those Croats whose generosity of spirit allowed me to probe their views, opinions, sentiments, and emotions.

There are many who have, over the years, contributed to refining and improving on the arguments presented here. I wish to acknowledge those close friends who provided me with a wonderful blend of support and criticism throughout the period of this research. The Bosnian scholar Amila Buturović, although not willing to endure my tortured Croatian, patiently corrected me on details of Yugoslav history and was always ready to share her opinions with me. I am also indebted to the Croatian linguist Branko Franolić, whose broad-based knowledge and keen insights into Croatian life, culture, and history were indispensable from the very start, in 1992.

The many scholars who have provided a rich body of work upon which to base my research are deserving of more than mere mention here, and I hope that I do justice to their exemplary scholarship in the coming pages. I am particularly indebted to the work of Robert Hayden of the University of Pittsburgh, whose work inspired me to think critically about the issues I encountered and, most importantly, to stick to my analytical guns. Loring Danforth's foundational work on transnationalism and diaspora in the Greek and Macedonian contexts guided me through the political minefield that is diaspora politics.

Many people in Croatia, most of whom I have not named, to respect their privacy, have shared their thoughts, hopes and dreams, frustrations and anxieties, as well as their boundless hospitality. The brilliant scholars at the Institute for Ethnology and Folklore Research in Zagreb were always receptive and helpful. In particular I owe special thanks to Renata Jambrešić-Kirin, who never allowed me to leave the institute without an armful of books and articles. The anthropologist Tanja Bukovčan-Zufika and Lyn Šikić-Mičanović in Zagreb and the late Dunja Rihtman-Auguštin have also always been generous friends and colleagues. Most important is the Croatian sociologist Zrinjka Peruško, whose efforts to help in every way, be it in procuring contacts and resources, invitations to conferences, finding good places to shop, or letting me bunk in her daughter Jana's room, deserve my warmest gratitude. The gracious hospitality and insights of Mirko Polonijo and Tanja Perić-Polonijo helped me to think more clearly about all issues Croatian.

Thanks to friends and colleagues Sandra Bamford and Teresa Holmes for their critical input at our 'book support group' meetings, to Naomi Adelson and Angela Bogdan for their unflagging support, and to Rosalind C. Morris, a dear friend and an inspiration.

I have been fortunate to have enlisted the help of Croatian research assistants in Canada and Croatia. The assistance, feedback, and critical comments of Danijela Vrdoljak, Ivana Polonijo, Paul Posilovic, Natalin Peros, and Ivana Pezer added much needed perspective to the results presented here. Thanks are also in order to Sam Dunn and Sandra Byers, who did wonders with the reams of statistics and documentation to code and analyse.

The guidance and encouragement of my colleagues in the Department of Anthropology at York University over the years have been critical to the success of this project. The many conference, seminar, and round table venues where I presented preliminary findings – some to tough but always gracious audiences – provided the feedback necessary for revisiting some of the assumptions that informed my thinking throughout.

This research upon which this book is based was made possible by funding from the Social Sciences and Humanities Research Council of Canada, Canadian Secretary of State – Department of Canadian Heritage, the Faculty of Arts Research Fellowships at York University, and the Centre for Research on Immigration and Settlement (CERIS). I also benefited greatly from a research leave funded in part through the Social Sciences and Humanities Research Council of Canada. Financial support for the publication of this book was made possible through the generosity of the Office of the Dean (Faculty of Arts) and the Office of the Vice-President of Research and·Innovation at York University.

Thanks to Virgil Duff, senior editor at the University of Toronto Press, whose support and encouragement saw me through the rough spots. The skilful and meticulous copy-editing of Kate Baltais and Harold Otto helped to make this manuscript clearer and more readable. My gratitude also goes to the anonymous reviewers at UTP who provided helpful, critical comments.

Parts of the Introduction and chapters 1 and 2 originally appeared in different form in 'Raising the Curtain: Transnationalism in the Post-Communist World,' p. 261–77, in Vic Satzewich and Lloyd Wong, eds., *Transnational Identities and Practices in Canada* (Vancouver: UBC Press, 2006); reprinted with permission. Portions of chapter 3 appeared in slightly different form in 'the Politics of Desire and Disdain: Croatian Identity between 'Home' and 'Homeland,' *American Ethnologist* 29(3): 693–718 (2002); reprinted with permission by the American Anthropological Association. Parts of chapter 4 appeared in different form in 'Ten Years Later: The Changing Nature of Transnational Ties in Post-independence Croatia,' *Ethnopolitics* 5(3): 295–307 (2006); reprinted with Permission by Taylor and Francis. Chapter 5 is a revised and expanded form of 'Claiming to Be Croat: The Risks of Return to the Homeland,' p. 201–20, in Vered Amit and Noel Dyck, eds., *Claiming Individuality: The Cultural Politics of Distinction* (London: Pluto Press, 2006); reprinted with permission.

Finally, to my family – my partner in all, Steve Gaetz, my brilliant sons Hillel, Sean, and Evan, and Yael, Susy, Roma, and Hanna, who have been forever supportive and unfailingly optimistic that I would finish what has been variously, albeit seldom affectionately, called 'the millstone' and 'the albatross.' In the end, this book belongs to my late mother Helen Winland, whose sharp wit and intelligence, wild abandon, and enormous capacity for love inspired me to believe that anything is possible.

# Croatian Political Parties

HDZ    Hrvatska demokratska zajednica (Croatian Democratic Union)
HNS    Hrvatska narodna stranka (Croatian People's Party)
HOP    Hrvatska oslobodilački pokret (Croatian Liberation Movement)
HSLS   Hrvatska socijalno-liberalna stranka (Croatian Social Liberal Party)
HSP    Hrvatska stranka prava (Croatian Party of Right)
HSS    Hrvatska seljačka stranka (Croatian Peasant Party)
IDS     Istarski demokratski sabor / Dieta democratica istriana (Istrian Independent Party)
SDP    Socijaldemokratska partija (Social Democratic Party)

# WE ARE NOW A NATION:
# CROATS BETWEEN 'HOME' AND 'HOMELAND'

# Introduction: On the Meaning(s) of *Hrvatstvo* – Croatness

*As a Croat, I am a brother of all men and wherever I go, Croatia is with me.*
Drago Ivanišević, Croatian poet (1907–1981)

As happened at the beginning of the twentieth century, transformations in Europe in the 1990s led many to rethink notions of nation, nationality, and ethnicity. The emergence of supranational institutions and structures, perhaps most spectacularly exemplified by the evolution of the European Union, caused many to anticipate the demise of the nation state as we have known it. Yet, contrary to its eclipse, we have witnessed the spectacular revival and rebirth of the national idea in Europe defined by boundedness and homogeneity, perhaps most strikingly evidenced through the drama that began to unfold in Eastern Europe in 1989 with the collapse of the Soviet Union. Seemingly overnight, the region was thrust into tumult at every level – political, economic, religious, cultural, and familial.

Events in the former Yugoslavia, dramatically reconfigured the existing nation state, which during the Cold War was often celebrated in the West for its experiments with 'soft socialism.' This period in Yugoslavia's history has been documented extensively (see e.g., Glenny 1999; Woodward 1995; Ramet 1996; Cohen 1993, 2001). Scholars, political leaders, and policy makers scrambled to make sense of the eruption of violence and nationalist fervour and fretted over the implications of the conflict for the European Union, pluralism and a democratic future for the region. Beginning with Slovenia's declaration of independence in 1990, and followed by that of Croatia in 1991 and then of Bosnia and

Hercegovina in 1992, the former Yugoslavia fragmented into separate new nation states.

The story of Croatia's independence from Yugoslavia began in much the same way as with most of the states that emerged or re-emerged after the Cold War in Europe ended in 1989. Various difficulties within Yugoslavia were becoming apparent by the late 1980s, and especially following the rise to power of Yugoslav President Slobodan Milošević in 1987. Apart from the looming political and economic crises facing Yugoslavia, the fragility of the state was evidenced in faltering support for the preservation of Yugoslav unity (Ramet and Adamovich 1995; Ramet 1996). With the erosion of Yugoslav federal institutions, steps were taken in Croatia to found independent political parties, all of which sought in different ways to deal with the Croatian national question. The threat of a Croatian multiparty democratic system to Milošević's hold on the federal Yugoslav state led to the rapid deterioration of relations. Milošević's truculence proved decisive in Croatia's course to pursue the path of independence rather than opt for the earlier Croatian offer of a compromise giving Croatia more autonomy under Yugoslav rule. The war that erupted shortly afterward caused untold damage, the human costs of which are inestimable.

There is now little doubt about the global significance of the Balkan wars of the 1990s. These events played out worldwide in the mass media – in newspapers and on radio and television – often graphically highlighting the violence of the conflict, while at the same time situating so-called ethnic tensions at the base of such struggles. A central theme, or lens through which these conflicts were popularly viewed was that we were merely witnessing the spectacular re-emergence of long suppressed ethnic hatreds (Ignatieff 1994; Kaplan 1994): That is, within the former Yugoslavia, communities were historically organized along discrete and bounded ethnic lines, and that the unravelling of Eastern Europe merely allowed for these distinct and conflicting ethnic identities to coalesce into new nation states. This controversial perspective found proponents both in and outside of the former Yugoslavia.

For researchers across a broad range of disciplines, these events spawned a great deal of inquiry. The literature is replete with debates on the issues of nationalism, the nation state and its future, ethnic conflict, civil society, and even the contemplation of themes of including the 'end of history' (Fukuyama 1993) and the 'clash of civilizations' (Huntington 1993; 1996).

These debates and the changes that inspired them demand a reconsideration of how we conceive of ethnicity and transformation, not only within the boundaries of newly emerging nation states but transnationally as well. The events of 1989 and 1990 highlight the need to complicate our understanding of nation states as bounded entities, where within defined spatial contexts ethnic and/or national identities are conflated with the state. For one can convincingly argue that parallel to the phenomenon of newly emerging nation states has been the deterritorialization of the borders and boundaries of such states, fuelled by war, migration and developments in global market culture and the ubiquity of transnational flows (Appadurai 1996a). We must now engage with notions of ethnicity and ethnic identity in ways that account for the transnational qualities of such concepts. Thus, the impact of the events in the former Yugoslavia, for instance, is felt not only by ethnic or national groups within the borders of these new states, but more broadly by people living in diasporas, and by the transnational communities now represented by these new national entities.

In cities like Toronto in the early 1990s, one could not help but notice an endless number of protests and demonstrations by people actively engaged in these processes of national reconfiguration. In the Toronto Croatian diaspora such protests and demonstrations were organized to raise national and international awareness of the plight of the Croatian homeland. Groups of Croats regularly protested at Toronto City Hall, the provincial legislature, and also in the federal capital in Ottawa.[1] Such activity was evident also at university campuses like my own, where Croatian students have a strong presence. Croatian information tables became a regular feature in the student centre, and speakers such as homeland politicians from Croatia were invited by the Croatian Student Association. During the first few years of Croatia's independence, approximately half a dozen Croatian students taking my courses requested academic deferrals and other accommodations for reasons such as Croatian army or national guard service, work in brigades to rebuild war-torn Croatia, and transfers to Croatian universities (to take up Croatian government-sponsored scholarships). In these contexts my interest in diaspora Croats emerged.

The analytical challenges posed by the confluence of global and often ethnically based nationalist forces are both daunting and invigorating for theorists of nationalism and identity. My main goal in writing this book is to explore the effects of war and independence from Yugoslavia on diaspora Croats, both in the diaspora and in the homeland. What interests me most about the transnational dimension of the post-socialist transition is how relationships and identities are characterized not only by upheaval and chaos but also by continuities.

By transnational, I mean not only the typical focus of diaspora–transnational studies, namely, the multiplicity of involvements and linkages sustained by diasporas in both homeland and diaspora societies (Basch et al. 1994:7; Rouse 1991, 1995; Tölölyan 1991, 1996), but also, and especially, the mutually constitutive relations *between* those in the homeland and those in the diaspora. The two, as I learned over the course of research for this book, are inextricably linked. Indeed, this is what makes the case of Toronto Croats so intriguing. Unlike most diaspora studies, where homeland is treated as a residual category, the Croatian case foregrounds both the changing place of homeland Croats in the lives of diaspora Croats and the changing place of diaspora Croats for Croats in the homeland.

The case of Toronto Croats is important for what it tells us about the role of diasporas in homeland nationalisms and for what it reveals about the continued relevance of diasporas for people and events in the homeland. Much has transpired in Croatia, in Bosnia and Hercegovina, and wherever else Croats have been living in the years since independence. Alignments, affiliations, and identifications, not to mention social and political conditions in the diaspora, have been changing continuously, as they have also done in the homeland. Diaspora Croats remain involved in homeland affairs. This is reflected in their political activities, for example, one of which is advocating on behalf of Croats accused of war crimes by the U.N. International Criminal Tribunal for the Former Yugoslavia (ICTY) and in calling for the removal of Carla del Ponte, the chief prosecutor, (see Chapter 4 on the case of General Ante Gotovina who was captured in late 2006). Despite strong political support in Croatia for the ICTY, largely because compliance is the main condition for eventual inclusion in the European Union, diaspora Croats are still lobbying intensively for the acquittal of all Croatian generals indicted by the tribunal. Diaspora Croats provide political and financial support for (mainly right-wing) Croatian political parties and their candidates, especially Hrvatska democratiska zajednica (HDZ, or Croatian Democratic Union), not to mention diaspora Croats (all HDZ) in Croatia's Sabor (parliament).

A telling example of the tenacity of diaspora Croat efforts to remain involved with events in Croatia is their declarated support in the 'War on Terror.' Citing Croatia's proximity to Bosnia and Bosnian Croats, who are currently advocating for sovereignty (since their recent rejection of amendments to the Dayton Peace Accords), there are diaspora Croats actively promulgating anti-Islamic rhetoric (see articles in the *Croatian Herald* of Australia, commentaries by Jeffrey Kuhner of the *Washington Times*, and recent pronouncements by the Croatian Catholic Union of America). On 27 October 2005, the Alliance of Croats of Bosnia and Herzegovina, based in Chicago, issued a statement asserting that Bosnia and Hercegovina now serves as a 'base for Al-Qaeda operatives, where numerous terrorist cells are active and plotting attacks on targets throughout Europe.'[2] Croatian President Ivo Sanader has frequently made statements to the effect that Croatia is a 'security provider in the War on Terror.' He did so, for example, during a speech given on 18 October 2006 at Johns Hopkins University that he had entitled 'Croatia: An Engine for Change – the EU, the U.S., NATO, and the War on Terror'. This has emboldened diaspora Croats to more aggressively demonstrate their support for the Croatian government and its policies. The legacy of the conflict therefore, lives on and all indications point to the fact that diaspora Croats will continue to be a force in Croatia and in Bosnia and Hercegovina well into the foreseeable future.

For more than a decade, I have been observing and examining dramatic shifts in the terms and conditions of relations within and between Croats in the homeland and diaspora Croats. My research for this book began in the heady days that followed Croatia's proclamation of independence in 1991, and my focus has been the impact of this milestone event on Croats in Toronto in the years that followed. Projecting unity is essential to any political cause (see, e.g., Boyarin and Boyarin 1992; Axel 2001), but as well as inspiring unity, Croatia's independence led to the emergence and/or exacerbation of often fraught or equivocal relations among diaspora Croats *and*, perhaps even more pointedly, between diaspora Croats and homeland Croats. Conflicts, over, for example, national imagery, ethnicity and other symbols and expressions of Croatness (*Hrvatstvo*) and what is a true, real, or pure Croat now proliferate.

The Toronto Croatian community is unique in that, despite its small size relative to other Croatian diasporas, it played a defining role in shaping the political vision and practices of the emerging Republic of Croatia. There are large and active Croat communities in the United States, Australia, Europe (especially Germany), and South America (see, e.g., Winland 2004; Skrbiš 1995, 1999; Čižmić 1996), yet the mobilization of relief and other efforts by Toronto Croats had a decisive impact on the political landscape of Croatia in the 1990s. Toronto Croats were instrumental in shaping the nationalist vision of the country's first president, Franjo Tuđman, leader of the HDZ. Darko Hudelist, writing for the Croatian political weekly *Globus*, observed that the 'seed of Tuđman's Croatia was created in a town or, more specifically, on a farm 40 kilometres from Toronto' (1999, no. 468:78).

The new government recognized Toronto Croats for their contributions to Tuđman's campaign. Gojko Šušak, a highly influential Ottawa Croat was appointed Minister of Defence, while several Toronto Croats were also given important political posts in Tuđman's government and others were afforded lucrative business opportunities in Croatia.

This level of engagement did not go unnoticed in Croatia. Virtually everyone I talked to in Croatia knows of the Toronto suburb of Mississauga (where many Croats live) and has an opinion on the Croats who live there. Thus, it is perhaps ironic that, given the significant impact of Toronto Croats on developments in Croatia, attitudes of the homeland Croats with regard to diaspora Croats are, at best, ambivalent. Indeed, it can be argued that Toronto Croats have acquired an unfavorable reputation among homeland Croats, and that they are often depicted as, among other things, too involved in the political and economic machinations of the government of Croatia. In the homeland media, Toronto Croats have been portrayed as nationalist zealots and profiteers (Hudelist 1999–2000; Pusić 1997a). In light of these developments, the complexity that defines Toronto Croats becomes lost, and the histories, tensions, and ambiguities that have shaped the lives of diaspora Croats are ignored and/or dismissed, in favour of characteristically essentialist portraits (see Anderson 1994; Kaplan 1994). This book, it is hoped, offers a corrective to such portraits and follows the lead of those who are committed to investigating the diversity of diasporas.

## Croatness and Home

Avtar Brah (1996), in her entreaty to examine local particularity when addressing transnational connections, that is, the formation of 'diaspora space,' draws our attention to the homeland dimension as more than just the object of diaspora imaginings and longing but as a crucial site of diaspora identity politics. Although Brah does not focus on the homeland as the subject of study per se, her distinction between 'homing desire' and 'desire for the homeland' is relevant to the experience of Toronto Croats. Although heavily laden with symbolic meaning and emotion, the idea of actually 'returning home' does not reflect the reality for the vast majority of Toronto Croats. For them, 'home' and 'homeland' are conceptual or discursive spaces of identification, nostalgia, and imagination, with no concomitant requirement to actually move to the homeland to live. Furthermore, for those who have moved, it has not necessarily been a return (since they were born and raised in Canada).

The inevitability of increased diaspora–homeland contact during crises in the homeland is perhaps axiomatic. For Croats, the nature of this contact has been shaped, and continues to be shaped, by the historical conditions that have produced Croatian diasporas. The responses of diaspora Croats to Croatia's independence, presented here, provide a context for re-examining the premises upon which notions of identity are based, notions that often hinge on the apparent fixity of these identifications. The diverse historical trajectories of Toronto Croat journeys *to* and *within* Canada, as reflected in regional, social, economic, and political specificities, suggest inimitable challenges for people who have either come together or been thrown together *and* into the spotlight by war in their – common – homeland. These developments are inextricably related to the currents of global change in which human populations increasingly transcend the temporal and spatial constructs of modern nation states. Croatian nationalism has been imagined, fought for, and is now practised in Croatia within the confines of centuries of regional conflict and imperial rule. The Croatian case challenges us to consider the ways in which nationhood, nationalism, and regionalism have been conceived of and understood by Croats both at home and abroad; it urges us to contemplate how these notions have been shaped by transnationalism and how they have been affected by and have influenced the politics of the homeland.

The key question that frames this analysis is why, given the momentous occasion of Croatia's (re)birth, do responses from both diaspora Croats and Croats in Croatia range from joy and exhilaration to ambivalence and even distrust of one another? Croats everywhere are implicated in each others' lives, hopes, and imaginations in ways that demand attention to what I refer to throughout as the paradox of desire and disdain. Croats at home and abroad, whose origins and histories are diverse, are at once attracted to and repelled by one another. Terms such as vulgar, peasant, romantic, communist, or patriot are not just thinly veiled criticisms, but rather, they reveal the dynamics of embedded and/or emerging personal and identity politics among Croats. The politics of desire and disdain draws attention to the vicissitudes of certainty and doubt about who is a 'real' Croat and more importantly, what constitutes Croatness.

## The Croatian Homeland and 'Ethnic Conflict'

The views and images that dominated media accounts of atrocities and incomprehensible destruction in the former Yugoslavia, particularly in places like Croatia and Bosnia and Hercegovina, depicted a region condemned to endless cycles of violence due to 'age-old ethnic hatreds.' Proponents of this viewpoint include scholars, both within and outside of the former Yugoslavia, who favour explanations based on historically determinist notions of 'national character' – that is, that Croats, Serbs, and/or Bosnians are somehow historically predisposed to violence (see, e.g., Kaplan 1994; Fukuyama 1994, Tomašić 1948; Todorova 1997, 2004). According to Andrew Wachtel, conventional wisdom about the collapse of Yugoslavia falls into one of two explanatory frameworks – the deterministic-historical and the fiendish-political (1998:14). The lens through which the wars of succession and the struggles for independence were viewed was largely shaped by prevailing views of ethnic groups in conflict and a rendering of ethnicity as essentialized and historicized in often simplistic ways. Unfortunately, the power of the images of these wars for the collective imagination made such explanations not only plausible, but convincing. Nevertheless, such explanations are misleading.

There is therefore merit in exploring the recent history of Croatia leading to independence, especially given the degree to which this history has now become central to the narrative structure of both Croatian national discourses and the dynamics from which Croats, including those in the diaspora, gain their inspiration. The Croatian past in all its national, political, regional, and historical permutations, has been an endless source of discussion and debate among scholars whether of Croatian and non-Croatian origin. But in the past fifteen years or so it has become a hotly contested site for all those interested in and/or anxious to understand or to legitimate the Croatian past and present. Attempts to simplify the history of a remarkably complex region like the former Yugoslavia, specifically Croatia, are problematic, because of not only the extensive historical sources from which to draw but also the legitimacy which they are accorded by politicians and scholars. In setting the stage for the immediate events that led to independence and, more importantly, how they played out for diaspora and homeland Croats, a brief introduction to Croatian history is necessary.

The challenge of providing a snapshot of a '1,000–year history' presents difficulties, not the least of which is weighing the multitude of historical accounts of the region, although, as the Croatian historian Ivo Goldstein argues: 'books dealing with the entire span of Croatian history, detailing its major periods, were few and far between' (1999:v). Furthermore, as is often the case with the historical record of conflict-ridden regions, national(ist) historians all too frequently take on the role of guardians of memory (Hobsbawm 1990). For Croatia, this was particularly the case after 1990, as many of the scholarly debates focused on responsibility and/or culpability for the Yugoslav wars of succession. The frequency and intensity with which Croatian history is discussed, debated, and marshalled as evidence of, for example, a history of oppression or the justice of actions taken during the recent conflicts, necessitates pointing out some of the major developments in Croatian history, especially those in the nineteenth and twentieth centuries.

## Croatia: A Brief Historical Tour

Aviel Roshwald has observed that 'nowhere in Europe was the project of constructing national identity plagued by more ambiguity than among the South Slavs. Serbs and Croats were divided by their identification with distinct historical state traditions, different churches, and different alphabets. Yet the Serbs and Croats spoke the same language, as did Bosnia's Muslims' (2001:13; see also Banac 1984). The historical borders of Croatia have shifted many times in response to political changes (see, e.g., *Historical Maps of Croatia: From the Penguin Atlas of the World*. 1992. Zagreb: Croatian Information Centre). Throughout the history of this region, the issues of territory and sovereignty have been at the centre of disputes between numerous key players, few of whom were indigenous to the region. Shortly after the establishment of an independent kingdom of Croats, in the eleventh century, Croatia began a long history of domination by foreign powers, beginning with the Hungarians and followed by the Ottoman (in parts of Croatia) and Habsburg empires. In 1867, after its defeat by Prussia, the Habsburg Empire was transformed into the dual Austro-Hungarian monarchy, which divided the empire–and Croatia–into two. This constitutional arrangement remained in effect until 1918.

A review of the past several hundred years of Croatian history reveals a profile of an area marked by a series of invasions and wars. The twentieth century, however, was the most turbulent.

The idea of a pan-South Slav (Yugoslav) state, championed mainly by Croats in the nineteenth century (as a way of resisting domination by the empires), came to fruition at the end of the First World War. However, Serbs and Croats (the two largest ethnic groups in the region) differed in their visions for this state from the start. Croatian nationalism has had numerous incarnations. In the nineteenth century pan-South Slavic identification was epitomized in the Illyrian movement led by the Croat 'nationalist awakener' Ljudevit Gaj (Raditsa 1977:94), while other Croats preferred union within the federalist Austrian monarchy or with Hungary (favoured by the Croatian nobility, anxious to preserve the feudal order from which it benefited). Others still, such as the radical nationalist Ante Starčević (1823–1896), provided the inspiration for twentieth-century Croatian political movements. The political philosophies of Croats, inspired largely by Enlightenment ideals, reflected influences including liberalism, romanticism, nationalism, and pragmatism.

Competition over nationalist visions was most pronounced, however, between Serbs and Croats, and with the creation of the first Serb-dominated–Yugoslav state in 1918 took a discernible turn towards greater emphasis on *ius sanguinus* (law of blood) and common ethnic origin (Holjevac 1999). The assassination, ten years later, of the leader of the Croatian Peasant Party (HSS), Stjepan Radić, by a Montenegrin deputy, exacerbated these differences. The following year the name of the country was changed from the Kingdom of Serbs, Croats, and Slovenes to the Kingdom of Yugoslavia in 1929. King Aleksandar introduced a dictatorship suspending all political parties, the constitution, and individual rights (Glenny 1999; Banac 1984, 1992a; Sekulić and Šporer 1997; Sekulić 2004; Jelavich and Jelavich 1977; Biondich 2000).

Despite efforts to remain neutral, by 1941 Yugoslavia was drawn into the Second World War, during which it was divided among Germany, Bulgaria, Italy, Albania, and Hungary. Croatia was declared an independent country (1941–45), although it was little more than a fascist puppet state under Axis influence. This period has left a dark and seemingly indelible stain on Croatia's reputation abroad (Ramet 1996; Tanner 1996; Banac 1995, Granić 1998). Led by the ruling Ustaša – the

Croatian separatist organization founded by the exiled Croat Ante Pavelić and later installed by the Germans – the Independent State of Croatia (NDH) implemented a program of virulent anti-Serbianism, and anti-Semitism, that included forced expulsions, massacres, and forced conversions to Roman Catholicism.

At this time, two resistance movements formed in Yugoslavia: the Četniks, a Serb-based monarchist movement, and the Partisans, comprising members (Croats, Serbs, Slovenes, and others) of the outlawed Communist Party of Yugoslavia under the leadership of Josip Broz (a Slovene and Croat by birth whose nom de guerre became Tito); eventually the latter became the country's dominant resistance force. The Second World War ended with a Partisan victory, and Tito formed a provisional government in accordance with arrangements worked out at the 1945 Yalta Conference. The power of the terms Četnik and Ustaša is revealed in the fact that Serbs and Croats both in Croatia and in the diaspora to this day continue to chastise each other using them. During my twelve years of research, I heard the term 'Ustaša' used often and sometimes in an unapologetic manner, including once by a graduate student whose father had served with the Ustaša from 1941 to 1945. This young man's conversation did not betray any hint of the controversy surrounding the term. More typical however, Ustaša elicits from Croats reactions of defensiveness or regret.

The new state founded in 1945 was called the Socialist Federal Republic of Yugoslavia, and it consisted of six republics: Montenegro, Serbia, Croatia, Slovenia, Bosnia and Hercegovina, and Macedonia, as well as the autonomous provinces of Vojvodina and Kosovo. Over the years, Tito's model of a socialist state included extensive economic liberalization and political decentralization, as evidenced in numerous experiments the most significant of which was workers' self-management. But these changes did not satisfy various nationalist groups, particularly the Croats. Furthermore, Tito's promises of national equality and 'unitarism' were overshadowed by his efforts to appease royalist Serbs, resulting in measures that further entrenched Serb influence in key military and government posts, the police, and the diplomatic corps.

Nationalist activities among Croats increased markedly in the late 1960s and early 1970s. One of the most important was the publication of the 'Declaration Concerning the Name and the Position of the Croatian Literary Language' in 1967, which was a direct repudiation of the 1954 Novi Sad Agreement on the Serbo-Croatian language

(Greenberg 1996). These and other measures, which included economic policies unfavourable to Croatia (e.g., the siphoning off of foreign currency to Yugoslavia's capital, Belgrade–in Serbia), changes in language policy, and restrictions on cultural or nationalist expression, culminated in the 'Croatian Spring' (masovni pokret or *MASPOK*) of 1971, a movement comprised mainly of Croatian students and intellectuals who sought to challenge Tito's regime. Tito reacted to this uprising by purging liberal and/or nationalist Croatian politicians and scholars from public office and academic posts and arresting hundreds of students and intellectuals (Ramet 1996; Čuvalo 1990). Tito's reaction may have quelled the rebellious activities of Croatian nationalists, but his crackdown in 1971 also served to revive and, in some cases, radicalize nationalist sentiments and to drive further a wedge between pro-Yugoslav forces and Croatian nationalists. The chain of events that was precipitated, in part, by Tito's death in 1980 – particularly the hostile measures undertaken by his successor, Slobodan Milošević – led in Croatia to the May 1990 elections, the 19 May 1991 referendum on secession from Yugoslavia, and the declaration of Croatia's independence on 25 June 1991. With the 1990s the Socialist Federal Republic of Yugoslavia was no more.

While the history of Croats has been marked by political turmoil and uncertainty, one of the main continuities as suggested above, has been the consistent efforts, especially of particularly nationalist Croats, to reinforce the notion of a singular national ethos. The promotion of a unique and distinctive Croatian identity has been most intensely espoused or commemorated during or immediately following times of political upheaval or renewal – the Illyrian movement of the nineteenth century, the assassination of Stjepan Radić in 1928, the Bleiburg massacre in 1945 of Croatian soldiers, collaborators, and civilians sympathetic to the NDH (Nezavisna Država Hrvatska – Independent State of Croatia) by Tito's Partisans in 1945,[3] the Croatian Spring in 1971, the Yugoslav wars of succession, and most recently, the positioning of Croatia as a bulwark of Western European traditions (read as liberal democratic and Christian) in the Balkans. The dissolution of the former Yugoslavia in 1990 and Croatian independence have been by far the most significant events, not only from a regional historical point of view but also in terms of how they have affected scholarship on nationalism, the state, identity, the symbolic centre of politics, and forms (increasingly transnational) of solidarity.

## The Breakup of Yugoslavia

Although the literature on Yugoslavia's pre-1990 history provides the student of this region with a relatively comprehensive picture of its past, nothing can compare with the explosion of literature since the breakup of the former Yugoslavia. Such titles as *Balkan Tragedy* (Woodward 1995), *Balkan Babel* (Ramet 1996), *The Tragedy of Yugoslavia* (Seroka and Pavlović 1992) *Broken Bonds* (Cohen 1993), *Balkan Ghosts* (Kaplan 1994), *The Death of Yugoslavia* (Silber and Little 1995), and *The Destruction of Yugoslavia* (Magaš 1993) betray the tenor of shock and dismay. Scholarly perspectives on changes in the former Yugoslavia since 1989 range from geopolitical and policy-oriented analyses to personal accounts and reflective essays. Many, however, also are caught up in conflictive narratives of responsibility (see Kennedy 2002; Wachtel 1998), sometimes characterized by accusations of guilt and blame, as evidenced in the arguments and critiques of Thomas Cushman (1997), Thomas Cushman and Stjepan Meštrović (1996), Bogdan Denitch (1994), Bette Denich (1994), Stjepan Meštrović (1996), Robert Hayden (1992, 1996, 1997), and Branka Magaš (1993).[4] Thus, for some like Slavoj Žižek, it is pointless to even try to understand the Yugoslav conflict (2001).

Susan Woodward's 1995 analysis falls in with those who attribute the fall of Yugoslavia to economic factors, specifically the inability of the Yugoslav state to cope with the economic crisis afflicting pre-conflict Yugoslavia. She also places debates about the breakup in a wider theoretical context by, in part, examining localized interpretations and meanings associated with the Yugoslav state. As Woodward points out, conventional wisdom on the breakup of the former Yugoslavia is usually represented in one of two schools of thought. The first attributes the hostilities to Serb aggression, in accordance with the goal of a Greater Serbia (through the annexation of territory). In this version, leaders such as Slobodan Milošević and Radovan Karadžić are portrayed as the rogue heads of renegade states. The second is a perspective of the wars of succession as the inevitable product of forty years of communist suppression of ethnic conflicts (1995:7–14). Thus, ethnic identity was transformed in the late 1990s from a marker of cultural and regional characteristics into a principal political motive. However, as Woodward argues, those who hold to either of these two positions accept the claims of nationalists in the former Yugoslavia, 'giving credence to the war propaganda of politicians and generals who sought national states and accepted the necessity of war to that end' (1995:14).

Analyses of the dissolution of the Yugoslav federation overwhelmingly devote most of their attention to internal causes. External factors are framed mostly within the context of macro-political precipitants, with little regard for the processes associated with the broader context of globalization. There is, however, compelling evidence that points to the important role of global forces in hastening Yugoslavia's disintegration. For example, the drastic decline in living standards and austerity measures brought on by international pressure to resolve its foreign debt crisis in the 1980s, contributed greatly to the disintegration of government authority and to the government's inability to perform its function of preserving local political and civil order. The difficulties in rapidly transforming a socialist state into a democratic market economy (a transition demanded by foreign creditors and Western governments) exacerbated the region's vulnerability – one based on decades of dependence on Western powers. (But, the end of the Cold War undermined Yugoslavia's strategic position as a bulwark against the Soviet Union; the two Yugoslavias (1918–41 and 1945–91) were both shaped by the postwar settlements negotiated by Western European powers and the United States, let us recall.) Competition and conflict among leaders of the federated republics, particularly over their commitments to the terms of the debt repayment package in an already highly decentralized Yugoslavia, further weakened the social order. The very foundation of communities, namely, the protections and rights guaranteed under the state system thus became seriously compromised.

Regionalism in Croatia has a long history, as revealed in its heraldry and insignia and now found even on Croatia's national flag. Thus, 'to explain the Yugoslav crisis as a result of ethnic hatred, is to turn the story upside down and begin at its end' (Woodward 1995:18), in essence, confusing consequences with causes. Nonetheless, the deterioration of the former Yugoslav state was accelerated by the 'ethnification' of politics (Offe 1997:51), which resulted in the escalation of ethnic (and other) tensions that eventually culminated in civil war. After 1989, separatist nationalist politicians skilfully played the 'ethnic card' in their bids for sovereignty and explicitly conflated the nation, ethnically defined, and the state as *narod* (nation; see Schöpflin 1996). This, by definition, meant that members of the national majority (no matter by how large or small a margin) had sovereign status, while other national groups within the new state's boundaries had de facto secondary status, with the result, according to Hayden, that the much heralded transition from state socialism to democracy resulted in state chauvinism (1996:700). The salience of these and other explanations of the dissolution of Yugoslavia will be debated, perhaps vociferously, for a long time yet to come, providing further testimony to the difficulties in isolating specific causes and evidence of lasting grievances.

There has been much discussion as to the sustainability of these explanations (Cohen 1993; Ignatieff 1994; Verdery 1996; Ramet 1992, 1996; 2005; Magaš 1993); however, few have investigated how these ethno-national conflicts have affected or been affected by transnational processes, particularly those that occur 'below the radar' of international politics, such as the Vance-Owen Plan in 1993 or the Dayton Peace Accords of 1995 for the partition of Bosnia and Hercegovina. Those who do acknowledge the importance of transnationalism focus mostly on the refugees who fled their homes. Seldom does the discussion gravitate towards consideration of the role of diasporas before, during, or after the wars of succession, which, in the Croatian case, were formidable.

## Croatian Homeland Independence and Toronto Croats

Since the winter of 1991–92, when Tuđman proclaimed the realization of the Croats' 'one thousand-year-old dream of independence,' Croats all over the world have rejoiced at the birth of the new Croatian state, declared in Croatia on 25 June 1991, and internationally recognized in 15 January 1992. Croats both in the homeland and in the diaspora have been actively engaged in the recuperation of Croatian traditions through pageantry, public displays of unity, and a reinvigorated sense of Croatian identity – with cultural and folk festivals, the introduction of new Croatian studies courses,[5] the revival of Croatian cultural associations, and the establishment and renaming or resurrection of Croatian icons, monuments, and folk songs. In the midst of the convulsive changes throughout the 1990s, Croats have been trying to (re)create a new/old state. The collapse of socialism and the resulting war in Croatia set off an avalanche of personal and political questions and reflections on Croatian tradition, history and identity (see, e.g., Rihtman-Auguštin 1995).

The establishment of the Republic of Croatia has had a profound impact on diaspora Croats, many of whom had anxiously awaited independence. Narratives of displacement and disarticulation from the homeland have been largely supplanted by those of purpose and pride. Toronto Croats have revelled in the new state's fortunes, both privately and publically. Despite this openly celebratory mood, however, numerous signs of discord and tension among and between Croats in the diaspora and in the new homeland have emerged. Theodor Adorno noted, in his writings on exile, that distance is not a safety zone, but a field of tension' (1974 [1951]:127). This latter dimension – tension – is of central importance here.

Prior to the Homeland War,[6] it can be argued that Croats in Canada maintained a low profile, their identity as Croats at times withheld from non-Croats in favour of a Yugoslav identity. The reasons for this are complex and include among them fear of communist authority in Yugoslavia on the one hand, and the absence of official Canadian recognition of Croatia as a nation state, on the other. Since the Homeland War, however, diaspora Croats have vigorously asserted their ethnonational pride, primarily by identifying with the political cause – independence – of their compatriots in the former Yugoslavia. As Marcus Tanner submits: 'It was extraordinary to think that only a few years previously, the very notion of an independent Croatia had been the dream of a few befuddled right-wing émigrés, who spent their lives peering over their shoulders in case their activities should attract the attention of the Yugoslav secret police' (1996:301).

For Croats in the diaspora, the combination of images of war, fears and anxieties over the fate of family and friends in Croatia, and the sense of urgency, as well as their interest and/or involvement in homeland affairs, have all had a significant impact on the ways in which they 'remember, reconstruct, and lay claim' to Croatia as their homeland (Hannerz 1992). Although scholars have acknowledged the role of the diaspora in the ascent to power in 1990 of the first Croatian president, Franjo Tuđman (Pusić 1995, 1997a, 1997b; Tanner 1996, Goldstein 1999), only the journalist and political analyst Paul Hockenos (2003) has gone beyond but a brief description of the influence of specifically right-wing, specifically Toronto, diaspora Croats in Croatia during the early 1990s.[7]

Whatever their specific relationship to the homeland, Toronto Croats now speak of their transformation as a people – from what they represent as a historically repressed minority group in the former Yugoslavia to a proud nation that successfully tore off the yoke of socialist rule and asserted its new sense of destiny. The intensity of this sentiment is repeatedly verified in the comments I heard from many Toronto Croats. In a sense, one of my interviewees spoke for all Toronto Croats when he said: 'We have our own country – Croatia! A long dream come true' (engineer, age 51, 17 November 1992).[8]

Out of a diaspora history characterized, in part, by fragmentation and discord, stemming from such differences as political cleavages and viewpoints, economic status, regions of origin, and time of arrival in Canada, Toronto Croats were galvanized by the issue of independence in unprecedented fashion. Many worked tirelessly in mobilizing support for Croatian relief through fundraising and volunteering services, such as organizing student brigades to work in areas destroyed during the Homeland War and to serve in the Croatian military. This revitalization of identifications and the intensification of transnational links, as a direct consequence of the war and independence, has resulted in a movement among diaspora Croats to reclaim and redefine their Croatian origins and affiliations.

Outward displays of unity among diaspora Croats and a reinvigorated sense of identity did not, however, conceal cracks beneath the surface of this renewed community vitality and confidence. All diaspora groups, and particularly those with a long settlement history, are characterized by some form of social differentiation, and these differences can take on new and profound dimensions when change – often of a radical and destabilizing nature – occurs in the country of origin. Thus, despite the claims by leaders and other members of the Toronto Croat community that the emergence of the Croatian nation state has only strengthened and unified Croats, I suggest otherwise. Apart from fostering an overall sense of unity, Croatia's independence has reinforced or even created contestations over notions and expressions of Croatian peoplehood.[9] It is not surprising that some schisms have been de-emphasized in the wake of nationalist fervour. What is interesting is the extent to which differences rooted in both the diaspora Croat experience *and* political events in the former Yugoslavia have been in some cases, re-emphasized and in others given new form and meaning.

## The Politics of Desire and Disdain

While the series of changes that propelled Croatia towards its independence may be found in the long and turbulent history of the region itself, one important force in fuelling the momentum of these changes is to be found elsewhere. Central to Tuđman's success in 1990 was his ability to drum up considerable financial and political support in the diaspora and to recruit its representatives for his new national cabinet. The impact of Croatia's independence on diaspora Croats' identitifications may be best understood in the context of current theoretical debates around transnationalism and diaspora and the politics of location and representation. My analysis begins, therefore, with recognition of the importance of wider political contexts as well as local sociohistorical particularities in the formation of transnational connections, in an effort to make sense of the 'entangled tensions' (Clifford 1994:307) produced in and through diaspora–homeland relations. My focus thereafter is on the issues of representation for Croats in Toronto and in the homeland, since 1992, and their impact on diaspora–homeland relations through, what I am calling the politics of desire and disdain, for that is how I would characterize the processes and emotions set in motion by the experiences of Croats in the diaspora and homeland Croats since independence.

The newly realized dream of independence introduced many challenges to Croats everywhere, not the least of which is 'getting along.' Independence did not and could not produce a whole, unified, and undifferentiated, people. An examination of the Croatian state cannot rely on an essentialized portrait of an ethnic community. Croatian homeland discourses are replete with inter-regional, class-based, and other distinctions, and sometimes prejudices, which diaspora Croats carried with them to wherever they settle. Regional differences continue to matter as reflected, for example, in the variety of community associations and clubs in Toronto that are regionally based. Class is a persistent factor. Of a group of fifty-seven students that I surveyed across four universities in and around Toronto (York University, University of Toronto, Ryerson University, and McMaster University), the vast majority (93%) were children of parents who were born in Croatia or Bosnia and Hercegovina and who were employed as manual labourers in skilled and semi-skilled trades. More than half worked in factories, the rest in trades and the service industry. The four exceptions were children of professionals (e.g., medical doctors) or owners of businesses (e.g., construction).

The tremendous symbolic, personal, and political capital invested in the (re)crafting of a distinctively Croatian identity implicates Croats, both within and outside the boundaries of the new state, irrespective of their interest, enthusiasm for, or involvement in the Croatian nation-building project itself. Inevitably, innumerable efforts to map the conceptual terrain of new Croatian identities are at odds because the identities envisioned by Croats, and the histories and experiences that shape them, are formulated in contextual and relational terms that invariably mitigate against consensus or unanimity.

Early in the research, it became clear that dynamics that could only be explained as conflictual, dominated relations among Toronto Croats. Much of what was occurring could be explained as a response to events in the homeland, for example, euphoria over independence and the flurry of activity around fundraising, political lobbying and the jostling for an authoritative voice for diaspora Croats, but also as the personal anguish of relatives of Croats at war in Croatia.

Toronto Croats, many of whom had dreamed of homeland independence for decades, feel that they have a personal stake in the fate of the Republic of Croatia. The imagined homeland has become a site where Toronto Croats might reconcile their personal histories (and those of their forebears) with their lives in the present. Homeland Croats have been necessarily implicated in this process. That tensions and identifications *within* Croatia are relevant to Toronto Croats in highly specific ways reflects not only the contemporary centrality of the homeland to Toronto Croats but also the historical relationships developed between the diaspora and the homeland throughout a century of emigration to and settlement in Canada.

## Suffering and Croatian Peoplehood

One of the most potent forces in uniting diaspora Croats behind the homeland cause has been the suffering of homeland Croats, not only the suffering resulting from the Homeland War, but also the suffering that preceded it. Croats are well versed in the dates and details of the traumatic events in Croatian history, and the resentments borne of this suffering have had a lasting impact on Croats wherever they might live. The suffering of homeland Croats at war is a factor that led diaspora Croats to feel as one with them. Most Toronto Croats have family in the former Yugoslavia, many in places that were heavily bombarded during the war. Toronto Croats uniformly expressed personal anguish and trauma over the war, and the outpouring of grief and the degree of emotional distress, especially during the period between 1992 and 1996, was palpable. Although I initially did not factor the suffering of homeland Croats directly into the analysis of diaspora–homeland relations, it became inescapably obvious that 'the modes of experiencing pain and trauma can be both local and global' (Kleinman et al. 1997:x).

Suffering, as both an individual and a socially experienced phenomenon, has had a significant impact on the public presentation of a singular Croatian experience, for example, in conveying victimhood and/ or mobilizing people for political or moral purposes (Bauman 1995). Croatian historians routinely foreground the suffering of the Croatian people throughout the centuries in their accounts, and the Homeland War continues that legacy – albeit with a different purpose. Popular cultural and historical representations of suffering through images, commemorative art and literature, and collective memories are powerful communicative devices. Toronto Croats have felt compelled to give me many videotapes, photos, medical and other journals, and miscellaneous other documentation chronicling the tragedies of war in Croatia. The emotional impact of these sounds, images, metaphors, and memories of tremendous suffering resonate very deeply for many Croats, regardless of their proximity to Croatia geographically, temporally, or experientially.

The experience of trauma and suffering for homeland Croats during the war differs greatly from that of diaspora Croats, of course, primarily in the proximity of terror, death, and loss, all in the context of trying to cope and recover the everyday. Even so, according to the Croatian writer Slavenka Drakulić (1996), the *only* unity among homeland Croats was the pain and suffering brought about by the Homeland War. The argument for unity brought about as a result of the war, then, falls short. The significance of suffering for Croats transnationally lies in the differential impact and interpretation of suffering, and most importantly on how suffering has served to both unite *and* divide Croats, both during and after the war. Many Toronto Croats shared in the pain and grief of homeland Croats and some even went to Croatia to help in the war effort between 1990 and 1995. But they did not experience the war in the same way as homeland Croats, who at times expressed antagonism towards what were often derided as hollow overtures of compassion from diaspora Croats. This is not an unusual sentiment among homeland peoples, as is well known from reports of the experiences of Israelis compared with diaspora Jews (see, e.g., Shain 2000). Expressions of grief and guilt by diaspora Croats speak to their deeply held commitments, memories, and desires, but also their ambivalence and uncertainty, about the homeland. Nevertheless, the desire of Toronto Croats to connect with homeland Croats in a deeply felt reaction to the suffering experienced in the homeland was, by and large, neither acknowledged nor reciprocated.

How then, are we to understand desire in the context of the Croat diaspora? The Lacanian scholar Slavoj Žižek's (2001) perspectives on the 'reflective nature of desire' are helpful in the Croatian case, as they convey the conflicted nature of desire – read here through political change. Žižek's analysis of the relationship between desire and politics in post-communist Eastern Europe is captured in the following: 'Eastern Europe is returning to the West the "repressed" truth of its democratic desire' (1990:58; 1991). Rather than fulfilling 'narcissistic' Western desires for the fruits of its fantasies of freedom, enthusiasm for a new democratic future in Eastern Europe was repeatedly disrupted (for the West) by the brutal civil war in post-socialist Yugoslavia and its aftermath. For diaspora Croats, desire is paired with its corollary, disdain, underscoring the necessary tensions and ambiguities that characterize the process of subject formation. One of the most surprising findings from discussions and interviews was that Croatia's independence has not succeeded in fulfilling diasporia Croats' desires for the Croatian homeland. In other words, the new Croatian state does not measure up to the expectations of many diaspora Croats, collectively or personally, and it arguably, never will. Desires for the homeland are irreconcilable with the needs of diaspora Croats for the Croatian home that they envision and long for.

Following Lacan's critique of Freud's 'wish fulfilment,' Žižek argues for the 'constitutive reflectivity of desire' (1991:144); that the desire is precisely *not* to satisfy the desire, but to keep it alive. There are a number of processes that contribute to this outcome for Croats. Through their actions, attitudes, and ways of being Croatian, homeland Croats thwart the efforts of diaspora Croats to inscribe their desires onto them. Disdain, then, can be seen as the converse of desire. It is the rejection, revulsion, and/or judgment of people and their actions. Disdain becomes a necessary impediment to the fulfilment of desire, as evidenced in the relationships between Croats in the diaspora and in the homeland. Croatian national imaginaries, as they have been conceived and cultivated, shared and contested over time by diaspora Croats, are ever-changing and always in process, both personally and politically.

Desire regarding Croatia and Croatness, for Toronto Croats describes a reconfigured imagined relationship to Croatia, while disdain is a sentiment that I locate more centrally among homeland Croats. That is, homeland Croats often express a degree of resentment and/or ambivalence towards diaspora Croats. This disdain is manifest in a range of sentiments, such as the view that diaspora Croats retain a vulgarized and/or romanticized ethnic culture and obsolete political ideals that are not representative of the lived reality of Croats who are experiencing more directly the transformation from socialism and, more specifically, have lived through the Homeland War. Other diaspora Croats are criticized for capitalizing on investment opportunities of questionable benefit to Crotia and for meddling in Croatian internal political affairs.

Desire for homeland Croats manifests itself primarily in the elusive idea of the (Central or Western) European subject and the imagined prosperity and 'civilizational' status that membership in the European Union, in particular, promises to bestow. A liberal-democratic counter-narrative to that of the nationalist state has always been present in Croatia, but it was suppressed, side-lined, or forgotten in favour of ultra-nationalist discourses promulgated by right-wing political parties such as the HDZ particularly in the early 1990s. The mainly ethnocultural emphasis of diaspora Croat nationalism, then, is not easily compatible with what operates in Croatia's sociopolitical realm. The complex and multi-stranded nationalisms of homeland Croats, in turn, cannot be fully appreciated or understood in the Toronto diaspora context. Whatever overlap there is does not coincide with diaspora purposes, since the interests and sensibilities that feed into diaspora Croats' aspirations for Croatia reflect memories, sensibilities, and lived experiences that have accumulated over lifetimes spent in Croatia, Canada, or elsewhere. Although problems at home (Croatia or Bosnia and Hercegovina) may be on the minds of many diaspora Croats, the more accessible and familiar languages of identification and the contingencies of life in the diaspora, often produce a disregard for the complexities of life for the homeland Croats. The dynamics revealed through a focus on the tensions that desire and disdain produce, bring into focus the centrality of relations between the diaspora and the homeland, with necessary emphasis on the homeland.

There is also the case of returnees for whom Croatia is 'home,' that is, Canadian citizens of Croatian descent who return not only to visit, but to settle in Croatia. The question that arises is why, given returnees' knowledge of the continuing political and economic instability in Croatia that has caused many homeland Croats to emigrate, have these people decided to return to Croatia? What are the individual and collective motivations of returnees, and what is the role of Croatia's government that has courted them? Furthermore, what has been the reaction of homeland Croats to the return of diaspora Croats?

Although the increased traffic in images, goods, and people to-ing and fro-ing between the Croatian homeland and the diaspora has been greatly enhanced since independence, this has not necessarily translated into greater affinities between the two. Neither overtures of pan-Croatness nor broad-based condemnations of diaspora Croats as extremists address the multiplicity of revived, imagined, and/or emergent bases of compatibility or differentiation, understanding or misunderstanding, agreement or disagreement among and between Croats. The nationalist aspirations of diaspora Croats and homeland Croatian nationalists do reinforce each other at some level, but they cannot easily be generalized beyond the level of political rhetoric, polemics, and ideology.

## Bringing It All Back Home

In introducing her most recent compilation of articles on contemporary research on Eastern Europe, the anthropologist Daphne Berdahl points out that anthropologists have been working against Cold War binaries and macropolitical and economic perspectives that have dominated the field of 'transitology' to provide ethnographically informed analyses of people's everyday lives in post-socialist societies, that is, 'what happens to memory, identity and personhood in the aftermath of rapid social change' (Berdahl 2000:1). Such ethnographically informed perspectives have typically provided insights into the vagaries of life after socialism through a more focused exploration of the everyday lives of people in the former Yugoslav republics. Efforts to understand post-socialist transitions in the Balkans have primarily looked at the impact of the rampant and often deleterious effects of global capitalism manifested most often in consumerism and commodification, impoverishment, and ubiquitous crime and corruption. Myriad studies chronicle the general breakdown of the social, economic, and political order of post-communist societies in this region and the efforts of local populations to make sense of the past and of contemporary realities. The contributions of anthropologists in studying the region since 1990 have been ethnographically rich and theoretically challenging, as well as innovative, but such efforts to 'explore the construction and contestation of new cultural landscapes' (Berdahl 2000:1) invariably have been localized, and they focused on the impacts of transition, however defined, on local populations (Kideckel 1995; Verdery and Burawoy 1999; Wanner 1998; Ries 1997; Halpern and Kideckel 1993, 2000; Grant 1995; Berdahl 1999; Rethmann 2001; Lemon 2000). The literature that does deal with the transnational dimension, specifically on relations between the diaspora and the homeland of post-socialist societies is found largely outside the field of anthropology and focuses primarily on diasporic efforts to influence foreign policy, the creation of 'near-abroad' diasporas of Russians in post-Soviet successor states (Motyl 1998; Hyman 1993), or external national homelands in borderland states, for example, Latvia and Lithuania (see, e.g., Brubaker 1996).

The politically charged and often violent circumstances of Croatia's independence that have drawn both homeland and diaspora Croats into often intense transnational contact are revealing of how Croatian identification processes *in both sites* are informed by desire and disdain. Although this book focuses on a unique case of diaspora–homeland relations at a particularly volatile moment in time, it does demonstrate the importance of working against the notion of a 'unified subject ... engaged in identity quests and struggles in diverse places' (Marcus 1998:7) and the need to specify the dimensions, contexts, and idioms that constitute a particular diaspora. Furthermore, the Croatian example also challenges the inclination to juxtapose diaspora and homeland contexts and points to the need to investigate the struggles of the people in each context to define their often tenuous yet increasingly intimate relationships with one another within, across, and between borders. Most importantly this book demonstrates that the politics of *Hrvatstvo* are constantly changing and responding to the contingencies of local, national, and international political shifts. The current repositioning of Croatia (and Croats) as an ally in the 'War on Terror,' poised at the 'ramparts of Christendom' in a region now defined by prominent diaspora and homeland Croats as in danger of being dominated by Eastern influences and *mujahedin*, is just the most recent incarnation of ongoing efforts to remain visible and relevant.

## Chapter Overview

The next chapter presents the central argument around which this book is built, namely, the need to draw attention to the centrality of homeland Croats – their sentiments, practices, and relationships – to the views, imaginings, connections, and formation of diaspora Croats' identifications, past and present. I draw attention to the multifaceted ways in which the homeland has been woven through the material and sociopolitical conditions of life for Croats in Toronto. Over the years, they have inscribed their presence in Toronto as Croats, Yugoslavs, Canadians, by region of origin, and/or all of the above within the shifting contexts of the possibilities and constraints afforded by life in Canada. These, combined, have not only contributed to the political socialization of diaspora Croats but also fostered particular kinds of diaspora imaginaries. Many of the observations here also foreground Canadian master narratives of immigration and liberal discourses of multiculturalism that have been integral to the politics of representation for Croats in Canada.

Croatian independence and war provide the context for a discussion of diaspora Croats' responses, both personal and political in Chapter 2. They are examined through an analysis of domestic (Croatian) nation-building efforts by the ruling party, Hrvatska democratska zajednica (HDZ) or Croatian Democratic Union, under Franjo Tuđman, how they have affected the cultural politics and conditions of everyday life for homeland Croats, and the relationship of these developments to diaspora Croats' involvement in Croatia's affairs. But while the analysis begins with diaspora Croats, it does not remain there. Chapter 3 examines the political engagement of Toronto Croats in homeland affairs, specifically that of self-selected elites in redefining Croatness. Homeland Croats have been drawn into the politics of diaspora identity by virtue of their newly found status as members of the new Croatian nation state. But, while many homeland Croats have embraced Western practices, ideals, and imaginaries, they do not look to diaspora Croats for guidance in achieving their goals. They, by and large, do not share the views of diaspora Croats on the future and direction of Croatia. By contrast, diaspora views of homeland Croats reflect not only frustration with the lack of progress towards the goals that they had envisioned for Croatia, but resentment towards the indifference to or rejection of diaspora imaginings of the new homeland by Croats in Croatia. Key to understanding the relative lack of a rapprochement between Croats 'here' and 'there' is that neither understands nor has patience for the complexities inherent in the experiences and personal or political histories that have shaped the other's outlooks on the meanings of Croatia as a homeland or more importantly, of Croatness.

Nonetheless, Croatia's independence has been a powerful catalyst for the revitalized self-image of diaspora Croats of all ages, back-grounds, and affiliations, regardless of the strength of their ties to the homeland. Independence not only rejuvenated the sense of Croatness but also created and/or exacerbated conflicting personal and political sentiments and loyalties. Independence also made possible the prolif-eration of disparate and often contradictory ideas and feelings about what it means to be Croat, despite efforts from within the diaspora Croat community, specifically its elites, to contain them.

In Chapter 4, the focus shifts to the contemporary Croatian national context and diaspora–homeland relations since independence. Croats have experienced independence for over a decade but diaspora Croats are not yet confident in their relationship with the new homeland. Changes in government composition and priorities, especially since Tuđman's death in 1999, have meant lessened influence of diaspora Croats on homeland affairs. Many fear that their involvement during the fight for independence is being increasingly overlooked and that they are being marginalized. As recently as July 2005, the National Federation of Croatian Americans (NFCA) sent a formal request to the Croatian Ambassador to the United States to introduce absentee ballot-ing, which would allow Croatian citizens living abroad to participate in Croatia's elections. However, diaspora involvement in the home-land has not been as radically compromised as some Croats have expected, given the continued dependence of homeland Croats on diaspora support and the ubiquity of far-reaching and sophisticated forms of information dissemination, commerce, and communications linking Croats globally. The re-election of the Croatian Democratic Union in November 2003 pleased many of the diaspora Croats who feel strongly about their role in the future of the Croatian state and speaks to the continued significance of diaspora involvement in Croatia's politics (see, e.g., Čuvalo 1999; Šoljak 2002). Nonetheless, conflicting messages from the Croatian government, due largely to the exigencies of Croatian realpolitik have left many deeply concerned about their continuing role and stake in the homeland.

In the final chapter (Chapter 5) the phenomenon of return from the diaspora is explored, specifically the contexts within which the return migration of diaspora Croats has been made appealing and possible, by analysing the structures and organizations, networks, and symbolic processes that have promoted, facilitated, or impeded these transna-tional movements and the factors that compel some to return to Croatia. The ubiquitous 'myth of return' embedded in diaspora narratives of homeland is seldom addressed in terms other than those that speak of either its symbolic importance or romantic delusion. What motivates diaspora Croats to return to the homeland? Once in Croatia, do returnees adjust their notions of belonging and/or loyalty to conform with the contingencies and demands of life in Croatia, and if so, how? Moreover, why do some abandon their dream of return to the homeland and go back to Canada?

I conclude with a summative discussion of the book's findings, both in terms of its contributions to contemporary debates on identity and politics and in terms of the ethnography of post-socialist European societies, in this case Croatia. Croatia has been a site of suffering and of struggle, but also of promise for Croats, wherever they have settled. For diaspora Croats, the country was invested with iconic status for generations, indeed, centuries. Perhaps the dreams and hopes for Croatia outstripped the reality that presented itself with the realization of Croatia's independence in 1990. Throughout I foreground the tensions and ambiguities, continuities and disjunctures that characterize the often-fraught relationships among and between Croats both in the homeland and in the far abroad diaspora home of Toronto. These are illustrated through memory, discourse and imagination, political manoeuvring, celebration and commemoration, all in the service of something called *Hrvatstvo* – Croatness.

# Chapter 1

# Locating Croatia in Diaspora

'Naša Vjećna Domovina' – Our Eternal Homeland

In the winter of 1992, while walking through the student centre of the university where I teach, I noticed a large group of students gathered around one of the many student club information tables. The commotion began with an altercation between Croat and Serb students over the war in the former Yugoslavia. Accusations and name-calling – Četnik and Ustaša – began to fly and it wasn't long before a shouting match ensued. At that point, campus security was called in and order was restored, for the moment. This incident was repeated on several occasions on campus between 1991 and 1995. The passion and commitment for the Croatian homeland of these students – mostly part of the second and third generations in Canada – piqued my interest. What was it that inspired such devotion, not to mention displays of vitriol and contempt for Serbs and for Yugoslavia more generally? While there are parallels aplenty among campus student groups advocating homeland causes (Palestinians, Jews, Macedonians, Greeks, etc.), some of these young Croats came from families where intermarriage (with Bosniaks or Serbs, for example) was not uncommon. According to those I interviewed, there had been also little or no personal family history of overt (ethnic) hostility either in Croatia or Toronto.

These events, combined with a broader interest in the rise of ethnic nationalism globally and in the destruction of Yugoslavia, spurred me on to examine the impact of the Homeland War, as it has come to be called by Croats. The processes that were unfolding and their relationship to the newly independent Croatia initially drew me to the theoretical possibilities presented in the emerging literature on transnationalism and diaspora. However, it was not only the intellectual challenges or even the empirical fit of research on diaspora with the experiences of Toronto Croats that inspired me to pursue this line of inquiry.

What also made this research compelling was the extent to which I had been encountering the term 'diaspora' in the course of my personal and professional dealings with Croats. *Dijaspora* as a term has for some become emblematic of purpose and pride and, for others, of ignorance, corruption, and vulgarity. It is found in the language of politics, commemoration, community festivities and publications, religious sermons, and public speeches. Diaspora is also a common personal identifier for Toronto Croats. While doing research in Croatia, however, I found that the mention of diaspora Croats aroused sentiments of ambivalence, antagonism, or derision. It didn't seem to matter who I was interviewing or speaking to in Croatia, mention of diaspora Croats elicited comments such as that from a computer analyst (age 45) in Zagreb: 'Those diaspora peasants don't know what they want or what they are talking about' (14 April 1997). Homeland Croats' impressions and expectations of the diaspora (i.e., of privilege and ignorance of homeland issues) have had a strong impact on their largely negative or ambivalent views and relationships towards them, regardless of their personal connections with family and friends abroad. Diaspora is not a neutral term.

As a concept, diaspora has been widely championed as a transnational social formation that transcends the territory of the host nation state and embraces the analysis of global processes associated with fluidity, fragmentation, and movement. Its scholarly significance is reflected in myriad contributions to the analysis of economic, political, and cultural modalities of dislocation and migrancy (Glick Schiller et al. 1992; Clifford 1994; Hall 1990; Gilroy 1987, 1994; Appadurai 1991, 1993). While Croats have actively participated in those processes typically associated with diasporas, the conflicts, tensions, and ambiguities that have come to characterize their involvements, affiliations, and loyalties are embedded in relationships and events that have continuously put the homeland front and centre. I begin here by setting the historical context for Toronto Croats, as it is crucial to understanding how and why the political has always figured so centrally in their lives. The task, then, becomes how to define the meaning and the parameters of the political in the context of diaspora. This is taken up in the latter half of this chapter.

## The Making of a Diaspora: Toronto Croats

Judged by the standards set by most scholars in the area of diaspora studies, Croats are identifiable as a bona fide diaspora as evidenced in the conditions of their dispersal and resettlement and, most importantly, the long-term maintenance of political, familial, material, and symbolic connections to the homeland (Safran 1991; Tölölyan 1991). Predictably, however, efforts to define them according to selected criteria run into difficulties. Croatian consciousness of kind has never been reflected in 'consistently organized protest' (Tölölyan 1996) and agreement regarding the fate of Croatia. Until the Homeland War and independence, Toronto Croats appear to have shared only a vague sense of peoplehood, despite commonplace assumptions about their vigorous and continued struggle for an independent Croatian homeland.

The term 'diaspora' itself is also, in some respects, a misnomer in the case of Toronto Croats. Diaspora and homeland Croats are not inherently and eternally discrete groups, because many homeland Croats have been, at one time or another, diaspora Croats and vice versa, due to the exigencies of labour and return migration. Thus, while many homeland Croats may not have identified themselves as diaspora Croats during their often lengthy sojourns in Western Europe, North or South America, or elsewhere, their experiences have invariably affected their affiliations, identifications, and ways of thinking about and being Croatian. Thus diaspora is not simply a theoretical concept or heuristic tool, but rather a meaningful category of self-representation and political discourse, not just for diaspora Croats but also for those homeland Croats who have inhabited that space and been drawn into diaspora spheres of influence – symbolic, political, or otherwise. The multivocality of the term *dijaspora* in Croatian discourse thus undergirds a complexity that is revealing of numerous impressions and expressions of Croatness (*Hrvatstvo*), of community, peoplehood, location, history, and politics.

A place to begin is by thinking about the localized practices and contexts through which Toronto Croats, in particular, define Croatness for themselves. This entails their historical experiences as immigrants, displaced persons, refugees, or temporary migrants. It also involves looking at how Toronto Croats have been positioned in relation to the changing Canadian state and polity, that is, through their insertion historically into 'axes of differentiation' (Brah 1996:182). These combined have had a significant impact on the politics of representation and recognition for Toronto Croats, namely, the ways in which they have negotiated the terms and conditions under which recognition has been extended or denied through changing practices of citizenship, belonging, and contexts of (in)visibility in Canada. 'Diasporas always leave a trail of collective memory about another place and time and create new maps of desire and of attachment' (Appadurai and Breckenridge 1988:i).

As the Toronto Croatian case demonstrates, even the most patriotic responses to developments in the Croatian homeland have been mediated and disciplined through the 'lived experience of locality' (Brah 1996:192). Attention to the relationship of situatedness to diaspora draws on the importance of what Avtar Brah refers to as the 'entanglement of the genealogies of dispersal with those of staying put' (1996:181). Diaspora is not simply a signifier of transnationality and movement, but of settlement, dwelling, and the struggles to define the local. Thus, Toronto's outlying areas such as Oakville and Mississauga, as well as neighbourhoods in the Kipling and Rexdale avenues area in the west end of Toronto, and Bloor and Dufferin streets in the downtown core are not just locations where Croats reside, but also sites that signal status, origins, generation, loyalties, and politics among Croats.

Although Croatia's independence has forced many Toronto Croats to re-evaluate long-held sentiments about their regional, national, religious, or ethnic identities, this is a process that is not new to them. Toronto Croats have long worked hard to establish formal and informal networks and institutions that celebrate Croatness, and these have all been shaped by life in Canada. Nonetheless, transnational processes have been central in reinforcing the conditions through which Toronto Croats have developed identities embedded in networks of relationships and systems of meaning that have connected them simultaneously to the homeland and to Canada. Links to the homeland have been maintained over the years through informal familial and economic networks of family and friends, visits 'back home,' and involvement in Croatian political and cultural life. Whether through picking up the occasional Croatian newspaper, listening to Croatian radio programs, participating in online Croatian chat rooms or in regular Saturday protests in front of the Yugoslav consulate in midtown Toronto (before 1990), the homeland has always been in their field of vision. Croatia has always been central to their senses of Croatness, and not a temporary symptom of post-independence euphoria.

The sense of continuity, both positively and negatively perceived and experienced, shared memories and collective destiny derived from connections to the homeland is evidenced in the everyday lives of Toronto Croats. Just about every interaction I have had with Croats of all generations has involved some evocation of a shared Croatian past. Whether this has taken the form of personal narrative or didacticism, history has played a central role in the ways in which Croats relay their Croatness.

The role of history according to theorists such as Michel de Certeau (1988), Hayden White (1987), and Maurice Halbwachs (1980) is to create order out of the past, to authenticate its existence and legitimate actions, and finally, to retrospectively reconcile diverse elements into a meaningful, comprehensive, and accessible narrative or story. Diaspora Croats have made concerted efforts to create a common history framed in accessible discursive styles that highlight, among other things, the (Christian) teleological trope of suffering, pride in origins, and commitment to continuity. The tone and presentation of these histories reflects efforts to authenticate Croatian existence, to convey legitimated notions of traditions, and most importantly, to produce a distinctive Croatian identity. Although Croatia's independence has generated and intensified interest in and celebration of all that is Croatian, the organization of life history narratives centred on Croatia permeates the history of Croatian migration and settlement in Canada.

Dominant discourses of early Croatian experiences in Canada present the past as one of flight and suffering, punctuated by personal and collective memories of displacement and persecution. The story arc is a familiar one beginning with struggles to overcome seemingly insurmountable barriers and culminating in testimonials of progress, achievement, and triumph. Titles such as *For a Better Life* (Rasporich 1982) and *Unknown Journey* (Scardellato and Sopta 1994), as well as the 1996 Canadian film *Hardship and Happiness*, all convey the essence of the prototypical immigrant experience (see also Eterovich 1987; Godler 1981; Grubišić 1984; Čižmić 1994b, 1996).

Croatian immigrants, like others from Eastern Europe at the beginning of the twentieth century, experienced restrictive policies that privileged migration from northern European destinations. They soon became the target of scorn and racist tensions as 'inferior' Eastern Europeans, an attitude prevalent in Canada at that time. As former subjects of the Austro-Hungarian Empire, though, Croats were also branded as hostile enemy aliens by the Canadian government (Rasporich 1994:17; 1978a, 1978b). These experiences were compounded by the indignities of poverty and discrimination. One first-generation Croat in Toronto said: 'Work was not so hard to get but it was very hard and little pay' (retired foreman, age 74, 20 May 1993).

Throughout the years of hardship and their efforts to build a 'better life,' the Croatian homeland was the most powerful and persistent theme around which an abiding sense of identity revolved. It always provided the benchmark for crafting the narrative foundations of diaspora Croatian identity. Because it was a magnet of group identification, Croatian social and political organizations in Toronto were moulded largely by homeland concerns. They responded intensely to all political developments beginning during monarchist-era Yugoslavia, especially after the 1928 assassination of the leader of the Croatian Peasant Party (HSS), Stjepan Radić. In fact, the HSS was established in Toronto in response to Radić's assassination (Herman 1994). He soon became a folk hero for many diaspora Croats and came to symbolize the struggle against their perceived Yugoslav/Serb oppressors. But even during these early years, Croats were divided in their political points of view, with most of their organizations having either right-wing nationalist or left-wing political orientations.

Most early Croatian immigrants were politically left-leaning (Bubrin 1994, Rasporich 1982; Godler 1981), but involvement in leftist politics was frowned upon by the Canadian government during the early decades of the twentieth century, and the Yugoslav government of the time worked closely with the Canadian government to rid itself of communist and anti-Yugoslav agitators. The Yugoslav monarchy took an active interest in the affairs of its emigrants in a determined effort to stifle the development of dissident political movements overseas.[1] These actions led to abiding feelings of mistrust of governments among Toronto Croats, particularly as a result of the complicity of the Canadian government with Yugoslav authorities in discrediting and harassing them. Ultimately they began to lose faith in government, as a rule to close ranks, and to develop an anti-statist attitude relying on each other through Croatian institutions and support groups.[2] However, the ties that bind can also rend, and political differences were not the only source of tension among Toronto Croats.

The internal dynamics of most diasporas are seldom harmonious, and in this way, the history of Croats is not unusual. One common source of difference has been regionalism. When Croats first emigrated to Canada, they frequently identified their regions of origin such as Dalmatia, Slavonia, or Istria, rather than their official citizenship (e.g.,

Austro-Hungarian, or Yugoslav after 1918). These locally specific logics of self-identification often translated into the establishment of discrete social and political networks that continue to the present, and, for
example, many fundraising events during the Homeland War were
organized along lines of regional origin. One of the most significant
regional differences that has influenced affiliations, political views,
and Croatian national imaginaries over the years, has been that
between Croats originating in the geographical territory of historic
Croatia and Croats originating from other territories in the former
Yugoslavia, in particular Bosnia and Hercegovina. While Croats from
both territorial regions share a great deal, their experiences in and of
the Croatian homeland vary in key respects. Thus, the history of Bosnia and Hercegovina, marked by four hundred years of Ottoman rule
followed by that of the Austro-Hungarian Empire, meant that the historical identities of Bosnian Croats differ from those of Croats in what
is now Croatia. However, as with others from the region, the migration
trajectories of Bosnian Croats did not differ greatly from those of other
Croats. Many emigrated from the former Yugoslavia largely because of
economic pressures or in response to political turmoil. The politics of
diaspora Croats of Bosnian origin differed from other Croatian emigrants, if not in the focus of their political interests, then in the intensity of their commitments to these goals and their resolution. As in
Croatia, regional differences between Croats are substantial. Hercegovinian Croats in both Bosnia and Hercegovina and in the diaspora
are noticeably more nationalistic than those in Croatia. Many Croats of
Bosnian origin have never lived in Croatia, although the more nationalistic among them consider Croatia their homeland.[3]

Inevitable fault lines of class have had an impact on relations among
Toronto Croats. Post–Second World War immigrants, for example, who
were trained in Yugoslavia in such professions as engineering and
administration often made a successful economic transition to Canada
as entrepreneurs in fields like real estate, engineering, and construction. They were better educated than their predecessors and were more
inclined to live in urban centres, where their professional skills were in
greater demand.

Nonetheless, the most visible and vociferous form of difference
among Toronto Croats has been ideological, sharply revealed in relation to homeland concerns. Over the years political differences pitted
some diaspora Croats against others. It seems that Toronto Croats have
always thrived on any political engagement that concerns the home-

land. 'Everyone has a political opinion' is a comment I have heard over and over again, and one exemplified in the history of Toronto Croat political involvements. From early on, Croats were divided along political and ideological lines as to the fate of Croatia. Although most were united in their opposition to the pre–Second World War Serb-led Yugoslav government, conflicts erupted over the events leading up to that war, and opinions did not necessarily all point to independence from Yugoslavia. The political turmoil of the Second World War in Yugoslavia, which resulted in civil conflict and the short-lived Nazi occupation of Croatia under the fascist Croatian Ustaša, served to only exacerbate these tensions.

This period has been an enduring source of controversy among Croats and has continued to dog them all these years later. Because of the large number of Croats who escaped Tito's Yugoslavia and emigrated to Canada, many were often mistakenly associated with the Ustaša. Thus, the role of Croats during the Second World War became a source of resentment and frustration for Toronto Croats.[4] Accusations of pro-fascist or communist sympathies were exchanged in a diaspora Croatian milieu comprised of a volatile mix of royalist Yugoslav immigrants, Austro-Hungarian war veterans, and refugees from post-1945 socialist Yugoslavia.[5] On the one hand, Croats who settled in Canada in the early twentieth century (many of whom had leftist leanings), clashed with post–Second World War Displaced Persons, whom they often labelled Ustaša, a term that for early immigrants was virtually synonymous with 'war criminal.' On the other, postwar immigrants resented earlier settlers for what they saw as their naivety concerning the political and social realities of life in socialist Yugoslavia under Tito.

Even Croatian pride over their famed 1976 win of the North American soccer championships by Toronto's professional soccer club, named curiously, 'Toronto Metros-Croatia' revealed rifts and dissension among Toronto Croats. For one thing, the name 'Metros-Croatia,' which signalled ethno-national loyalties, created problems for the team both within and without until it was sold in 1978 (Sopta 1994b). The club's decision to import players from Yugoslavia also met with resistance from those opposed to any cooperation with Yugoslavia. Cases such as this were by no means atypical in that they underscored the overall climate of divisiveness over the political fate of Yugoslavia. Bitter organizational disputes for control of Croatian social facilities were also common. Competing visions of an independent Croatian state continued to create the conditions for political factionalism in Toronto, evidenced in part by the large number of Canadian branches of Croatian political parties (Rasporich 1982; Winland 1995). The legacy of political activity in Croatian social clubs and associations is revealing of the strains among Croats within and beyond borders.

## Going Public: Visibility and the Politics of Representation in Canada

The ascendance of diaspora Croats in high-profile efforts to support the emergence of the Croatian state must be understood in part in terms of the place of Croats in the context of multiculturalism, race, and representation in Canada, and how these have had an impact on expressions and presentations of Croatness. A key factor in negotiating a sense of place and belonging for immigrants and diasporas in Canada has been the issue of visibility (see, e.g., Dyer 1997; Frankenberg 1997; Jacobson 1998). In a country long dominated by a staunchly Anglo-Protestant political and economic presence, visibility has been *the* standard against which all Canadians have been valued and evaluated. Thus, the power of whiteness lies in its normative character (Dyer 1997:45), its unmarked character (Mackey 1999), and this has been central to identity politics in Canada for generations of newcomers. For Croats who arrived in Canada in the early years of the twentieth century, the obstacles or opportunities that they encountered upon arrival defined their experiences, as did their positioning in relation to others. For most early immigrants, the terms and conditions of recognition in Canada were negotiated in terms *not* of their own making.

The politics of difference in Canada for Croats, beginning almost a century ago, meant discrimination and marginalization. A first-generation Toronto Croat explained: 'Being East European meant many things here were not very good. I have been here many years. People used to put down my accent all the time. I was treated like a second-class citizen. It made me feel very bad' (retiree, age 76, 18 November 2000). Furthermore, Croats struggling over the years to establish a presence in Canada have been at the margins of wider debates on the Canadian nation-building project, in large part because of their changing and often equivocal relationship to the former Yugoslavia. The Canadian state routinely bestowed identities upon immigrants that were often not of their own choosing. Croats were identified as Yugoslavs, first and foremost. In the case of Yugoslavia, national, ethnic, regional, historical, and myriad other differences made this reality difficult for some to bear.

Such tensions were not unique to immigrants from the former Yugoslavia. Matsuoka and Sorenson have demonstrated that, even now, in the case of Eritrean and Oromo diasporas in Canada being classed as Ethiopians: 'Regardless of their own identity affiliation, all members of the diaspora were administered by the Canadian government as if they belonged to one category, based on their origin within the boundaries of a state that many rejected as illegitimate' (2001:200). Similarly, Sikhs have been regularly identified as Indian, much to their dismay (Van der Veer 1995a).[6] The same was true of those Croats who rejected their designation as Yugoslav, Balkan, Eastern European, or from the Eastern Bloc. Thus, in the early decades of the twentieth century, Croats were still distinguished from the 'we' (read as Anglo, northern European) of the Canadian nation state.

The introduction of multiculturalism and shifts in Canadian immigration policies marked a turning point in defining the relationship of Toronto Croats to the Canadian state and to each other. The relaxing of barriers to immigration and the introduction of the Multiculturalism Act in the early 1970s coincided with the introduction of legislation resulting in a huge influx of immigrants from non-traditional source countries of the Caribbean, Central and South America, South Asia, and Southeast Asia (Elliott and Fleras 1992). Toronto Croats saw their ethnic status improve relative to that of more 'visible' newcomers, and they were progressively becoming part of the white invisibility of the social mainstream of Canada. The result was increasing demographic diversity and greater attention to issues of difference, discrimination, and identity politics.

Changes in the hierarchies of difference in Canada meant that Croats were able to identify more easily as European, allowing them to begin to negotiate the terms of privileged English/white equivalence. Croats were no longer vilified (publically or politically) as members of – inferior – Eastern European stock. Among the available strategies that Toronto Croats embraced was the terminology and historical precedents of ethnicity (either as Yugoslavs or as Croats, *culturally* defined) to construct themselves as an ethno-cultural group within the Canadian political and cultural landscape. Thus, from the early 1970s until the outbreak of war in the former Yugoslavia, many Croats cautiously relaxed strategies of invisibility to take advantage of heritage language programs and to publicly celebrate their *Hrvatstvo*, sense of being

Croatian, and living a 'multicultural life' (*multikulturni život*; see, e.g., *Folia Croatica-Canadiana* 1995). Canadian Croats were extremely proud when in 1981, Awde Street in downtown Toronto was renamed Croatia Street. However, even these relatively innocent endeavours at culturally 'coming out' were complicated by the need to play the 'politics of recognition' (Taylor 1992;[7] Pusić 1995) on terms set by the state – terms that did not find universal favour among Croats. Canadian policy and discourse primarily recognizes national cultures that are connected to independent states and this has meant that official recognition was accorded solely to the Yugoslav state by the Canadian government.

Since nation state origins have traditionally formed the basis for Canadian multicultural classifications, over the years Croats have responded in ways that reflect their acceptance of, ambivalence towards, or rejection of the terms under which recognition has been extended. Thus, despite the ability of Croats to list their backgrounds as Croat in the official Canadian census, that Croatia was still part of Yugoslavia continued to compromise the legitimacy of their claims to Croatia.[8]

Until Croatia's independence, Croats were routinely referred to as Yugoslavs by those unfamiliar with the religious and cultural differences within the former Yugoslavia or with the geopolitics of the region. Nonetheless, throughout this period, Toronto Croats were thrust into the spotlight in one way or another and not always in a positive way. In the early 1970s, for example, Croats were subjected to crude caricatures as Balkan 'terrorists' and 'troublemakers' because of isolated, incendiary acts of violence and vandalism committed in protests over Tito's regime.[9] This had repercussions in Canada. Some still remember when Croats in Canada were accused of terrorism by Canadian government leaders. In a 1975 speech the Canadian Minister of External Affairs Allan MacEachen promised to control 'the activities of right-wing groups opposed to the Belgrade government.' Political scientists George Klein and Patricia Klein are among those who emphasized the terrorist threat posed by Croatian extremists in the diaspora. At one point they wrote: 'Yugoslavia faces a constant threat from exiled national Croatian organizations which have proved their ruthlessness and determination during the past few decades' (1981:272; see also Clissold 1979). Milton Esman also used the term 'terrorist' to refer to diaspora Croat smuggling operations (1986:341). According to Croatian-American historian Ante Čuvalo, Anglo-American writers were never sympathetic to Croats and always critical of Croatian concerns (1989). Croatian historian Ivo Banac, observes that the 'perceived barbarism of the Croats has been a greater source of misidentification' (1992b:9).

These comments, although considered inflammatory by Croats, reflected an uncomfortable reality. Since the early 1950s, small groups of radical anticommunist and nationalist diaspora Croats in Europe, South America, and North America, were preparing for the overthrow of the Yugoslav regime through clandestine paramilitary training, targeted assassinations of Yugoslav officials, bombing campaigns, and the hijacking of Scandinavian and Trans World Airlines flights.[10] During this time, tracts and publications from radical nationalist groups, such as *Drina*[11] and *Otpor*, made their rounds throughout the diaspora calling for revolt against the Yugoslav regime. The title of one of their pamphlets that was circulated by the Canadian-Croatian Club in 1951 read, 'Please Don't Call Me Yugoslav.' It was distributed internationally and published in several languages. The activities in Canada of such organizations were extensive, and they found their most radical expression in the diaspora publication *Otpor*, the Croatian term for resistance.[12]

One infamous ultra-nationalist Croat in Canada was Gojko Šušak. A native of Siroki Brijeg in the Croat-dominated southwest region of Hercegovina, Šušak lived in Ottawa and Toronto from the mid-1960s until his return to Croatia in 1990. He was a continual source of concern for moderate Croats in Croatia and abroad not only because of his ultranationalist views but also for the radical image that he conveyed. For example, in his efforts to bring media attention to Croatia on Yugoslav National Day in Ottawa in 1979, he staged a publicity stunt that involved painting the name 'Tito' on a piglet and putting it in a closed coffin in front of the Yugoslav embassy. This stunt drew media attention of course, and as a result, swift public condemnation (see, e.g., *Ottawa Citizen*, 30 November, 1979, 5–6). Later on, as Croatia's defence minister (1991–98), Šušak favoured close ties between Bosnian Croats and Croatia proper, but moved away from the idea of annexing territories inhabited by Bosnian Croats because of pressure from the United States and its allies.

The Yugoslav government had, for years, branded Croatian émigrés as Ustaša and as agitators bent on undermining the Yugoslav state; at times it even resorting to targeted assassinations. Rumour and suspicion were, therefore, not uncommon. Fear and intimidation were recurrent reference points for Toronto Croats, reinforcing the insular patterns of earlier years. A Croatian physician related his experiences while he was working in the emergency ward of a Toronto hospital. Frequently, when he recognized a patient's name as Croatian, he would address her in Croatian; however, he was usually greeted with suspicion. For example, when he posed the question: 'Where are you from?,' such a patient would often cautiously respond with 'Yugoslavia.' Although this response was officially the correct one at the time (pre-1990), this interviewee felt that despite his Croatian name and his facility with the language, he was not trusted. When I asked other Croats why this might have been the case, some confirmed the physician's sentiment and stated that it was the result of negative stereotypes and fear generated by years of monitoring by the Yugoslav government, as well as damning portrayals of Croats as fascists and extremists by the Canadian media and by some Canadian politicians. A retired contractor said: 'We just knew that we were looked at that way' (age 74, 15 June 1993). Another, somewhat younger one stated: 'You have to understand that we didn't have an easy time of it during those times. People were nervous about the Cold War, and even though we were very against it – we demonstrated – they were suspicious of us. Bad press didn't help' (age 61, 7 April 1999).

Many participants also pointed out that before independence they had confined their pride in their ethnic or national origins to their fellow Croats out of fear or pressure generated by conditions in the former Yugoslavia. On many occasions, I was told stories about how the UDBA (the post–Second World War Communist Yugoslav State Security Administration) used Croatian informers and intimidated Toronto Croats, and their families during their visits to Yugoslavia. An insurance broker recalled: 'I remember when they would take us into a room when we went home and asked us who our family was and where they lived. It was frightening especially for my kids' (age 57, 11 June 1993). Another contractor explained: 'The UDBA you know, they scared us. They told us that if we did anything or said anything that our family in Croatia would suffer. How can you know for sure?' (age 61, 14 May 1997). Although the repressive tactics of the UDBA abated considerably with time, diaspora Croats remained wary. Many mentioned the surveillance of Croats by Yugoslav operatives. Several, for example, referred to the employees of one Toronto tourist agency as Yugoslav 'spies.' This concern for repercussions meant that, as a researcher, I too was sometimes the object of suspicion. One of my interviews was conducted in a public library because the subject was wary of my credibility or credentials and, therefore, would only meet me in a busy public place.[13]

Although Croatia's independence and the Homeland War that followed had a major impact on Toronto Croats, events in the 1990s should not be viewed as *the* defining factor in diaspora Croats' interest and involvement in homeland affairs. Nor should their activities during this period be taken as evidence of the historic unity of Croats. Rather than uniting diaspora and homeland Croats, independence and the developments that followed, actually, increased already existing bases of differentiation *among* diaspora Croats and *between* Croats in the diaspora and homeland Croats. Given the problematic nature of the conventional fiction that groups share common origins, politics, and statuses, it is important to specify the dimensions, contexts, and idioms that constitute particular diaspora groups. It is in light of these factors that what came to be a central question for Croats – 'What is a Croat?' – takes on a significance that is at once personal and political.

The events that led to the collapse of the former Yugoslavia, the first Croatian democratic elections, and the ensuing war alleviated some long-standing conflicts in the Toronto Croatian diaspora, exacerbated others, and set the stage for new ones to emerge. Croatia's independence and the Homeland War fundamentally transformed the lives of many Croats and generated or revived new forms of association, identification, and reputation for Croats internationally – as tortured and torturers, oppressed and oppressors, war victims and warmongers. In addition, the appellation 'Balkan' linked with stereotypical and orientalist assumptions of ancient ethnic hatreds and tribal animosities gained currency in the early 1990s and resurrected unwanted associations for diaspora Croats.[14] This had the effect of complicating efforts to publicly promote their vision of Croats as democratic, peace-loving Central, even Western, Europeans. Croats were once again made visible on terms not of their own making.

The effects of this were discernible in Toronto, in the sense that Croats were angry at the inadequate international response to Croatia's plight, specifically international sanctions preventing the shipment of military aid to Croatia during the Homeland War. Croats were thus beset by more struggles for legitimacy and recognition. While Canadian Serbs have taken the brunt of much of the criticism for the war in the former Yugoslavia, Croats have also been negatively implicated.

In the early stages of the Homeland War, Croats emerged as clear victims of Serb aggression, as evidenced in the occupation of one-third of Croatia's territory and the high-profile destruction of Vukovar in 1991. But they soon became the object of international condemnation for their role in the conflict, particularly allegations of the cleansing of Serbs from the Krajina region of Croatia and their role in Bosnia and Hercegovina. Canada's role as U.N. peacekeepers in Croatia and in Bosnia and Hercegovina during the war did not do much to soften criticism of the Croatian government's policies and the actions of the HVO (Hrvatsko vijeće obrane, Croatian Defence Council) in Bosnia and Hercegovina. The subsequent naming of Croatian military commanders by the U.N. International Criminal Tribunal for the Former Yugoslavia (ICTY) in The Hague did not help to bolster the international reputation of Croats either.

Although diaspora Croats concerned with projecting positive public images and/or generating support for the war effort worked hard over the years to influence Canadian attitudes towards them – calling attention to their history as victims of 'tyrannical' communist (Serb) forces and their Central and Western European historical and cultural pedigree – these efforts were consistently frustrated by what many regard as negative attitudes towards Eastern Europeans and biased press coverage. The frustration of Toronto Croats with feeling misunderstood was directed particularly at international condemnation for military actions that Croats themselves saw as necessary measures of self-defence against Yugoslav military incursions into Croatia's territory. Many dispora Croats were also distressed by negative images that they speculated were being circulated by 'Serb propagandists.' Insofar as representational regimes go, this is one of the only areas upon which the Croats that I interviewed were agreed. Toronto Croats regularly sent letters to the editors of major dailies in Toronto complaining about inaccuracies and biases concerning the Homeland War.

The wars of Yugoslav succession and the events that followed unleashed not only tragedy on a monumental scale but also fundamental questions on Croatia's past, present, and future. The period since independence has raised questions over what representations of Croatness have been promoted, by whom, and to what effect? Toronto Croats have mobilized images, narratives, and institutional and associational bonds to constitute themselves as a group. These efforts are replete with conflict and tension over precisely what constitutes Croatness, and for whom. The political field, as we now understand it, has expanded to include the politics of the everyday, as reflected in the personal and the private, the nostalgic and emotional, the commemorative and consumerist.

## Engaging the Political in Diaspora

By all accounts, Toronto Croats have been and continue to be defined by their politics. The degree to which politics has dominated the history of Croatian life in Toronto and, most importantly, Croatian identifications, suggests the need for a perspective that can address the multiple ways in which politics insinuates itself into the lives of Croats. Although diaspora politics has been a popular field of scholarly interest for many years, the scope of analysis has been relatively limited. The involvement of diasporas in political activity geared towards homelands has long been recognized as a central factor in diaspora life, specifically in relation to its macropolitical effects. In recognition of the growing importance of diaspora groups on the national and international political stages, scholars have expended considerable efforts in defining the analytical parameters of what some identify as the complex 'triadic' relationships between ethnic diasporas, their host countries, and the homelands (Brubaker 1996; Sheffer 1993; Weiner 1993; Esman 1986, 1994).[15]

Many have been interested in exploring financial and political support for homeland regimes or insurgency groups and in homeland reliance on investment or remittances. Lobbying and fundraising are key areas of interest, specifically their effects not only on host governments, policies towards homelands, but also on homelands themselves. Host country governments vie for the loyalty of their ethnic communities and often exploit ethnic and nationalist sentiments for political ends. They are increasingly coming to rely on these communities for political and material support – diasporas are resources to be tapped. The Canadian context provides many examples.[16]

Although perspectives such as these provide a wider context within which to locate the influence of diasporas on host country and international politics, they adhere to rigid definitions of diaspora as a unified, homogeneous entity. Such perspectives also tend to promote a bifurcated model of diaspora positioning in relation to politics on the assumption that diasporas work in various ways either *against* the homeland or *for* homeland it (Sheffer 1986, 2003; Shain 1989).[17]

The analysis of diaspora politics has had tremendous appeal for cultural theorists who value, among other things, the implied critique of the nation (Gilroy 1991/92; Clifford 1994; Appadurai 1996a, 1996b, 1996c) and its ability to transcend modernist constructs and the discourses that emanate from them. My interest in the politics of the everyday for Croats resonates more closely with this perspective, but with one major exception. Diaspora Croats in particular, through their influence on, involvements with, and imaginings of the homeland, in effect, reproduce rather than disrupt the classic modernist logic of the nation state. The often nationalist activities and narratives that many, particularly influential Croats promote, actually reinforce a typically modernist conception and/or ideology of the nation state through transnational means. The national values that these diaspora Croats espouse place greater emphasis on ethnic pride, loyalty, and history than on themes of civil society and democratic governance. Indeed, multiple and even competing ideas of modernity and nationalism found among Croats actually have served to reinforce the notional and ideological foundations upon which they are based. Diaspora Croat identifications have been at the same time regional, imperial (Austro-Hungarian), republican (Yugoslav), religious, and only very recently state-based – holding meanings that differ for diaspora Croats of different generations as well.

This is not unusual, particularly in the contexts of Eastern European diaspora. According to the Russian critic Chelyshev's analysis of Russian émigré literature, rather than preserve Russian 'humanist scholarship,' the Russian diaspora has often expressed a neoconservative nationalist agenda (Slobin 2001:524; see also Raeff 1990). Witness the (political) conservatism epitomized in the exiled writer Alexander Solzhenitsyn's (1991) critiques of Western values. The conservative and nationalist leanings of, for example, North American Jewish and Hindu diasporas are well also documented. It does not necessarily follow that diaspora patterns of identification lead to a transnational essence that functions to undermine, if not subvert, the cultural and territorial goals and political vision of the nation state (Ong 1996; Guarnizo and Smith 1999; Clifford 1994).[18]

Although such factors as regional origins, migration, and/or settlement experiences have been suggested as parameters for assessing the political in the diaspora, some argue that diaspora politics is best understood as constituted in acts of philanthropy, community celebration, and commemoration (Werbner 2000; Tölölyan 2000). The rationale behind this latter argument is that representational regimes are not constituted only in formalized and often ritualized forms. The majority of diaspora populations are not involved in the high-profile activities of cultural producers or interlocutors or in politics, formally defined. Rather they are engaged in the 'routine behaviours' of life (Tölölyan 2000:124), the semiotics of public and private spaces – fields generally outside the traditional structural realm of politics.

Pnina Werbner (2000) focuses on what she refers to as the aesthetic underpinnings of diaspora life emanating from schools, churches, celebrations and festivals, radio programs, film, videos, and photography. These may involve 'persuasion, the courting of constituencies to join community institutions, status, shaping of consciousness, loyalties and commitment' (Werbner 2000:6), particularly by elites and other community leaders. They often include managed and scrutinized cultural productions in artistic, literary, and other expressive forms – from the traditional and folkloric to the digital and experimental and in literary productions ranging from the crude and polemical to the philosophical and intellectual.

These insights are instructive in the case of Toronto Croats whose 'calendar' regularly includes such opportunities to congregate and share Croatian history, traditions, customs, of course, politics. Picnics (e.g., the Saint Anthony's Day Feast) are held, as are art exhibits by Croatian artists, choir and dance performances, and musical events. Naive art, depicting 'genuine life in the countryside,' has become increasingly popular among Croats everywhere. Galleries and art shows in Toronto and elsewhere in the diaspora regularly feature this kind of art, which portrays motifs replete with imagery of 'typical' Croatian countrysides – ploughmen, day labourers, cattle in the fields, and seasonal scenes. Although associated by some with a Croatian social protest movement (against the former socialist regime), these art works contribute to the creation and/or reinforcement of an idyllic, pastoral Croatian imaginary. Throughout the years, Toronto Croats have gathered to commemorate political milestones such as the anniversary of the assassination of Stjepan Radić, the Day of All Souls at a Croatian cemetery in northwest Toronto (to commemorate friends and family killed in Croatia), the Annual Memorial Day in May to commemorate the Bleiburg massacre, and finally, the controversial 10 April 1941 'anniversary' of Croatian independence. This date is celebrated with religious masses, banquets, and picnics, often at Father Kamber Croatian park in Mississauga.

Such community activity is also where the complexities and contradictions inherent in ways of being Croat are revealed. These include volunteering in local Croatian cultural, religious, and other associations, supporting local Croatian businesses, eating at Croatian restaurants, travelling to the Croatian coast for the summer, and consuming Croatian media – activities that are not necessarily overtly political acts defined by a conscious political sensibility or volition regarding things and activities explicitly Croat. Through these practices, diaspora Croats are afforded the opportunity to inscribe themselves in contemporary and/or historical worlds of Croatness. Their combined political effects though are also clear, especially when viewed in light of diaspora – homeland relations.

## Where Homeland and Diaspora Meet

The intensification of relationships between diaspora Croats and the homeland, marked by Croatia's independence and the Homeland War that galvanized diaspora Croats but also challenged pre-independence practices, loyalties, and politics, has thrust the issue of diaspora – homeland relations to the forefront of this research. Numerous correctives to the concept of diaspora have been proposed (as evidenced above in the interventions of scholars like Werbner and Tölölyan); however, few focus on engaging the political in a way that recognizes the broad range of activities and sentiments that may be thought of as political and the multiply inflected relations between the diaspora and the homeland. The mutual imbrication of diasporas and homelands has been simply assumed, with diasporas receiving the lion's share of theoretical and ethnographic attention. The research for this book differs in that it directs attention to the centrality of homeland Croats – their sentiments, practices, politics, and relationships – to the views, connections, and formation of diaspora Croat identifications, past and present. The importance of this perspective is evidenced in the partiality of perspectives that claim to be presenting a comprehensive focus on transnationalism without fully taking into account the significance of homelands and their inhabitants.

While there has been a great deal of interest in the ongoing and complex positioning of diaspora communities between host countries and homelands, little is available on the roles of homeland peoples as such – other than the political and economic elites – on diaspora identities. Analytical and empirical emphasis is invariably on the diaspora experience, specifically that associated with conditions of migrancy, marginalization, and alterity.

At their most basic, analytical perspectives on relations between the diaspora and the homeland are premised on the assumption that diasporas *need* homelands. The focus is typically on links to family forged through overseas communication, periodic trips 'back home,' financial support through remittances sent to family members, and interest and sometimes involvement in political affairs in the homeland. Symbolic representations, nostalgia, customs, and diaspora narratives that speak to the homeland are also identified as central. 'Mother country,' then, is a highly notional concept within diaspora communities, even though people's relationships to their countries of origin vary according to the exigencies of time and place (Gold and Paine 1984). Just as the context of usage changes, so too does meaning. Thus, it is argued, remembered places often serve as symbolic anchors of community for dispersed people (Gupta 1992). Identifying the original or ancestral and often idealized homeland as constitutive – as the core metaphor of diaspora identity (Appadurai and Breckenridge 1988; Rushdie 1991; Axel 2001) – has become central to discussions of diaspora. Highly affectively charged, the meaning of the term 'homeland' can arouse many emotions such as nostalgia and pride, inferiority, insecurity, ambivalence – and even shame.

Although the syntactical differences between the terms 'home' and 'homeland' do not appear to vary all that much, the contexts discussed here draw attention to significant variations in their uses and meanings. First, it is acknowledged by specialists in diaspora studies that the use of 'home' as a conceptual or discursive space of identification is integral to the diaspora experience (Fog Olwig 1998; Jackson 1995; Rapport and Dawson 1998; Brah 1996). The idea of home 'brings together memory and longing, the ideational, the affective and the physical, the spatial and the temporal, the local and the global, the positively valued and the negatively' (Rapport and Dawson 1998:8). More specifically, home is simultaneously a 'mythic place of desire' as well as the 'lived experience of a locality mediated by the historically specific everyday of social relations' (Brah 1996:192).

The effects of Croatia's statehood then have not just manifested themselves in diaspora–homeland relations but in ideas of homeland and diaspora – ideas shaped by experiences and memories of hardship and suffering, pride, nostalgia, and anger, and also ambivalence. The importance of the distinction between home and homeland becomes clearer when examining the roles that these notions play in the lives of Croats. The imagined, remembered Croatian *domovina* (homeland) has been variously woven into Toronto Croats' experiences over the years in the course of (re)establishing new grounds of identification and belonging. Homeland has, at the very least, provided an ontological sense of security for Croats living in the diaspora and has always been a potent personal and political referent. For example, the positively valued connotations of patriotism expressed in love for one's homeland – a long-standing and standard refrain for many diaspora Croats – reinvents and reinforces personal relationships with the homeland in affective terms. It also avoids the often negative connotations that have come to be associated with ethnic and nationalist sentiments and loyalties and the sometimes unsettling politics of the homeland. Thus, despite the overwhelming support of the majority of Toronto Croats for the ultra-nationalist President Tuđman, the invocation of homeland expressed through personal and familial referents, aesthetic and nostalgic imagery, symbols, and memories, frames the terms through which most diaspora Croats claim their stake in the new nation. The preferred use of the term 'Homeland War' by diaspora Croats says a lot about their relationship to Croatia, employing 'homeland' in a strategic and spatial, yet also symbolic sense (Holy 1998).

Over time, Toronto Croats have built up an inventory of narratives, memories, and practices, personal and shared, that are distinctive to their experiences and relationships. Furthermore, the sudden increase in contact between different and, in many ways, incompatible traditions between homeland and diaspora Croats is having a definitive impact on how diaspora Croats imagine or reflect on the homeland. Thus, many Toronto Croats had come to see themselves as a victim diaspora and, by extension, to view Croats in the former Yugoslavia as their oppressed brethren.

But what of homeland Croats' notions of home? How is the language and meaning of 'home' or 'homeland' used by them and to what effect? Unlike other countries under communist rule in Europe, Yugoslavia was relatively open to the outside (Dyker and Vejvoda 1996; Ramet 1992; Kennedy 2002). Despite this history, Croats in the past decade have been increasingly (and rapidly) enveloped in capitalist-consumerist and other global influences. Increased and more immediate contact with the West since 1990 has meant that homeland Croats have been able to re-evaluate their lives in ways that not only open them to the possibilities and opportunities previously unavailable under communism, but also serve to demystify life abroad. As the Croatian case demonstrates, diasporas construct notions of the homeland in ways that are often very different from those of homeland peoples, and this can lead to ambivalence and/or tensions between them. Indeed, the collapse of the former Yugoslavia and the aftermath has unsettled and, in many cases, disrupted already unstable and ambivalent bases of loyalty, affiliation, and identification.

Homeland Croats, who have had to endure enormous upheaval due to the war, have been faced with the task of not only coping with the toll of the transition from communism, but of reconceptualizing themselves as citizens of the newly established Croatian nation state. Not surprisingly, they have not always responded positively to diaspora Croats' efforts to insert themselves into Croatia's political and economic affairs. Indeed, homeland Croats often hold negative views of diaspora Croats, often expressed in personal, professional, and political contexts. Therefore, it is not surprising to find that for those Toronto Croats who have made the commitment to return to the homeland – whatever their motivations – their reception has been quite different from what they might have anticipated. Nevertheless, the mythic destination – Croatia – has for many become the place of return.

Return to the homeland represents the culmination of decades, indeed centuries, of longing for many Croats. Croatian literature is replete with examples of writing on exile (Krleža 1969 [1932]; Baričević 1993; Matvejević 2005; Ugrešić 2005; see also Grubišić 1991). For the Toronto Croats profiled here, the myth of return has insinuated itself into Croatian life and thought in ways that defy attempts to explain it away, for example, as a political or ideological tool or romantic obsession. The myth of or desire to return to the homeland for Croats has a long history. While for many, return was a pragmatic economic goal, it first found its strongest expression during the First World War, when Toronto Croats began to coordinate their political activities in response to developments in the homeland. The politicization of Toronto Croats, which manifested itself in lobbying, organizing, and fundraising, was motivated in part by the desire to return home, even for those who favoured a federal Yugoslav state. The establishment of the Kingdom of Serbs, Croats, and Slovenes after the First World War, Italian rule over Istria and other coastal areas, as well as the elimination of the Croatian parliament, however, led to widespread disillusionment, not only for those who remained in the diaspora but also for those who returned. The idea, dream, or desire to return went through numerous incarnations in the diaspora in the years that followed, and these were deeply attuned to political and economic fluctuations in the homeland.

A careful assessment of the multiplicity of factors that shape myths or aspirations of return (examined in Chapter 5) illustrates their power and ability to both inspire and/or to mobilize diaspora Croats to nourish, if not realize, their dreams of going home.

## Homecoming, Memory, and Nostalgia

> To articulate the past historically ... means to seize hold of a memory as it flashes up at a moment of danger.
> Walter Benjamin, *Philosophy of History*, 6th thesis, 1968

Among the most powerful influences in sustaining homeland imaginaries is nostalgia, the structured feeling towards the past. Memories that variously authorize versions of Croatian selfhood have combined to produce or reproduce images of and desires for Croatia. Aside from the material links that many Croats have to Croatia, belonging is lived at least partially through nostalgia and memories. Gillis (1994), perhaps echoing Benjamin's statement, argues that new forms of 'memory work' appear at times when there is a break with the past, an observation that has direct relevance to the experience of diaspora Croats dealing with the new reality of Croatia's independence. As Svetlana Boym argues, 'nostalgia is not always about the past; it can be retrospective but also prospective. Fantasies of the past determined by needs of the present have a direct impact on realities of the future' (2001:xvi). State propaganda and national memory build on these, but there are also discrepancies and tensions between the two.

Since independence, the state (supported by right-leaning diaspora elites) has been actively renovating selected memories and emblems of the Croatian homeland through the restoration of (ethnic) origins. The replacement and renaming of statues, the reinstatement of Croatian heroes, and the rewriting of Croatian educational and historical texts are selected examples of the state's efforts to rehabilitate Croatia through the development and intensification of a grand narrative of Croatian nationhood (Matković 1993). Indeed, most schoolchildren's books have been distributed through *Skolska Knijžara* shops, which were run by the Croatian Democratic Union (HDZ). The nostalgia of many Toronto Croats I have interviewed over the course of this research however, has subsisted on the 'emotional topography' of cherished fragments of personal memories (Boym 2001). Thus, for example, efforts by diaspora and/or homeland Croats (e.g., elites, politicians, ethnic entrepreneurs) to meld these together though the process of regulation and the erasure of inevitable 'gaps and discontinuities' (Boym 2001:53) in favour of a coherent national vision and identity, have encountered resistance.

The passage from the desire for the Croatia lived and/or imagined and conveyed through family memories, myths, and commemoration has, for some diaspora Croats, been transformed into bitterness and disappointment, but not as in the past. Disillusionment in the past was directed largely towards foreign powers, empires, and monarchs. Since independence equivocations and reservations expressed by Toronto Croats have been directed at the pace and direction of Croatian nation-building, Croatia's government policies, and homeland Croats themselves.

The processes instigated by events beginning in 1990 demonstrate that one can neither presume the Croatian diaspora itself nor even, for that matter, the homeland or the Croats who live there. Their self-evident qualities need to be scrutinized through detailed attention to the material practices, commodified, institutional, aesthetic, and ideological forms and discursive formulations, as well as the 'realpolitik of everyday life' (Comaroff and Comaroff 1997:410–11).

The debate over public identity takes place on many levels and in different settings. The radical, destabilizing nature of change in the former Yugoslavia has reverberated throughout the diaspora in a manner that demonstrates, among other things, the contingency of Croatian identifications. One of the many things that emerges from debates about the diaspora is a recognition of the importance of context in accounting for those processes that contribute to the reproduction of identities over time. As Stuart Hall notes, 'at different places, times, in relation to different contexts, the boundaries are re-sited' (1990:228). Thus, despite Croats' claims to the contrary, Croatness is not a monolithic category of identification.

The politics of contemporary Croatian identities point to the need to extend the analytical reach of transnationalist constructs such as diaspora by problematizing not just the creative diaspora tension between 'where you're from' and 'where you're at' (Gilroy 1991/92; Ang 1993:13) but also how diaspora and homeland relations and identities are mutually constituted. This entails the analysis of the diaspora subject-in-process caught up in transnational 'flows,' and an investigation of the politics of representation and recognition for Croats within *and* between those socio political and historical landscapes variously identified as home, homeland, and host country.

When viewed in light of the particularities that have shaped Toronto Croats' experiences over the years, the actions of the Croatian university students that were initially perplexing to me begin to make sense. These young people were not only responding to taunts and insults but also to the stories and personal histories they have carried with them – stories that they have learned from their families, their teachers at Croatian Sunday school and church, and their peers. Whether their actions were connected to the contexts of their upbringing, to strongly held personal and political commitments to Croatia and all that is Croatian, or simply to their baser instincts (i.e., to carp), what is clear is that the debate on identifications must be widened to include the possibility of all of the above, that is, one that foregrounds the politics of the everyday.

*Chapter 2*

# 'The War Made Me Croatian':
## *Independence, War, and Identity*

The above comment was made by a Canadian-born woman (age 35) during an interview in the spring of 1995. It is striking not because of its novelty. Many Toronto Croats have made similar proclamations. But, underlying this woman's defiantly patriotic tone was a sense of newly found commitment and urgency. Although neither she nor her family had suffered any personal losses during the Homeland War, it did awaken memories and feelings of suffering, victimization, and helplessness. One man I interviewed became very emotional during our discussion and stated that 'holocaust is happening before our eyes, and here we can do nothing. What can we do? Hitler then, Milošević today' (engineer, age 51, November 1993). How does war make one a Croat?

Toronto Croats are not unique in their connections to the homeland. Numerous parallels to specific dimensions of the experience of Toronto Croats can be found in cases of both new and well-settled diaspora communities for whom war or other crises have been central – consider, for example, non-resident Indians (Rai 1995, Appadurai 1993; Shukla 2003), Jews (Jacobson 1995; Sheffer 1986; Shain 2000), Sikhs (van der Veer 1995; Axel 2001; Dusenbery 1997 Barrier and Dusenbery 1989, Irish (Akenson 1993), Vietnamese (Bousquet 1991), Macedonians (Danforth 1995), and Greeks (Constas and Platias 1993). Croats are also not alone in experiencing trauma, anguish, and/or exhilaration in times of homeland crisis such as war, genocide, and oppression. The experiences of Tamil, Jewish, Sikh, Somali, Iraqi, and other diaspora communities in Canada are testimony to what, for many originating in war-torn regions, is often a daily fact of life. Although united in their concern for their homelands, the degree of their involvement and the forms that their involvement may take, vary widely from fundraising and political lobbying to volunteering for local militias in the homeland. In this chapter and the next, these themes are explored in detail. Virtually all Toronto Croats have been affected in some way by events in the former Yugoslavia. Early on in my research, it became clear just how variable the impacts have been. On the one hand, there were efforts by various groups and institutions, including local churches, to partake in forging a sense of Croatian unity. Language became a tactical device for producing and reproducing a sense of Croatian identity.

A key argument of this book, however, is that Croat claims of unity and cooperation and of a singular Croatian identity are quickly to be challenged by the historical and political evidence. The veracity and accuracy of historical and other details gleaned from interviews and conversations with Toronto Croats, at times, conflict with historical and other sources of documentation. While this may not be unusual insofar as identity politics are concerned, these persistent inconsistencies and discrepancies point to the need to understand the contexts within which they arise. Internationally, diaspora Croats have endeavoured, most intensively since independence in 1991, to create discourses of commonality that would help meld a disparate population and project a favourable image to the world. What began to emerge in my interviews, however, was a pattern pointing to sometimes competing efforts to present or to disrupt particular images of both Toronto Croats and the events preceding and following Croatia's independence. My attention turned to how these images and sensibilities around Croatness (*Hrvatstvo)* were formulated, contested, or contained.

In a diaspora where differences of political opinion are routine, the question that comes to mind is: Did a particular political vision of Croatia and Croatness prevail after independence, and who was behind the shaping of such a vision(s)? That is, which aspects of the Croatian past and present were being explored, revised, and suppressed to this end, by whom, in what contexts, and to what effect? In this chapter, many of the factors that have shaped the emergence of the varying and divergent discourses of Croatian identity are examined, including language, memory, and relations between Toronto Croats and Toronto Serbs. A central theme is the significance of generation as a point around which such differences coalesce. Generation became a common ground for articulating and working through changes in the cultural and social life of Croats in Toronto – changes influenced mainly by the events in the former Yugoslavia.

For older first-generation Croats in Canada, the imagined Croatian homeland is shaped by a different set of experiences, memories, and desires than is the case for younger second-and third-generation Croats, whose sense of self and identity has perhaps been more strongly influenced by the Homeland War and its aftermath. These tensions have affected not only issues of identification for Toronto Croats, but between them and others from the former Yugoslavia, particularly Serbs. Because the wars in the former Yugoslavia thrust persons of Croatian descent into the spotlight, the issue of how not only Croatia but also the diaspora has been represented became the subject of debates and action in Toronto in the 1990s. The schisms and shifting allegiances that characterized Toronto Croats prior to the war have continued to shape the scope and nature of these debates, making impossible the emergence of a singular, shared, and endorsed perspective on Croatia and being Croat.

## Independence, War, and Their Effects

The period between 1992 and 1996 enabled, among other things, the proliferation of disparate and often contradictory knowledges about what it means to be Croat. Even at a time when the collective show of unity and peoplehood could have been expected to be at its peak – when Croats were at war – there were numerous indications that this was not the united community that Croats often professed it to be. Croatia's independence not only revitalized sense(s) of *Hrvatstvo*, but also created and/or exacerbated conflicting personal and political sentiments and loyalties. The sudden changes precipitated by the events of the early 1990s consumed the thoughts and actions of many Toronto Croats. An analysis of Toronto Croat responses to the war could not help but become intertwined in political discourses about the Croatian homeland. Predictably, political views dominated discussions and generated the most debate. Indeed, almost all of the Croats that I encountered seemed compelled to share their views on the political situation in Croatia and to tell me what they had done or planned to do to contribute to the war effort. Some sent money, others wanted to or, in fact, did volunteer for Croatian military or National Guard service.[1] When three young Toronto Croats from Mississauga volunteered to serve in Croatia, their story was even profiled in the *Toronto Star* ( 15 August 1991, A15).

The homeland became *the* dominant reference point overriding other grounds of identification for Toronto Croats in the 1990s. It also became the prism through which most expressions of Croatness were refracted, and its effects were ubiquitous. These were manifested in public forms of discourse, commemoration and celebration, allegiances and loyalties, and also through everyday practices and relations. This period, more than any other in their history, has affected the ways in which Toronto Croats see and represent themselves and, most importantly, relate to each other. Although Toronto Croats had always expressed the hope that some day Croatia would proclaim its independence, most were not psychologically or emotionally prepared for the consequences of this eventuality. As a result, the homeland became not only *the* imagined topos through which many Toronto Croats expressed their unity and purpose as a people but also, and significantly, it became a lightning rod for conflict and tensions concerning their relationships to the homeland and, more importantly, to each other.

At one level Croatia's independence has been a powerful catalyst for the revitalized self-image of Croats of all ages, backgrounds, or affiliations, regardless of the strength of their ties to the homeland. The international media began to notice Croats, and this resulted in a visibility that they had never had before. The sudden interest of the press in Canada in all things Croatian was fuelled by the violent conflict in the former Yugoslavia. With the advent of CNN around-the-clock international news coverage, audiences were continually exposed to graphic images of the brutality of the Homeland War. Reports of the destruction of Vukovar in the eastern part of Croatia and of Dubrovnik on the Adriatic coast (the latter, a popular tourist destination) in 1991 put Croatia on the map for many who had hither to been unfamiliar with the region. These scenes captured the imagination and the sympathy of many and helped Croats in their efforts to communicate the message that they were victims of Yugoslav/Serb aggression. While these images propelled the idea of a Croatian people and nation onto the world stage, there were, of course, concerns within the Croatian diaspora about the accuracy of media reportage. As a result, Toronto Croats increasingly came to rely on Croatian sources of media (e.g., radio and videos) and the Internet for up-to-date and more extensive information.

Croats were concerned not just with the accuracy of information about the war, but with how Croatness was being represented. As a result, Toronto Croats busily tried to project a positive image of Croats to non-Croats through the celebration of Croatian culture, a noble past, and the portrayal of idealized political and social values. The new context of an independent Croatia allowed for the emergence of positive public displays of ethnicity in Canada, including annual public celebrations such as, for example, Croatian Heritage Day (recently at Canada's Wonderland theme park north of Toronto). Croatia's independence made this not only possible but necessary; *possible* because independence provided the conditions for the freedom to express ethnic and nationalist sentiments without fear of potential repercussions for family back home, and *necessary* as a counter to what they felt was an unjustly negative image of Croatia and Croats. Toronto Croats reacted vociferously to accusations of Croats' Nazi tendencies and their alleged reputation as terrorists, and to what most Croats regard as smear tactics by Serbs both in Canada and in the former Yugoslavia.

It can be argued that the negative associations that Croats were exposed to were amplified by the Homeland War. Many Croats in Toronto expressed frustration with what they saw as flagrant exaggeration, exacerbated by an inordinate amount of media emphasis on several isolated incidents, however, these images endured and did not go unnoticed by a wide range of commentators, who reflected on the flowering of nationalist sentiments among diaspora Croats in the early 1990s. Even Benedict Anderson describes long distance nationalism with reference to Croats, 'as a probably menacing portent for the future' creating a serious but radically unaccountable politics often of the extremist kind (1994:327). Anderson goes on to proclaim that 'the malign role of the Croats not only in Germany but also in Australia and North America in financing and arming Franco [sic] Tudjman's breakaway state and pushing Germany and Austria into a fateful, premature recognition' (ibid). According to Croatian-American historian Ante Čuvalo (1989), however, Anglo-American writers have never been sympathetic to Croats and have always been critical of Croatian concerns. Croatian historian Ivo Banac also observes that the 'perceived barbarism of the Croats has been a greater source of misidentification' (1992b:9).

With the knowledge that they had an uphill public relations battle ahead of them, Toronto Croats organized aggressive information campaigns through the distribution of press releases and leaflets, the production and dissemination of videotapes and photos chronicling the war in Croatia, and lobbying activities to gain public and political support in Canada for Croatia. They raised awareness within and outside the community by organizing protests and rallies.

Figure 2.1. Protest in Ottawa organized by the Croatian-Canadian Information Congress (Toronto), 4 December 1991.

In their efforts to present a salubrious image of Croats to the world, diaspora Croats funded numerous publications highlighting their historical and cultural contributions to art and literature, but most of all defending the principles of freedom and democracy in Croatia. Members of various organizations such as the Toronto chapter of the University of Zagreb alumni association Alma Matris,[2] and the short-lived Croatian Canadian Information Congress (CCIC) also monitored Toronto-based newspapers for 'anti-Croatian bias' in their coverage of the war.[3] Letters to the editors of various Toronto daily newspapers were regularly submitted by members of these organizations, pointing out perceived biases and unbalanced reporting.[4] Newspapers such as the *Toronto Star* were filled with complaints about media bias and the defamation of Croatian character. Among the many submissions by Tor-

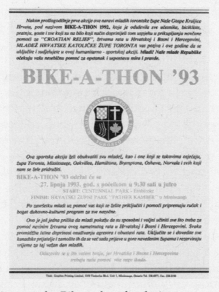

Figure 2.2. Advertisement for Bike-a-thon fundraiser.

onto Croats to the *Toronto Star*, Peter Granić criticized the constant links made between the government of Franjo Tuđman and the Ustaša: 'It is both a malicious and deliberate lie to suggest that the strong anti-fascist conviction of today's government is equivalent to that of the fascists of World War II' (2 September 1991 p. A12).

Toronto Croats undertook additional strategies both to counter negative stereotypes and to lobby the Canadian government to recognize the new Croatian state. Committees and organizations invited Croatian homeland politicians (primarily from the HDZ) to give speeches in Toronto. They organized aid drives and took part in programs and initiatives organized by national and international Croatian agencies. For example, young Toronto Croats participated in 'Task Force 1992' (since then an annual event), which was organized by the Croatian International Youth Corps to help rebuild war-torn areas in Croatia (e.g., hospital and school reconstruction). This form of 'volunteer tourism' (Wearing 2001) has been attractive to young Toronto Croats who want to 'make a difference' in the new homeland. Toronto Croats also sponsored several programs in Croatian studies that provided opportunities for youth to learn more about their heritage, especially in the context of a new Croatian independent state.

In addition to the high-profile lobbying activities there was a proliferation of small-scale and less visible grassroots activities by diaspora Croats. When the war in the former Yugoslavia broke out, frequent fundraising and relief efforts were organized by informal groups of Croats whose common base of affiliation was either formally or informally identified through local and/or regional, religious, recreational, and other ties. Members of local churches and regionally based clubs and associations initiated clothing drives and collections of food and medical supplies for the homeland. Church basements and clubs became makeshift depots for food, medicine, and goods to be transported to Croatia and to Bosnia and Hercegovina. Aside from direct financial and other support for their relatives in the homeland, individuals and families devoted a great deal of time and energy to various initiatives for the homeland generally.

Fundraising efforts and support from various postsecondary institutions resulted in a Chair in Croatian Studies at both York University and the University of Waterloo, in Ontario, course offerings in Croatian language and history at two universities in Toronto, and academic conferences and special sessions devoted to Croatian history and culture. For many, including younger second-and third-generation Toronto Croats, the family – the traditional locus of knowledge about the homeland – was supplemented by the cultural production of identity beyond the traditional local, often church-based *tambouritza* folk dance groups to include sponsored events and trips to the homeland, Croatian-themed events, the proliferation of Croatian art, radio, and television programming, and the Internet.

The establishment of political and relief organizations and associations such as Bedem Ljubavi (organized by a Croat women's group called Mothers for Peace),[5] Croatian Family Relief Fund, Croatian National Fund, Croatian International Youth Corps Canada, Toronto Croatian-Canadian Congress, as well as local representation of international organizations such as the Croatian World Congress, not only mobilized Toronto Croats but also provided avenues through which many of them could channel their energies and resources towards the homeland cause. Many of the Croats that I interviewed were members of boards or were otherwise active in these associations, which provided an outlet for publicly articulating and expressing Croatian nationalist sentiments and pride.

Overall, the Homeland War and its aftermath had the effect of leaving many Toronto Croats emotionally exhausted and financially

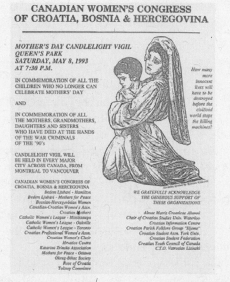

Figure 2.3. Advertisement for vigil in support of Croatian victims, 1993.

drained. One said: 'We are worn down' (volunteer, age 48, 14 September 1998). Nonetheless, these local efforts facilitated communication and cooperation among Toronto Croats from all walks of life and also offered new opportunities for those who had seldom or never actively participated in Croatian activities. Although many Croatian organizations sprang up in response to the war, interest and involvement in older, more established cultural and social organizations and clubs (e.g., Croatian Fraternal Union; see Čižmić 1994a) also increased, albeit temporarily for most.

The Croatian Homeland War and independence also had the effect of shaking the foundations of some long-established diaspora institutions and charitable organizations that, in the face of radically changed circumstances in the former Yugoslavia, had to quickly reassess the direction of their work and their goals. Most diaspora political party associations were the first to feel the effects, as their pre-independence mandates (primarily to oust communist rule in Croatia) soon became obsolete. Although some have continued to maintain a presence in Toronto, such as the Croatian Democratic Union (HDZ) and the Croatian Peasant Party (HSS), others such as the Canadian Croatian Information

Congress, have faded away. Their success at sustaining a sense of Croatness has been tempered by the everyday realities of Croatian identifications.

## The (Un) common Ground(s) of Identity

The tumultuous period in Croatia that began in 1990 fostered a plethora of opinions and views – some vitriolic, many tinged with emotion and some thoughtful assessments of Croatia's future. According to Pnina Werbner, 'the superior mobilizing, financial, and organizational capacity of diaspora ethnic nationalists determines which kind of transnational visions ultimately become hegemonic' (2000:7). But, given the history of diaspora Croats' politics and relations, it would be unrealistic to presume that consensus on issues relating to Croatia is possible. The Croatian case demonstrates that even in the event of long – sought-after homeland independence, competing versions emerge and rapidly become the subject of contestation making a hegemonic vision unlikely. Impressive displays of unity and commitment did not mask the difficulties in presenting a common front and defining an image acceptable and meaningful to Toronto Croats as a whole.

Evidence of the multiplicity of tensions among Toronto Croats became clear almost immediately, ironically at a time when they were still basking in the glow of the post-independence honeymoon. At one level, these difficulties were manifested in political differences of opinion concerning the conduct and policies of the HDZ government of Franjo Tuđman and differing and/or competing imaginings of the homeland. This is not surprising, given the historical complexity not only of Croatia as a territory and Croats as a people, but the divergent visions of Croatian nationhood. Indeed, before independence, this was the rule. It was only after independence that multiple versions and visions became problematic. At another, more symbolically charged level, there were conflicts over the ownership and stewardship of Croatian culture, history, and heritage. These were reflected in reactions to the efforts of often self-appointed interlocutors to restrict the discourse(s) of Croatian identity to those Croats they considered acceptable. It is in these contexts, namely, in articulating the public face of Croatia and Croatness, that contested meanings and images emerged.

The moral economy of identity representation revolving around attributes considered appropriate to the 'new Croat' was at the forefront of many of these discussions and debates, both formally (in local

Croatian newspapers and radio programs) and informally. Since independence, Croatian attempts to establish common grounds of identification have encountered obstacles stemming from differences that are as wide as they are deep. The Homeland War and independence provided Toronto Croats with a new context within which the terms and conditions of belonging were mobilized and expressed. These were variously defined in terms of the Croatian immigrant condition (configured in terms of suffering and sacrifice), nationalist consciousness, and the identification of the new/old homeland with local, regional, and historical particularities. More specifically, responses by Toronto Croats to Croatia's independence have been through the familiar spaces of church and clubs and the fault lines of class, generation, and regional origins, among others. Viewed together, these contexts provide numerous opportunities for playing out Croatness.

Although the Croatian Catholic Church in Canada has been unsuccessful in overcoming the 'regional and sociological differences within three generations of Croatian immigrants' (Rasporich 1982:204), it did assume a central role as a local and a transnational institution in fostering and reinforcing connections with the homeland, and it quickly became a central space for the Croatian politics of identity and desire. Croatian churches in Toronto (downtown, in the west end, and in Oakville and Mississauga) have, like most immigrant churches, had a long history of involvement with local Croats and, as a result, they became natural locations for the coalescing of Croats' efforts and opinions about many issues that affected their respective congregations and constituencies.

Croatian churches in Toronto became centres of political activity and debate during the war. Sunday sermons regularly dealt, at least in part, with the political situation in the homeland. The church newsletter, *Župni vjesnik* (Parish Messenger), frequently included excerpts from Croatian newspapers and carried features on the war. Croatian churches featured centrally during the period of war and independence, but other forms of diaspora Croat sociality, too, became contexts for asserting membership or belonging by those interested in or compelled to define an essential Croatian identity. With independence, language once again became a key vector of identification.

## *Jezik i Narod* – Language and Nation

A central barometer of interethnic relations in Toronto has been the issue of language Serbo-Croatian, Bosnian, Serbian, or Croatian (there

Figure 2.4. Illustrations from the Toronto church bulletin *Župni vjesnik*.
Reprinted with permission, *Župni vjesnik*.

are now dictionaries for each).[6] Debates over language have had a long
history in the region but, during the Homeland War and following the
establishment of the new state of Croatia, the language issue became
not only a rallying cry but also a lightning rod for debates over the distinctiveness of the Croatian language, and more importantly, heritage
and culture. Thus, the Illyrian (cultural–linguistic) movement of the
nineteenth century, spearheaded by Ljudevit Gaj (1809–1872), quickly
became the focus of contemporary claims to the autochthonous nature
of the Croatian language and culture (Holjevac 1999).[7]

Gaj's name was increasingly cited in discussions of the uniqueness
and historical pedigree of the Croatian language, not only among specialists and scholars but also among Croats in general. Knowledge of
Gaj's influence became a common reference point in discussions of the
Croatian language and culture among Toronto Croats, and from 1990
onwards the politics of affirming linguistic superiority became para-
mount.[8] In his analysis of language, ethnicity, and power in Eastern
Europe, George Schöpflin acknowledges this movement and points to
'the determined efforts of the Croatian authorities to make the Croatian language as different from Serbian as possible' (1996:8). Emily
Apter's insights are also appropriate here. She notes that 'when war is
at issue, it makes more sense to define it as a translation no-fly zone, an
area of border trouble where the lines dividing discrete languages are
muddy and disputatious; where linguistic separatism is enforced by
high surveillance missions' (2001:68).

The post-independence promotion of new language identities through language fragmentation (i.e., from Serbo-Croatian to Serbian, Croatian, or Bosnian) led to calls for a return to Croatian literary forms (*čavakian, kajkavian,* and *štovakian*) and other dialects. Despite their best efforts, Stallaerts and Laurent, authors of the *Historical Dictionary of the Republic of Croatia* (1995), refer to the 'rigid' or 'harsh' *ekavian* variants of the Serbian language, further conveying the politically tinged nature of the debate around language. There are numerous, often state-sponsored efforts to eliminate Serbian references, dialects, and terms in school textbooks and other publications (Baranović 1999; Kalogjera 2001; Katičić 2001; Katičić and Novak 1987), although there is general agreement among linguists that, aside from their alphabets (Serbian Cyrillic and Croatian Roman), the two languages are virtually indistinct (see, e.g., Kačić 1977). Nonetheless, the narcissism of minor differences became the stuff of tireless discussion and debate.

There has been criticism of revitalized Croatian national symbols, as well as grammatical changes that Sabrina Ramet argues has been done for 'the purpose of building differences with Serbians' (1996:209). Several Croatian dailies (such as the then state-run *Vjesnik*) regularly produced columns identifying out words that purportedly do not have Croatian origins. 'Prominent linguists are given special columns in the state-run papers to teach the public which words are considered Croatian and should be used and which words should be avoided as non-Croatian' (Sučić 1996:10). Language was a frequent target of the Croatian nationalist project.

This was the case in the diaspora, too. Croatian language programs were launched in several Ontario universities in the early 1990s. Toronto Croats funded the three-year appointment of the respected historian and linguist Dr Branko Franolić at York University. A Chair of Croatian Language and Literature, also funded with the support of the Toronto Croats, was established at the University of Waterloo, under the stewardship of linguist Dr Vinko Grubišić. Through our numerous discussions over the years, Dr Franolić has been an invaluable resource concerning the Croatian language and its history. Nonetheless, even Franolić, who has written extensively on the historical roots of literary Croatian (1988, 1994) publically acknowledged that 'if there is a political frontier, there is a language' (*Globe and Mail*, 19 June 1993, A20).

The Department of Slavic Studies at the University of Toronto had for years offered courses in Serbo-Croatian. In 1993, at the behest of Toronto Croats, the program ceased to call its courses Serbo-Croatian.

According to Christopher Barnes, then chair of the department, 'the Croatian community has been on the boil. We had a lot of calls from students of Croatian origin and their parents, complaining that their children were having to learn the Serbian version of the language as well' (*Globe and Mail*, 19 June, 1993, A20). Students now have the choice of taking either Serbian or Croatian language courses. Currently, funding for Croatian courses is supported through donations from the Croatian community.

These issues also arose when I took a course in Croatian at the University of Toronto in 1999. The majority of students were of Croatian ancestry, but some had difficulty reconciling their parents' regional dialects with the Croatian taught by the instructor. Differences in dialects and colloquialisms made agreement on proper Croatian terminology problematic at times. Students frequently corrected each other or teased each other on their accents, fluency, pronunciation, and regional origins.[9] The instructor, a recent immigrant from Split (on the Dalmatian coast), told me that she found it difficult to teach students whose language was 'compromised' by major differences in comprehension stemming not only from different language competencies, but different dialects. Here, too, evidence of diaspora–homeland differences became noticeable. Young Toronto Croats, who had learned Croatian from their parents and in Croatian heritage language classes, were often made to notice how Croatian, as a language form, differs aside from its regional variants. It is as much a symbol of unity as a marker of difference. In Croatia, as well, linguistic terms and colloquialisms from elsewhere have crept into the Croatian language, especially among young homeland Croats with whom these young Toronto Croats often socialize when they are in Croatia. The experience of young returnees to Croatia (discussed in Chapter 5) further illustrates the linguistic challenges they face.

The issue of language as a central barometer of culture, class, and region continues to be the source of consternation in Croatia and in the diaspora. On 27 February 2005, Croatian Prime Minister Ivo Sanader gave his support to a Croatian school spelling guide, a move that stirred up some public criticism because of its exclusion of commonly used Croatian terms that were suspected of having Serbian influences. To some critics I have spoken to in Croatia, the language is in danger of being vacuumed of all contaminating (read Serbian and Bosnian) references. But to Toronto Croats, criticism of these efforts is seldom found or expressed. Thus, debates in Croatia and in the diaspora on these and other issues pertaining to the Croatian past, present, and future do not complement one another. With independence has come less harmonization and increased contestation. A key place to observe this was in discussions within and between different generations of Toronto Croats.

## Generation: Differences in Time and Place

Whether revealed in debates about Croatian homeland politics or the issue of Croatian continuity, generation emerged as a key site of mobilization and debate during the early 1990s. My use of the term 'generation' here is qualified by the recognition that, although suggesting a group often united by age and experience, discrepancies in (regional) origins, dates of migration to Canada, and other social differences make efforts to consider generations as discrete entities problematic. Moreover, it is the *language* of generation that has become ever more central to the ways in which many Toronto Croats make sense of themselves in relation to their histories, both personal and political, and to expressions of sameness and difference.

Generation has typically been used in ethnic and immigration studies to periodize the settlement trajectories of immigrant populations and to affix specific characteristics to each (see, e.g. Hansen 1952). Following this logic historians of Croatian settlement in Canada have posited that early generations of immigrants were insular and never fully mastered the English language, were suspicious of non-Croats, and had modest goals for themselves and their children (Rasporich 1982; Bubrin 1994). Many were committed to the preservation of Croatian culture and heritage for succeeding generations through local organizations and programs, although they were not united in their politics.

During the war that followed Croatia's independence, however, the language of generation as a discursive strategy became central in providing the rhetorical tools necessary for reaffirming the essential stewardship role of older, often first-generation diaspora Croats maintaining cultural continuity and reinforcing original or ancestral links with the homeland. Generational discourses provided a language for chronicling – and often lamenting – changes in the cultural and social life of Toronto Croats through images of successive waves of immigrants and the gradual movement away or estrangement from the Croatian homeland. This kind of talk fed into the rationale of those committed to reinforcing the terms and conditions of Croatness, but not in any clear and consistent way. Generation became central to the discussion of politics and not just to the reproduction of social and cultural forms and ideals.

Over the years, older first-generation Toronto Croats developed ways of expressing themselves that reflect experiences of displacement, struggle, and accommodation. Their rich repository of narrative expression reveals the conditions that characterized their experiences. A retired contractor (age 71) explained: 'When I escaped from the Communists, I ended up in a DP [Displaced Persons] camp in Austria and I had nothing. I came to Canada and worked hard to build a life for myself here. I am thankful for the opportunities I got here that I never would have had at home' (21 November 1995). A woman (age 67) told me 'that life was really hard for women back home. I grew up in a small village in Zagorje and we couldn't make any decisions for ourselves – just work, work, work. Here things were tough and I worked hard, but things were better than back home' (17 October 1998).

The pattern that emerged in my interviewees' stories and recollections was revealed in themes of social inequality (i.e., gender and class), economic hardship, and/or political persecution in Yugoslavia, followed by emigration to Canada and the struggles they faced as immigrants in a new and sometimes hostile environment. Croatia and Bosnia and Hercegovina, as points of origin and of departure, were referred to in personal, nostalgic (and not always positive) terms through memories of places and relationships in the past.

The experiences and histories of Toronto Croats have had a profound effect on the ways in which memories and sentiments have combined to produce or reproduce varied images of homeland and of Croatian identity. Although, at one level, Croats have been united in their endorsement of homeland independence, nationalist ideology as understood by Croats does not correspond to any one body of discourse – a point made similarly, and forcefully, by Richard Handler (1988) in his study of Quebec nationalism. This is because the texture and significance of the Croatian nationalist ideal has been filtered through personal and collective memories and experiences, both at home and in the diaspora.

How people navigate the limits of what is possible both within and between their worlds is fundamental to understanding responses to the changes brought about before and after Croatia's independence. During my interviews, I was routinely lectured by first-generation older Croats, in particular, about Yugoslavia's history of suffering under the

Serb-dominated communist regime and Croatia's 'long,' but in reality putative, history of democracy, given centuries-long imperial rule in Croatia. As my relationships with Croats deepened, their responses and comments became more personal and more often emotional, punctuated with memories of home, *selo* (village), and/or region.

These personal histories not only provided some of the bases upon which difference among Croats were established but also a moral economy of sorts through which one's worth as a 'good' or 'real' Croat (*pravi Hrvat*) was assessed. Thus, it was in speaking about more recently arrived Croats in Canada (e.g., those who immigrated after 1969), with whom longer established Croats felt they shared little, that critical views reflecting deeply held views of Croatness were most often expressed. Much criticism was directed at the Croats who came to Canada during the late 1960s and early 1970s. The substance of opinions concerning these newcomers often reflected sentiments based on perceived or real disparities in class, status, education, and opportunity in Canada. What makes these observations interesting is that they were usually accompanied by negative evaluations of the commitment of newcomers to the newly independent Croatian homeland. The comments of Croats who had arrived in Canada much earlier conveyed the sense that they, the members of the older generation, are the true guardians of Croatian integrity and tradition and that they have maintained their commitment since before the time that it became, in the words of one pre–Second World War immigrant, 'fashionable to be patriotic' (4 June 1996). What the older generation of immigrants deemed to be patriotic posturings on the part of some of the newcomers was a source of vociferous criticism and a sore spot for long-established, first-generation Croats who had been consistently involved in Croatian life in Toronto over many years.

The major failing of these newer immigrants was seen to be the lack of depth and sincerity in their commitment to Croatia and Croatian values of community and collective responsibility. These recent immigrants had become, in the words of their older critics, 'bandwagon' Croats, 'reformed' Croats, or 'Croats of convenience.' The following quotes from first-generation Croats convey the tenor of many such criticisms expressed in the 1990s:

You see a professional advertisement in the Croatian newspaper or *Župni vjesnik* of one of these guys and wonder how committed they really are to Croatia. (Retired factory worker, age 67, 17 December 1994)

The sudden awakening of these new patriots is a joke. (Engineer, age 62, 13 March 1993).

Everyone all of a sudden is Croatian. (Homemaker, age 66, 15 December 1994).

One elderly, retired informant, who has lived in Canada for more than fifty years, opined: '*Now* they are proud Croatians. They come to speeches and dinners, give money and talk so much about *our* Croatia. But where were they three years ago?' (retired mechanic, 12 July 1992). Another Toronto Croat, a businessman (age 62) who came to Canada in 1951 after escaping from Yugoslavia, castigated these newcomers in the following terms: 'They called themselves 'Yugoslavs' before the Homeland War. They came to Canada not because they had to, like us. Compared with us who have been here for a long time, they had it good in Yugoslavia, especially if they were Communists' ( 10 October 1994).[10] Invariably, the issue of a 'communist mentality' crept into comments reflecting, according to some, a betrayal of Croatness and more significantly, the minimizing of often painful experiences of loss and suffering in Yugoslavia. Other bases for criticism were couched in terms of old-country regionalism and class, and the two frequently overlapped.

Croatia has a long regionalist tradition, influenced by such factors as its geography and history under various imperial regimes. Regional characterizations are powerful sources of affiliation or exclusion for Croats, in both the homeland and the diaspora. Evaluations of other Croats are often couched in terms of regionalism. Early Croat immigrants to Canada originated in the mostly poor, rural regions such as Dalmatia and Western Hercegovina, while Croats who came to Canada later on were often better educated and from urban centres such as Zagreb and Sarajevo. These stereotypical depictions are quite commonly expressed. One interviewee from Lika (Ličko-Senjska Županija), a poor region of central Croatia, stated that she is from the 'heart of the country, not the south, not coastal, but in the heart of it. It makes a difference. I experienced a regional prejudice. "Likans" we were called. It's sort of like "Newfies" here' (office administrator, age 55, 24 April 2000).[11]

Zagorci Croats from the agricultural region of Zagorje north of Zagreb and the birthplace of both Tito and Franjo Tuđman, where the *kajkavski* dialect is spoken, have been portrayed as quintessential country bumpkins, a stereotype that has persisted in the diaspora. Barbs about them were typical in the interviews, but the more urbane Croats from Zagreb were not immune, either. Remarks were consistently made about their 'snobbish' behaviour and their tendency to socialize only among themselves. One Toronto homemaker said: 'They flaunt their wealth, their degrees if they have them, and the privileges they have. It's disgusting' (age 54, Toronto, 2 June 2000). An engineer I interviewed, a member of the University of Zagreb alumni association, stated that the association does not have much to do with the older, 'less educated' population from the south (age 58, 10 October 1993). Another Toronto Croat stated that people from Šibenik, the Dalmatian port city he comes from, organize themselves better than do Croats from other regions. According to yet another, a businessman (age 60) who arrived in Canada in 1969, 'the rural element that came many years ago has opinions that are out of touch with the new reality' (17 May 1992). The clubs named after regions in Croatia, such as Klub Karlovac and Klub Zagorje, are further testimony to the sustained relevance of regional affiliations.

Croats who emigrated to Canada in the 1980s were also faulted by Croats who came to Canada earlier – for dissociating themselves from other Toronto Croats, for holding 'consumerist' values, even for being 'communist sympathizers.' Such frustration was compounded by the high-profile efforts of some of these newer immigrants to isolate themselves from others advocating Croatia's independence:

> For years we fought for Croatia, but now we are shut out of the process. (Retired bricklayer, age 68, 21 October 1992)

> We built the community, the churches, the parks; we built it all with our own sweat and they ignore us! (Retired tradesman, age 69, 16 September 1993)

> They have money and now they have friends in the new [Croatian] government, so they are showing off. (Accountant, age 65, 7 October 1993)

Such comments reflect of the omnipresence of class and regional divisions, which rather than being obscured by national pride and belonging, surfaced with some degree of regularity in the early 1990s and even later on, despite the war's end.

Generational tensions also reflect the different views of some Toronto Croats from an earlier time, who believed in socialism and hoped for an independent, but reformed socialist Croatia, and those of younger generations, who supported not only the newly found independence of Croatia but also the opening of the economy to an imagined Western style of capitalism. The views that earned considerable invective included such comments as: 'Yugoslavia just needed some fine tuning' (contractor, age 54, 17 April 1997) and 'A federation without domination was a good idea until the killing started' (engineer, age 49, 6 October 1994). These invited harsh criticism. I interviewed a musician, who said: 'Being a Yugoslav and a communist was the least line of resistance if you wanted to hold onto a good job' (age 38, 17 May 1996). Another interviewee, a dentist, stated: 'Where do you think I got my education, here? It didn't pay off there but it did here eventually' (dentist, age 48, 17 October 1995). While these comments are not representative, they typically infuriated earlier immigrants to Canada who felt that their efforts at working towards a Croatia free of socialism were being diminished. But as time passed, and the socialist era became more closely associated with the brutality of the Milošević regime, these more recent immigrants equivocated on the redeeming features of life in Yugoslavia. Generous assessments of the former Yugoslavia were less frequently expressed, at least publically.

Nonetheless, these relative newcomers provided their own unflattering evaluations of the factors that differentiated them from their immigrant predecessors in Canada. Educational and regional differences (i.e., earlier immigrants came from poor regions of Croatia and Bosnia and Hercegovina) topped the list and the suggestion that those who emigrated following the Second World War were irrevocably tainted by their wartime experiences and life during the early years of Tito's fledgling communist regime. One newer immigrant to Canada said: 'The issue of old borders is useless to discuss. The rural element is too dominant here' (engineer, age 52, 18 April 1994). Another, an accountant, stated: 'Croats here have no clue as to post-1945 Croatia' (age 49, 7 May 1993). The predominantly held view of Toronto Croats who had arrived since 1969 was that the older generations were preoccupied with anachronistic and simplistic political opinions.

## The New Generation(s): Toronto Croat Youth

The early 1990s did a lot to expose both the rifts and the bases of unity among Toronto Croats. Virtually everyone I encountered during this

period was united in their commitment to the preservation and celebration of Croatian cultural heritage. While discourses around generation have traditionally served to 'consolidate solidarity' (Fortier
2000:89) around issues of change and loss, the task of recuperation and
revitalization has been placed on the shoulders of younger generations
of Croats. Young second-and third-generation Croats were charged,
more than ever, with the responsibility of not only upholding Croatian
cultural traditions (through traditional forms of continuity such as the
pressure to marry a Croat) but also of being the agents of change – of
reinvigorating old traditions and injecting new energy and ideas
suited to the needs and challenges faced by the modern Croatian
nation state and its constituents abroad. Their responses to this challenge, of course, have varied considerably, even among those who
were actively engaged in Croatian activities through the church, as
well as cultural and political involvements. These descendants of earlier immigrants did, however, introduce different dynamics into the
analysis of Toronto Croat identifications.

Early on, I had encountered young Croatian university students in
Toronto passionately defending Croatia as their own. I became
intrigued with how and why some second- and third-generation Toronto Croatian youth were responding so strongly to the Croatian
Homeland War and independence, and others were not. Some established or joined Croat youth organizations and clubs such as those at
the University of Toronto and York University. Some travelled to
Croatia to contribute to the war effort and to 'rebuild Croatia.' While
some of these associations were openly political (most significantly
HDZ Youth), others made a point of dissociating themselves from
homeland politics. The opening statement of one such organization
(now disbanded) claimed that it was a 'volunteer, nonprofit organization with no political affiliations' (CCIC 1992:2). The reasons for this
position were clearly stated: 'There are many Croatian political factions
in Canada. They do not satisfy the needs of the Canadian Croatian
community as a whole' (1992:12). Nonetheless, the opinions and activities of members of the CCIC were almost exclusively political in orientation.[12] Their political position most closely reflected the mandate of
the HDZ.[13]

One of the main goals of the CCIC, as expressed in its mission statement, was to 'provide an accurate depiction of Croatian culture and
heritage to the Canadian public at large' (1992:12). In December 1992,
the CCIC organized an eight-member Croatian delegation comprised

mainly of Toronto youth to travel to Ottawa to lobby federal politicians to support Croatia and Bosnia and Hercegovina. The Liberal Party of Canada responded by convening a caucus roundtable discussion on 7 December. 'This lobby trip further demonstrated the necessity of a strong Croatian-Canadian group which could bring the problems and perspectives to Ottawa as Canadians. By maintaining a loud and clear voice as Canadians, the Croatian community in Canada can ensure that our government continues to view the situation there with a profound interest' (quoted in *Župni vjesnik*, 29 November 1992, no. 49, 6).

During the time I spent with members of the CCIC, they were consistently involved in lobbying, media monitoring, and organizing Croatia-focused events. In 1993 the CCIC took it upon itself to protest the company Hallmark Cards Canada for publishing a calendar entitled 'Faraway Places' in which Dubrovnik was depicted as a city in Yugoslavia. Hallmark promptly withdrew the calendar from their displays. Other initiatives included letters to UNICEF Canada, taking issue with their purchase of Serbian products and transporting them via convoy routes and distribution networks to Bosnia and Hercegovina. It also organized fundraisers, some of which I attended or was asked to participate in.

Although organizations like the CCIC and the Croatian Youth Council achieved some success in mobilizing support among their peers, some members expressed frustration at the parochial politics that frequently undermined their efforts. One young person, who is a clerical worker, said: 'Everyone thinks they are a politician' (age 23, 7 July 1994). Other clubs organized social activities such as monthly dances, skiing excursions, and pub nights at Croatian-run hangouts with names such as the DA Dog Café and the Cro's Nest Sports Pub and Grill. Young people who attended these events and meeting places were provided the opportunity to socialize with others and to enjoy Croatian music. At special events, Croatian patriotism was on full display, beginning with the Croatian national anthem. Nationalist sentiments, regardless of their degree of sophistication, were expressed by Croats as young as fifteen. Invariably, I would find groups of young people at these events discussing the political situation in Croatia, commenting on biased media coverage, on 'Serbian aggression' – the term invariably used to describe the actions of Serb forces – their plans to visit Croatia, or even young women fawning over the Croatian actor, Goran Višnić of the American television show *ER*.

These young, mostly second- and third-generation Toronto Croats, swept up by Croatian nationalist fervour, were actively and publicly discovering their primary loyalties. Their comments indicated that they were looking outward and elsewhere for their definitions of self. When I asked them if they identified themselves as Canadians or Croats (or both), most said that they were first and foremost Croat. They stated that neither were they like their parents' generation, 'fickle and moody,' 'naive,' and 'quarrelsome,' nor did they feel a strong attachment to a distinctly Canadian identity. For many young Canadian-born Croats, the factional political tendencies that have characterized Toronto Croats for generations were seen as destructive. They did not want to be saddled with what they saw as irrelevant hostilities, anachronistic political divisions, and stale notions of Croatian identity. One student (age 21) said to me: 'I am not as militant as my parents. For example, I don't think that the anthem should be played in church because, even though the church is the centre of the Croatian community, I feel that it is first and foremost a place of worship and not a political bandstand' (15 October 1999). Another young Toronto Croat explained: 'I would like to make it very clear that Croatians in Canada are hardly the way Croatians in Croatia are. Croatians here suffer, for the most part, from a horrible peasant mentality. It makes them very narrow-minded and stubborn, many to the point of fanaticism' (clinician, 26 April 1997). One young man (age 24) cleverly summed up his frustration with political factionalism with the following comment: 'My mom's liberal and my dad's an extreme right-winger. So you might say I'm a liberal-fascist!' (18 November 2000).

The primary socialization for these diaspora youth took place in the cross-currents of social fields that differed substantially from those of their parents. Over half of those whom I asked to reflect on how they identified affiliation and belonging mentioned multiculturalism as a key reference point, although not necessarily positively. Intergenerational differences on the issue of multiculturalism and its impact on perceptions of its role in identity claims soon became clear. Multiculturalism does not factor heavily into the politics of representation for older, first-generation Croats. Said one: 'Multiculturalism has not affected our Croatian identity – we have survived through our own choice to uphold our heritage with our own sweat and expense' (contractor, age 64, 14 December 1998). Another, a middle-aged woman, said: 'We came before there was such a thing, and we had to try to get people to respect us without any help, you know' (homemaker, age 55,

17 October 1994). Second- and third-generation Croats, however, have grown up with the apotheosis of multiculturalism through exposure to multicultural instruction in school and the ubiquitous efforts of all levels of government, Canadian media, and popular culture to disseminate the message of mutual tolerance and respect for interethnic, racial, and cultural differences.

Multiculturalism is claimed to be central to discussions of Canadian identity, but the responses of second-and third-generation Croat youth, did not all demonstrate an unqualified embrace of multicultural ideals. For approximately one-third of the Canadian-born interviewees who were less than thirty years of age, the experience of Croatia's independence has heightened their awareness of Canadian pluralist ideals, but it has not led to a complete endorsement of the goals or outcomes of multiculturalism. One Canadian-born woman, (age 25) stated that being 'Canadian is *not* a nationality' (emphasis mine, 28 March 1998). Another, a student, said that 'there is too much multiculturalism, so we're not connected to one another as Canadians' (4 October 1994). I found this particular comment interesting, because she had indicated that before the crisis leading up to the 1990 elections in Croatia she had not socialized with any Croats outside of her own family. Significantly, however, not only did Croatia's independence lead many Toronto Croats to embrace their Croatian heritage, it also led them to question and re-evaluate their own identity as Croats. Their comments reveal a range of sentiments on the relationship between belonging and identity. A young receptionist stated: 'Before Croatia became independent, I felt I was a Canadian but, you know, not really strongly. But since all this happened, and I saw how little Canadians know and care about us, I feel like I am not at home here' (age 22, 4 February 1999). One of the student interviewees said: 'I couldn't care less about Canada' (age 19, 16 October 1996). Another agreed, saying: 'Canada doesn't give two shits about its different cultures' (age 18, 2 November 1996). One student (age 22) explained himself like this: 'I'm a Croatian residing in Canada. I have my citizenship through birth but given the choice, I would not have become a Canadian. I plan on moving back to Croatia to spend the rest of my days there a year or two after I graduate' (Kitchener, 2 November 1996). This man eventually did move to Croatia, in 1999, married a Croatian woman, and is currently living in Zagreb. The case for hybridity and the positive, indeed celebratory, aspects of multiple diasporic identifications is therefore a weak one in the case of these young Croats. Croatia's newly found independence and the possibilities it affords Croats, young or old, who are yearning for connections to the homeland, can stimulate exclusivist, ethno-national sensibilities. Transnationalism, in the Croatian case, can lend itself to the reification of modernist categories of identity rather than their contestation, which according to Brian Axel 'creates a specificity that comes into tension with its own formalized generality' (2001:199).

Another important defining feature for young diaspora Croats is that they have not built up an inventory of memories, symbols, experiences, networks, and connections that are as intensive, extensive, or closely linked to the homeland as are those of their parents' generation. The conditions that have characterized life for different generations of Croatian immigrants to Canada inform the ways in which notions and experiences of Croatian belonging and identity have been thought through and articulated. The juxtaposition of narrative themes of displacement from Croatia, and survival and success in a sometimes hostile host nation, accentuates the sense of continuity and connection with the past for older immigrants. These are mediated by memories of what was left behind and experiences of disruption, as they have tried to reorient themselves to a new home, form new social networks, and learn to negotiate new realities in Canada. Their links to the homeland, however strong, are grounded in lived experience and do not involve the same engagement with Canadian ideals, as is the case with their children. This does not mean that first-generation Croatian immigrants' appreciation of these ideals is any less enthusiastic, rather that they have experienced, processed, and understood things differently than have their children, who have grown up in an environment where, among other things, multiculturalism is promoted as central to being Canadian.

Location and familiarity prove to be central to the ways in which Croatness has been conceived, practised, and expressed in the Toronto Croat diaspora. Since independence, the homeland as location and as relation (de Certeau 1984) has become *the* central axis for plotting out new terrains of belonging for Croats. But Croatia and Bosnia and Hercegovina are particular kinds of places for older generations and are constituted differently by them than by their descendants. Similarly, for young people, selective imaginings of Croatia emerge from experiences and expectations that are far different from those of their parents. For young Croats in the diaspora, nostalgia, while also a readily available and often shared resource upon which they may draw, is not based on the reservoir of personal histories and experiences – good and bad – of their parents in the homeland. Younger generations of Toronto Croats now identify with Croatia beyond sensibilities derived from regionalisms and emigration. Thus, while the terms of the narratives of older generations of Croats are personal and historical, those of the younger generations are collective and circumstantial. First-generation Croats often recall hardships or persecution; their children recall summer vacations in Croatia and festivities celebrating Croatian heritage in their local churches or community halls in Toronto. This is not to say, however, that the differences in generational experiences mean that younger Croats are not at times influenced by the personal and often emotional impact on their parents of the upheavals in Croatia. The pain of second- and third-generation Croats is palpable and personal. During the Homeland War, many mentioned being deeply affected by it. In 1996, one student made this explicit when he said: 'It's very hard to see my parents feel the way they do – they are distraught' (age 24, 19 October 1996).

An illustration of the connection the war inspired for second-and third-generation Croats is the film *Freedom from Despair*, directed by Brenda Brkušić, a young Croatian American. The film chronicles her father's flight from communist Yugoslavia to the United States in the 1950s and his subsequent involvement in lobbying on behalf of Croatia during the Homeland War. I attended a packed screening at a Croatian church in Toronto in May 2005. Throughout the film there are numerous references to the suffering, persecution, and survival of the Croatian people. In her comments after the screening, Brkušić made repeated references to endorsements of her film by the Jewish Anti-Defamation League. Their praise would not have been remarkable or require further elaboration were it not for the continuous debates over Croatia's role in the killing of Jews during the Second World War. The symbolic capital gained is undeniable.

Interviews in the film with selected members of the American Croatian diaspora, and with authors Michael McAdams and Jerry Blaskovich, placed Croatia firmly as the victim of communist and later Serb aggression. Overwhelmingly, *Freedom from Despair* asserts a Croatia of rich cultural heritage, heroism, and purity of purpose. The continuing struggle to represent the 'true voice of Croatian history' continued after the screening, when I was told by several people in attendance, including the film-maker herself, that Croatian President Stipe Mesić had been trying to ban the film's release on Croatian state-run televi-

Figure 2.5. Publicity poster for Brenda Brkušić's film *Freedom from Despair* (2004). Reprinted with permission of Brenda Brkušić.

sion, and this was cited as further evidence of the hostility of Croatia's political regime to voices in the Croatian diaspora. On 14 December 2005, Dennis Kucinich, a member of the U.S. Congress (and former Croatian presidential candidate in 2004), and a passionate advocate for Croatia, spoke to the House of Representatives about the obstructionist actions that HRT, the Croatian state television station, had taken against Brenda Brkušić. Kucinich alleged that the difficulties encountered by Brkušić in seeking the rights to film footage for the documentary signalled state interference: 'Croatia desires to be in NATO to protect itself from outside enemies. But who will protect Croatia from threats to freedom of expression inside the country?'

The most compelling impressions of Croatia for young Toronto

Croats are those that convey a strong, united, and independent nation full of hope, possibilities, and opportunity. The power of these impressions also serves a more immediate purpose in allowing young diaspora Croats to reclaim and invent connections to a prior home and provide them with a sense of status beyond what some take to be 'just another ethnic group in Canada.' As Croats they are members of a nation (*narod*), and one that has in the course of their young lives finally established itself as an independent state – they have been witnesses to a momentous historical event. Thus, they can claim roots and destinies, as well as international recognition, that extend beyond Canadian boundaries and identifications.

A focus on generation reveals differences deeply rooted in time and place for Croats. It also draws attention to the struggles to belong to a society – Canada – in which the value of citizens appears to be measured through the establishment and reinforcement of arbitrary categories of inclusion and exclusion. Generations of Toronto Croats have had first-hand experience with the shifting terrains of belonging in Toronto – belonging that is increasingly mediated by difference.

## Croat–Serb Relations in Toronto

'I would not even consider having a Serbian as a friend.'
(Student, age 20, 6 November 1996).

The wars in the former Yugoslavia have had an impact not only on Croats, but also on relations with other groups such as Serbs. These relations reveal complex and shifting sentiments, moving between antagonism, resentment, and efforts at rapprochement. In contrast to the many Croats, who throughout the 1990s voiced an open hostility towards all things Serbian, I also witnessed efforts by some Croats, often students, to establish friendship associations and networks of Serb, Croat, and Bosnian youth. These were mostly informal, but once established, news of their existence began to circulate. Sanja, a student and initiator of one such group, made her intentions clear to me: to set an example for a new generation of young people and a new politics free of interethnic and nationalistic strife. Although there have been efforts to establish interethnic groups of youth, these have been sporadic and are mostly interpersonal and informal.[14]

Debates over the distinctiveness of Croats and Serbs are not new, as the previous discussion on language has underscored. They have been fodder for discussion and worse for generations among historians, linguists, and philologists, not to mention Croats and Serbs themselves. What accounts for differences in relations between Croats and Serbs in the former Yugoslavia and in the diaspora are not only the complexities wrought by a history of conquest and power politics but also the contingencies of everyday life wherever they live. Croats and Serbs have coexisted for centuries in the territories of the former Yugoslavia; in Toronto, however, Croats have historically remained relatively isolated from Serbs, whether by coincidence or by choice.

Although some Yugoslav clubs and newspapers existed in Toronto proir to Croatian independence, these were not often frequented by Croats. Many first-generation Toronto Croats may have, and indeed reported to me that they often did live in close proximity to Serbs in Yugoslavia, particularly if they lived in urban areas. Yet most relied on their memories of the past. Once the Homeland War erupted, however many Toronto Croats, who had had little contact with Serbs in Toronto, had no difficulty demonizing Serbs as a whole. Most Toronto Croats who were interviewed conveyed their bitterness over Canadian 'inaction' concerning aid to Croatia during the war, but I quite often heard Croats blaming Canadian policy in the region on the fact that the wife of the prime minister at the time, Mila Mulroney, was of Serbian ancestry. One retired interviewee said: 'Her father is a Četnik' (age 70, 17 October 1992). Although much criticism of Serbs was confined to the actions of the Yugoslav regime and to Slobodan Milošević, it often spilled over into vitriol directed at Serbs more generally. The war had a strong impact on people's loyalties and allegiances, and on Croat–Serb relations in the diaspora, at a more personal level; this has largely escaped critical attention.

Early in 1991 Toronto Croat and Serb leaders expressed concern about the possibility of confrontations between their respective communities and violence in reaction to the hostilities in Croatia and Bosnia and Hercegovina. Joseph Gamulin, then president of the Croatian Metropolitan Toronto Council stated at the time: 'I hope it doesn't come to [violence] but I can't preclude it' (quoted in the *Toronto Star*, 9 May 1991, A18). Toronto Serbs and Croats bombarded local newspapers with letters to the editor – often in response to taunts and claims of misinformation aimed at each other – and staged protests at city hall, particularly in the early stages of the conflict. Vandals struck Serbian and Croatian community centres and churches.

There is some literature that focuses on this issue in conflict zones in the former Yugoslavia, notably Sarajevo, with discussions of the repatriation of Croatian Serbs to Croatia; little, however, is available on Croat–Serb relations in the diaspora communities, other than the study by Skrbiš of marriage preferences among Australian Croats (2001). In this study Skrbiš found a 'strongly' negative position in marriages with their nationalist antagonists (2001:139). My research on marriages preformed in several Croatian parishes in Toronto demonstrated that between 30 per cent and 40 per cent of them, before 1990 were marriages uniting a Croat with a Yugoslav. I was, however, unable to learn much about these mixed marriages. My efforts to solicit such information, between 1992 and 1996, were problematic because of the nature of the topic, but I was able to learn something of the motivations for changes in Croat–Serb relationships.

In the course my research during the first ten years of Croatia's independence, I encountered several instances of family discord, specifically in cases of Croat-Serb (and sometimes Croat–Bosnian Muslim) marriages. The sensitivity of these situations made it extremely difficult to contact and/or interview Croats who had personally experienced this. But many with whom I spoke, both during and after the Homeland War mentioned how family or social circles where Serbs had formerly been involved had changed significantly. Several interviewees mentioned the case of Vladimir Badanjak. He is a Toronto Croat who, since having lost his parents and brother during a Serb assault on the village of Lovas near Vukovar (which was heavily bombarded in 1991) where they lived, has had nothing to do with his Serb brother-in-law, who also lives in Toronto. This example was repeated in other interview contexts, but it seemed that on more than one occasion people were avoiding my questions about their own personal experiences. Although the history of Croat–Serb coexistence in Yugoslavia is a long and rich one, few interviewees discussed *this* past. One young Croat explained: 'Since I have family members on both sides [Serb and Croat] I had a very hard time dealing with other Croats. I have mixed emotions toward the Serbian part of my family. I was going through great emotional pain. When the war started I was absent from work for two weeks' (office assistant, age 32, who has been living in Canada since 1987; 18 May 1993).

The extent of acrimony that was expressed by Croats ranged from the ambivalent to the vitriolic, regardless of age or personal history or experience. One influential Toronto Croat said that 'Serbs are allergic to democracy' (business owner, age 58, 17 May 1994). Interpersonal relations between Croats and Serbs occasionally betrayed varying degrees of antipathy, much of which, I was told, was not in evidence before the war. A young Croatian consturction worker said: 'Serbs do one kind of construction work, Croats do another one, so that they are not forced to work together' (age 29, 18 October 2000). Speaking of Serbs, a married Croatian woman said: 'My husband doesn't trust them. We don't want them to come to our house anymore' (office administrator, age 50, 17 November 1999). Explained a young dental assistant: 'After independence Croats and Serbs have broke [sic] up: my father used to meet a Serbian family, but now they just say "'hi'"' (age 25, 16 October 2000). A young factory worker stated: 'None of them are good friends to me. They are all the same [*Oni su svi isti*]' (age 30, 1 November 2000). One Toronto Croatian returnee whom I interviewed in Zagreb, asserted that 'even there, [Toronto] Croats prefer to live in the west end and Serbs in the east end. Serbs don't like to communicate, so we had to confront them at soccer matches. It is easy to guess how these matches would always end. It is enough to say that security had to be so tight, as if *Hajduk* and *Zvezda* were playing' (contractor, age 28, 13 October 2003).[15] The most telling comments, however, came from young second- and third-generation Croats who had broken off friendships with Serbs. One teen told me that she had been under pressure from her parents to end her friendship with a Serb girlfriend.

Among the most persistent difficulties that was pointed out in my interviews with Croats was the pressure to take sides in the conflict. Neutrality was generally considered a liability by other Croats and, in some cases, not tolerated. I was informed that marriages between Serbs and Croats at times had become so strained that one of the spouses had returned to Croatia, Serbia, or Bosnia to join family back home. Although these kinds of tensions appear to have decreased significantly since the war ended in 1995, it is not necessarily because opinions have changed; rather, they have been placed on the back burner. From what I was able to determine, rapprochement between Serbs and Croats, particularly at the Croatian end, has not gained any significant momentum.

Toronto Croats were confronted with numerous challenges to and/ or affirmations of Croatness on many fronts – personal and emotional, collective and political, to name but a few. The images of Croat peoplehood conveyed to Toronto Croats by Croatian politicians, and those diaspora Croats who supported them during the Homeland War, were based largely on an essentialist discourse of nationalism, culture, and ethnicity, one that imbued many Croats with strong and newly found feelings of pride and a sense of importance and destiny. At a certain level, this form of expression gave diaspora Croats a pedigree as a legitimate nation, but at another, it failed to acknowledge the importance and complexity of identity apart from that informed by official nationalist ideology, and a partisan one at that – that of the Croatian Democratic Union (HDZ). This essentialist discourse did not and, perhaps could not, acknowledge the multistranded relationships that Croats sustain within, across, and between borders. In addition, because transnational links have intensified primarily in the forms of travel, communication, and commerce since independence, some Toronto Croats have been at odds not only with the supporters of the principles of the first Croatian government over official versions of developments back home but also within and between generations and their peers. The combination of these differences and the effects of Croatia's independence have impeded efforts by some, particularly those who have a stake in doing so, to craft a shared and unqualified sense of Croatian peoplehood.

As the Toronto Croats' case indicates, the proliferation of basic schemes of lived experiences does not allow for the recuperation or definition of a unified whole. Narratives connecting Toronto Croats to Croatia, which often revolve around an irredentist theme, do not best describe these diaspora Croats' relationships to the homeland. Although narratives of national renewal and Croatian pride have predominated, efforts to reduce the multiple expressions of Croatness to one commonly shared identity tended to introduce and, in some cases, exacerbate controversy and discord. It is important to note, however, that these internal tensions have not seriously dampened the enthusiasm of diaspora Croats for and their involvement in political efforts involving Croatia. The complexities undergirding diaspora sentiments, sensibilities, histories, and relationships do not lend themselves to one specific set of attitudes that would result in a single and monolithic Croat identity.

The discussion has thus far pointed directly to the combined effects of region, politics, class, and other factors on Toronto Croats, some minimized and others amplified as a result of events in the former Yugoslavia. In the next chapter, I will examine the effects of these dynamics on the changing political sensibilities, loyalties, and alliances of Toronto Croats – that is, on engaging the political in the diaspora.

# Chapter 3

# 'We Are Not Fascists!' – Toronto Croats and the Making of Croatia and Croats

The Homeland War in Croatia has had a profound effect on Toronto Croats' identifications, relations, desires, and representations. But the reverse also needs consideration. What impact have these diasporia dynamics on the emergence and development of the fledgling Croatian state? Many Croats in the diaspora were deeply affected by the tragedies that unfolded and took active roles in fundraising, lobbying, and raising awareness about Croatia. Croats in the United States, Germany, Australia, and other countries, many of whom had shared similar emigration and settlement challenges, all experienced similar feelings of guilt, loss, and pain, and a similar desire to help out in whatever ways they could (see, e.g., Kolar-Panov 1997; Skrbiš 1999).

The involvement of diaspora Croats in the homeland is not new and not merely a product of the war. Indeed, it can be argued that Toronto Croats' response to independence and the Homeland war is but the most recent and dramatic instalment in a history marked by continual diaspora–homeland engagement – familial, social, economic, and political – in varying degrees of intensity. Although Toronto Croats' involvement reached its peak with the flurry of political activity around Croatia's independence, this was preceded by a great deal of advocacy of independence that had intensified in the late 1980s. Key diaspora figures from Toronto and elsewhere in Ontario, including Gojko Šušak, Ante Beljo, Marin Sopta,[1] and Fra. Ljubo Krašić (head of the Hercegovinian Franciscan Order), were involved not only in Croatia's independence and as strong supporters of Franjo Tuđman but also, prior to the war, in fostering a strong unified national vision for Croatia.

These individuals were largely responsible for consolidating a network of Croatian heritage schools (Croatian Immigrant Schools of Australia, America, and Canada, HISAK) whose goals went beyond promoting the commitment to strengthen the Croatian language, culture, and folklore for youth in the diaspora.[2] HISAK was concerned not only with affairs in the diaspora. Indeed it was primarily intent on communicating a nationalist vision for Croatia and establishing lasting contact with the homeland through its 127 schools. According to Čiro Grubišić, HISAK representative in Croatia, 'these individuals were the most influential for setting the stage from abroad for what Croatia came to be' (Globus 2000, no.472:74). Grubišić was a secretary for the Croatian Heritage Foundation and later vice president of the executive council of the Croatian Democratic Union (HDZ), and also the brother of the Croatian-Canadian linguist, Vinko Grubišić. He has close ties to Bosnian Croats and eventually became Croatia's consul in Mostar, representing the Tuđman government. Numerous other Toronto Croats were involved in advocating, raising awareness, and lobbying on behalf of Croatia.

The crucial support of diaspora Croats for homeland independence was acknowledged in the June 1989 draft of the HDZ's basic program, which spoke of the importance of diaspora Croats. Diaspora Croat nationalists strongly promoted the HDZ, providing financial aid and (often passionate) moral backing to facilitate its growth and eventual electoral success. In February 1990, diaspora Croats from all over the world showed the degree of their support for the HDZ by attending the first party congress, in Zagreb. They launched an energetic and well-funded election campaign, spearheaded in large part by John Zdunić, a wealthy businessman from Toronto and leader of the HDZ's North American coordinating committee. As I point out later on in this chapter, some of the diaspora Croats who campaigned for Tuđman's bid for the presidency subsequently benefited not only in the genuine satisfaction of seeing him win but also through lucrative business contracts and high political posts for themselves.

What was it about Toronto Croats that placed them so centrally in the politics of Croatia's independence? By the time Croatia received international recognition as a state, Toronto Croats were, in one way or another, implicated in Croatia's political affairs. But while the HDZ defined the course of Croatian politics for the first ten years of independence, it did not have the unequivocal support of all Toronto Croats. While many Toronto Croats are proud of the role they played in championing the cause of independence, most published opinions and analyses emphasize the damaging influence on Croatian national politics of key players, portrayed as radical, right-wing, and corrupt Toronto Croats (see, e.g., Pusić 1997b; Hudelist 2000; Hockenos 2003). These assessments, are simplistic and in some cases impressionistic, preferring to focus on and generalize from the activities of certain personalities, such as the mercurial and ultra-nationalist Gojko Šušak, and overlooking the local particularities that undergird diaspora Croat bases of differentiation and compatibility, agreement and disagreement. My task is to provide a more nuanced picture of the nature of Toronto and homeland Croats' involvements in post-independence Croatian affairs, of those who were central to these efforts and their effects. The involvement of Toronto Croats has been driven in part by a desire to shape how Croatia and Croatness are to be represented, both among Croats but also outwardly to non-Croats in Canada and elsewhere, and this issue is central to an analysis of Croatian politics internationally.

It is difficult to speculate here on how and/or the degree to which wider social changes in Canada contributed specifically to Croats' self-perceptions. Nevertheless, the past century of a Croatian presence in Canada has shaped a shared history of belonging among Canadians of Croatian heritage, one variously marked by inclusion and exclusion. Changes in the rhetoric of belonging have kept pace with the ever-changing status of newcomers to Canada, and their impact on Croats is evident primarily in their political life in Canada. New forms of expression – cultural, political, and otherwise – over time, became increasingly possible without fear of upsetting Canadian authorities.

Croatian identity politics in Toronto have come to be expressed within a context of security and confidence in Croats' entitlements as Canadian citizens of Central or Eastern European origin. What has not changed substantially and, indeed, has been exacerbated since independence, is the internal dynamics of Toronto Croats' politics. New voices emerged during the early 1990s to put in question already unstable and dispersed bases of loyalty, identity, and affiliation. Political viewpoints were, and continue to be, articulated from an array of conflicting positions. The emergence of self-selected Croat elites at the centre of such debates has introduced new challenges into the struggle towards a Croatness suitable for the new Croatia and, more importantly, for the reconfiguration of political hierarchies and allegiances.

## The New Wave of Political Involvement in Homeland Affairs

The contexts within which particular diaspora Croats gained influence in Toronto in the late 1980s and early 1990s is directly related to Franjo Tuđman's efforts to curry favour with diaspora Croats. As soon as the HDZ was formed, Tuđman travelled to Canada and the United States to rally support for his party. The Croatian state under the HDZ was instrumental in creating and reinforcing formal channels with diaspora constituencies in much the same fashion as other national governments, for example, India (Van der Veer 1995a), Italy (Fortier 2000; Harney 1998), and Israel (Taras and Weinfeld 1993), in the Canadian case. These linkages intensified in the period that immediately preceded independence and the Homeland War.

Tuđman had established links with the Toronto Croats well before his rise to power in 1990. Indeed, financial and political support from diaspora Croats was decisive in his first electoral victory. His first trip to Toronto in 1987, hosted by a Toronto Croat, Zlatko Čaldarević, was undertaken for the purposes of raising his profile, raising money, and consultations with Toronto Croats. On this trip, he met with a variety of people spanning the political spectrum, including moderates from the Croatian Fraternal Union and radical nationalists such as Gojko Šušak. He delivered lectures at York University and the University of Toronto, on topics ranging from Stjepan Radić to his views on ethnicity and nationalism and Croatian destiny. During this time Tuđman began to associate more intimately with far-right Toronto Croation nationalists. Tuđman's reliance on Toronto Croats was evidenced in repeated visits to Toronto, one shortly after his election victory in 1990.

Čaldarević, a political moderate, stated: 'I agree, today's Croatia is as per the Norval agreement, but it won't stay that way for long.'[3] Summing up the assessment of several Toronto Croats whom I asked about this statement, Čaldarević's rationale was that the Norval group, widely associated with nationalist Hercegovinian Croats, wanted to take credit for its role in Croatia's independence.[4] A number of moderate Croats I spoke to in the years between 1992 and 1996, who were involved in Croatian politics both before and after independence, confirmed this sentiment. Several stated that they feel the process leading up to independence has been, in the words of one, 'hijacked by the radical agenda' of some Toronto Croats.

The controversial role of right-wing, nationalist diaspora Croats in independence and in Croatia's political and economic affairs since then has garnered the lion's share of media and academic attention. Journalists, commentators, and various others have reinforced these largely unflattering images of Croats. 'Serbs scoff when you say Tuđman should have atoned for Jasenovac. 'Are you crazy?' they say. His party was financed by Croatians abroad, in Toronto and Melbourne. And who were they? Old Ustashe' (Ignatieff 1994:34). Darko Hudelist, then a journalist for the respected Croatian political weekly *Globus*, and editor of *Feral Tribune*, wrote a thirteen–part series in 1999 and 2000 profiling Šušak and those Toronto Croats responsible for much of Tuđman's nationalist vision for Croatia.[5] These largely unsympathetic portrayals of diaspora Croats have been reflected in the opinions of Croat and non-Croat commentators alike (see, e.g., Pusić 1997a;[6] Anderson 1994).

Such negative coverage reverberated among Croats sensitive to public perceptions (in Canada) of Croats as extremists. Similarities with the negative pre-1990 coverage of diaspora Croats as 'terrorists' (based on several incendiary terrorist acts in the 1970s) are striking. As a result, many Croats in the diaspora have lamented that their stories, and the specific conditions that have shaped Toronto Croats' experiences, have been overshadowed by a tendency to treat all Croats as members of an internally homogeneous and indeed unsavoury (read as radical and right-wing) national group.

As I have already argued, the response among Toronto Croats to Croatia's independence has been a strong one, but it has also been diverse. To characterize it in terms of sweeping generalizations such as 'right wing,' is overly simplistic, even if the key players in Croatia's independence were quite conservative and nationalist. Support for Croatia came from many quarters, in terms of financial and political support, engagement with established and newly emerging political parties in the homeland, and work on behalf of institutions with a range of different purposes and ideological orientations.

Key figures were prominent in the events in Croatia as they unfolded; however, their involvement took many forms, including volunteering, but mostly lobbying and fundraising. These important efforts greatly understate the diversity of diaspora engagements in the Homeland War and the newly emerging Republic of Croatia. Toronto Croats campaigned to secure medical and food supplies, as well as local and international support for key political parties and figures in the homeland. A good many returned to Croatia to live, in some cases to assume government posts. For those individuals who had the resources, relations between the diaspora and the homeland shifted from being largely personal, family, and regionally based ties to more public, economically and politically based involvements in Croatia.

Many diaspora Croats are strong Croatian nationalists,[7] and as such they represent sentiments and qualities valued by Croatian nationalist elites in the homeland. Sekulić and Šporer (1997) observe that the national composition of the political elite in Croatia changed after independence: from an over-representation of Serbs to their disappearance, as an increasing number of diaspora Croat returnees appeared on the scene. In addition to their direct presence in holding political posts in Croatia, members of the Croatian diaspora were active in the political transformation of Croatia.

As discussed in Chapter 2, most Croats were infuriated by the lack of Canadian government support for an independent Croatia, and some resorted to taking matters into their own hands. Several Toronto Croats were involved in arms smuggling to Croatia during the Homeland War due to the arms embargo that had been imposed on Croatia. Anton Kikaš had been a resident of Mississauga for twenty-nine years and was head of the Canadian-Croatian Professional and Business Association and a man with links to Gojko Šušak, when he took it upon himself, as he reported at a press conference in Toronto, to personally deliver weapons to the poorly equipped Croatian forces (*Toronto Star*, 30 November 1991, A17). To this end, he had arranged for a shipment of nineteen tonnes of arms and ammunition valued at $1 million, to be delivered on a Uganda Airlines cargo plane in 1991, but the shipment was intercepted, and Kikaš was arrested by the Yugoslav People's Army (JNA). He was held for three months before being exchanged for Yugoslav army general Milan Aksentijević, in Velika Gorica, on the outskirts of Zagreb. Despite being illegal, Kikaš's efforts for Croatia were applauded by many diaspora Croats, including the Canadian historian Anthony Rasporich, who writes: 'Anton Kikaš, for example, provided vital support in resisting Serbian occupation of Croatian territory' (1999:385).[8] Kikaš was not alone.[9] Others, including young Toronto Croats, participated in raising funds and transporting equipment and sometimes even small weapons to Croatia.

Internationally, diaspora Croats as a whole played a central role in the success of the HDZ (Kearns 1996, Thompson 1992, 1994). According to Misha Glenny (1992:63), $4 million was raised by emigrant Croats (primarily in Canada, the United States, and Australia) towards the HDZ's electoral campaign in 1990. By 1992, Croats in Canada were the first diaspora group to have raised more than $1 million for this purpose. According to one of my Croats contacts, someone well connected with the HDZ who had moved to Zagreb from Toronto in 1996: 'We bankrolled the revolution.'

Several investigative reports in Croatian magazines such as *Globus* and *Nacional*, though, argue that much more money than reported was raised in the Croatian diaspora. They point to the siphoning off of millions of dollars of party funds by key government officials including Tuđman and Šušak. Over the years, numerous accusations of pilfering and corruption on the part of the HDZ and their diaspora supporters appeared in Croatian dailies such as the Split-based *Slobodna Dalmacija* and were made by various diaspora organizations such as the International Club of Croatian Emigrants, Returnees, and Investors from the Diaspora (discussed in greater length in Chapter 4).

It is common knowledge among Toronto Croats that the money raised in Toronto was instrumental in putting the HDZ in power in Croatia (see, e.g., Sopta (1994a:78) and Sunić (1999), both of whom have close ties to HDZ). According to Sunić, 'one must underline the crucial role of diaspora Croats and single out particularly massive help from American and Canadian Croats, who played an essential role in establishing, defending, and consolidating a new, independent, and democratic Croatia' (1999:48). Some went further and suggested that the involvement of Toronto Croats was decisive for Croatia's independence. One prominent Toronto Croat stated: 'If it was not for the diaspora, Croatia would not be independent today' (age 57, 7 December 2000). Another told me: 'We expatriates helped to save Croatia' (bank officer, age 40, Toronto, 7 November 2000).

The HDZ enjoyed a broad base of diaspora support primarily because it was seen as responsible for shepherding Croatia towards independence and, unlike the other Croatian political parties, it actively and effectively lobbied the diaspora Croats. In recognition of their vital political and financial support, the Croatian government incorporated its nationals abroad into both the Croatian national market and polity through a variety of measures such as supporting homeland associations (for Australian examples, see Kolar-Panov 1997, and Skrbiš 1995, 1999) and the extension of citizenship rights and voting privileges.[10] Diaspora Croats were also frequently featured in the state-supported press in Croatia.

In a 1999 published interview with Ruža Tomašić, then speaker of the Croatian Party of Right (HSP) in Dubrovnik (and a returnee from

Canada where she had lived for twenty-five years), entitled 'The Diaspora Should Not Be Treated Simply as Bag of Money,' she criticized the HDZ and Tuđman for their treatment of diaspora Croats solely as a source of personal financial support. A similar rebuke came from Simun Šito Ćorić, president of the Croatian World Congress. In early 2003, one newspaper paper, *Slobodna Dalmacija*, ran an eight-part series of articles on Croatian publications in the diaspora, called 'A Century of Croatian Emigrant Periodicals.' Croatia's politicians, particularly those from the HDZ, made frequent visits to Canadian cities with large Croatian populations (e.g., Vancouver and Toronto) to solicit both political and financial support, reinforcing this perception.

According to Tanner, 'Tudjman was not afraid of emigres and was tempted by their wallets' (1996:222). He personally recruited several key supporters from members of the diaspora who returned to live in Croatia after independence. By far the most influential such individual was Gojko Šušak, an Ottawa-based Croat originally from Hercegovina.[11] He was the most celebrated Croat expatriate (William Perry, then U.S. Secretary of Defense, gave a eulogy at his funeral), adept at tapping the hearts and purses of the tight-knit Hercegovinian diaspora. In Šušak, Tuđman had a direct line to the right-wing nationalist diaspora. Šušak was the subject of much attention internationally, and in Canada of feature articles such as one in the current affairs magazine *Saturday Night*, entitled 'Canadian Warlord' (Graham 1997). He was a prominent personality in Paul Hockenos's 2003 profile of Croat, Serb, and Albanian diaspora politics during the early 1990s. Šušak has been severely criticized in both Croatia and abroad as a profiteer, hard-line nationalist, anti-Serb, anti-Muslim, and promoter of a Greater Croatia (incorporating parts of Western Hercegovina). Hockenos observes that the 'radical emigres fit squarely into Tudjman's plans, a factor he astutely recognized in the 1980s. Tudjman not only relied on their money to finance his campaigns: he also relied on their extremism to help create the conditions for his rise to power' (2003:101).

The continued importance of diaspora support was evidenced in the steady stream of Croatian government officials who showed up to give keynote addresses at fundraisers in Toronto. This strategy has been widely used by leaders of countries that have large expatriate communities, who often 'actively [engage] in nation-building projects that [bind] transmigrants into the body politic of their states of origin' (Basch et al. 1994:267). Rather than focusing on the efforts of Croatia's politicians to gather support for their efforts in the homeland, I concentrate here on the varied responses of key players to these overtures to the diaspora and the broader responses of Toronto Croats.

## The Rise of Toronto Croat Elites

How elites come into being is critical in understanding not only their composition but also their impact and effects. In the case of Croats the emergence of a diaspora elite and its level of influence involved ongoing processes of in-group contestation. Since Croatia's independence, and indeed, even prior to that time, certain members of the diaspora have assumed a prominent role as self-appointed leaders and interlocutors for Toronto Croats by virtue of their education and/or financial and social status. In the late 1960s, large numbers of professionally trained Croats began to settle in Canada and to take on leadership roles in their ethnic communities in Toronto and elsewhere. This contingent consisted mostly of successful entrepreneurs, engineers, and church leaders, together with some academics, writers, and artists. Some of the most vocally nationalistic among them were from Herce-govina.[12] All in all, most of the elites were either of the generation who had emigrated to Canada immediately after the Second World War or the 'newcomers' who had done so during the 1960s and 1970s. A Croatian artist, who arrived in Toronto in 1980 and who did *not* consider himself part of the privileged few, sardonically referred to those who were successful as the 'drywall intelligentsia,' alluding to the success many Croats have had in the construction industry and related trades in Canada.

The impetus for redefining the essence of Croatian identity through the return to a nationally (rather than locally) defined 'tradition' was largely the result of a representation driven by these elites and the intelligentsia.[13] The endeavour was to create and/or convert particular diaspora discourses and images into constructs emblematic of Croatian nationhood – to promote a single Croatian identity. These business-men-philanthropists often founded, funded, staffed, and ran nationally oriented institutions, largely through the associational bonds (based on village, region, or common ethnic origin) provided by older groups. While the latter were initially enthusiastic, they soon became suspicious of the elite's motives.

Aesthetic and intellectual production of this sort are dependent on both philanthropic means and political motives. Toronto Croatian elites contributed a lot of the resources that sustain the spaces where

Croatian cultural producers publish and perform, and they therefore have sought public acknowledgment and the benefits that accrue from such recognition. This was the scenario that played out among Toronto Croats. The images the elites promoted championed Croatia as a Western European nation, one directly linking the identity of diaspora Croats to selected political and almost exclusively cultural and nationalist images of the homeland. Funding for Croatian events in and around Toronto and for travel (to Croatia and elsewhere) for Toronto Croatian politicos and dignitaries, as well as dance and musical troupes, was to a significant degree provided by Toronto Croat elites. The collective experiences that were publicly promoted were defined by specifically ethno-nationalist markers of Croatness.

The spate of iconographic and literary representations of Croatian heritage, inspired and funded by diaspora elites and the first post-independence Croatian government, is another manifestation of the efforts to direct discourses of Croatian identity. A steady stream of publications (in English and Croatian) has come out of Croatia and from Croatian diaspora presses in Canada, the United States, Australia, and elsewhere. Many were fully or partially financed by diaspora Croats. These publications chronicle the horrors of the war in Croatia and present treatises on Croatia's claim to statehood; they also articulate the new sense of nationhood through glossy, illustrated coffee-table books that contain ethnic and other maps that celebrate the cultural and historical heritage of Croatia. Such books have titles like *Our Lovely Croatia; Croatia and the Croatians* (Čuvalo et al. 1991) and *Two Thousand Years of Writing in Croatia* (Katičić and Novak 1987). The reclaiming and celebration of old conquests and heroes became commonplace, and more importantly, these were catapulted to new heights and presented as authentic symbols of the Croatian past.[14] Sabrina Ramet refers to the like as 'restored archaicisms' (1996:210). A primary motivation for the proliferation of such nationalist images and commemorative symbols has been to reinforce the sense of Croatia's 'triumph of nationalism' and the integrity of Croatia's past (Banac 1993:216).

A rich national past is important in the forging of a legitimate and viable identity in the present. Croatian historians have extensively chronicled the history of Croats, beginning with their migrations across the Carpathian Mountains in the seventh century. This history is marked by invasion and occupation by often hostile forces including the Magyars, Tartars, and Ottomans, and it culminates late in the turbulent twentieth century. Croatia's independence has generated a great deal of Croatian popular and scholarly research on the theme of Croatian history (*povijesan Hrvatska*). The Croatian World Congress (which claims to represent Croatians worldwide) has published an online book, entitled *The Croats: Fourteen Centuries of Perseverance* (Mijatović and Bekavac 2005). The production of Croatia as a place of origin through a definitive link to the past has been accomplished through the presentation of benchmark events and dates that coalesce into a story of suffering and perseverance. The year 925, for example, marks the beginning of the medieval Croatian kingdom ruled by Tomislav, but that soon after was taken over by foreigners. From then on, the history of Croatia is presented as one of oppression by a long succession of foreign imperialist rulers.

The recitation of historical milestones chronicling the suffering of the Croatian people is presented as a continuous progression of events leading up to the present. These historical markers have been effectively mobilized to generate support for homeland political causes. The 1945 Bleiburg Massacre, committed under Tito, is cited in generating criticism of what most diaspora Croats feel was a dictatorship. The 1971 Croatian Spring is regularly recalled as a heroic manifestation of sacrifice for the nationalist cause. Suffering is a major trope in Croatian histories, and it features centrally in Croatian publications. Croats capitalized on the opportunity brought about by the Homeland War to shift discourse away from negative portrayals of Croats (i.e., as Nazis and terrorists) to images of Croatia as a nation under siege with its citizens tormented by foreign oppressors. Titles (in English) such as *The Suffering of Dubrovnik* (Obradović 1992), *The Holocaust of Croatians* (Omrčanin 1986), and the *YU-Genocide: Bleiburg, Death Marches, UDBA* (Beljo 1995),[15] among others written by diaspora Croats, are readily available not only to diaspora Croats but also to interested others. The Torontonian Stan Granić has stated that Croats are commonly represented as 'humiliated and repressed by others' and as 'the victims of not only other national groups, but also of history' (1998:48). Rhetorical and discursive connections between historical events and the suffering endured by Croats have become the driving force behind post-independence productions of history.

These selective and often renovated images of Croatian history and the homeland, heavily politicized since independence, are not shared by all diaspora Croats. The freedom of the broader population of Toronto Croats to tell their own stories on their own terms has been compromised by the efforts of Toronto elites to highlight selective versions of the past. Historically, diaspora Croats have enjoyed sometimes vociferous debate on the fate of Croatia, and a multiplicity of visions and opinions prevailed. This was all challenged with the coming of independence and the push by elites to define the parameters of what constitutes Croatness. High-profile diaspora supporters of Tuđman's government, who had the financial and political resources to influence discourses and representations of Croats, took on the role of interlocutors for Toronto Croats. This aroused some suspicion and resentment among those who feel that their voices have not been heard and their experiences not considered relevant.

For many Toronto Croats I interviewed, whose identities and allegiances have been nurtured and negotiated in the diaspora, the efforts of elites to narrowly define the essence of Croatness – past, present, and future – in effect, has meant minimizing the importance of their personal or collective memories and experiences. The meaning of the ties they maintained in the past or present, locally and transnationally, has been challenged by elites, in favour of one, specific narrative of Croatian national unity, identity, and purpose. Although there are prominent moderate Toronto Croats who objected to this increasingly strident, right-leaning political vision championed by Tuđman's supporters in the diaspora, their views and priorities were soon eclipsed.

Croats have always maintained a strong and active interest in political developments back home, and as a result they have had their share of political associations that have ranged across the ideological spectrum from ultra-right to radical left, and they have often represented political parties or interests in Croatia. Political differences were an accepted part of the dynamics of diaspora Croatian communities before independence. But Toronto Croat elites, in particular those who supported the post-independence HDZ government, began to see such diversity of opinion as undermining their efforts to unify and represent all Toronto Croats, and more importantly, as encouraging negative public perceptions of Croatia and Croats. These elite-driven efforts have run into some resistance from Toronto Croats. The elite's attempts to establish their authority and control over selective narratives have been perceived by moderate Croats as acts of discursive violence, obliterating difference through stifling alternative views and expressions that had for generations been a source of vitality.

The opinions of many Toronto Croats differ from the assessments and/or expectations of the elites among them. Elite efforts were aimed at lifting discussion and debate out of the world of the everyday. In explaining the early support and/or lack of resistance to the efforts of elites to stake out the parameters of Croatness, comments similar to the following were heard: 'People respect them because of their money and they have influence' (contractor, age 28, 8 October 1993). While their elites were initially a source of prestige and pride, their close connections to the new ruling party and to Tuđman himself soon became the focus of concern. This was not necessarily a reflection of dissatisfaction with the political regime in Croatia (which began to surface further into Tuđman's mandate) but rather of dissatisfaction with the desires of elites to be accorded enhanced status among Toronto Croats and to promote their own particular ethno-nationalist vision. It became clear to those who were dissatisfied that, in the words of a Toronto Croat long active in local politics, 'only the rich or the well-connected can participate. They like the ego spotlight' (office manager, age 52, 25 March 1996). Another stated: 'They sold their souls to the devil, like Judas' blood money' (retired factory worker, age 72, 17 July 2003).

Emerging discontent was reflected in frustration that the new, well-placed diaspora Croats were being rewarded for their fundraising and other efforts while those who had worked long years towards independence and had expended considerable efforts through their local networks and associations, were being sidelined. I often heard derogatory comments about those who received plum political appointments in the new Croatian government (three from Ontario alone, including Ivica Mudrinić, minister of transportation and later director of the state-run television station HRT), the suggestion being that they were rewarded for their financial assistance and lobbying efforts. Some claimed that these elites were capitalizing on the situation in Croatia by seizing upon investment opportunities in the new Croatia and attempting to gain prestige both in Canada and Croatia for their role in raising awareness and funds for Croatian relief efforts.

Several prominent Croatian businessmen in Ontario initiated a variety of ambitious projects in partnership with the Croatian government to build housing and shopping complexes (e.g., Importanne Centar in Zagreb) in Croatia. Indeed, in the words of one of my interviewees, a successful businessman and major fundraiser: 'Tuđman is good for business.'[16] Toronto Croat entrepreneurs welcomed the new climate of privatization, one made especially attractive by Tuđman (evidenced in the Croatian Privatization Fund based in Croatia and headed by a former Toronto Croat). Diaspora Croats who were politically well-connected were able to purchase factories and businesses that were in financial trouble, at discount prices.[17] One Canadian entrepreneur I interviewed in 1999 bought a Croatian processing plant and began importing Croatian food products to Canada. He said that he had been approached to take on a position in the HDZ government but had declined the offer.

In the long run, the effectiveness of such investments is open to question, and they are not without problems. Some Croat entrepreneurs from Canada have had some success (e.g., in construction and tourism), but few (particularly large-scale) projects have actually transpired, because of concerns over the burdensome and inefficient Croatian bureaucracy, the troubled banking sector (a sizable part of which has been taken over by the Austrian and Italian banking industries), and the largely unfavourable investment climate that Canadian businessmen have encountered. Nonetheless, diaspora efforts to play a role in Croatia's economy, especially the post-independence privatization of national industries, has encouraged the development of investment consortiums. The Global Alliance of Croatian Investors, or Grupa 100, comprised of wealthy diaspora entrepreneurs was established in 2002. This association has members from Argentina, the United States, Australia, and Canada, and its executive vice president, John Zdunić, is from Toronto.

Reaction to these and other efforts to invest in Croatia, framed as a nationalist strategy, has not been unequivocally positive. According to an accountant (age 29) in Toronto: 'Croatian politicians and some corrupt businessmen divided them and misled them. There is a lot of competition, mistrust and rivalry going on' (7 April 1999). Toronto elites, for their part, have often chastised those critical of the HDZ government and its strategies to encourage investment (particularly from the diaspora) with accusations of meddling in the internal affairs of Croatia and, more importantly, of not being 'loyal Croatians' or being 'troublemakers.' The views of the critics have been often derided as obsolete or, in the words of one influential HDZ supporter, 'washed up.' These comments are as revealing of the existence of differing political points of view as of the socioeconomic gulf that separates some Croats from others. Many Toronto Croats, however, regardless of their politics, think that Tudman rewarded diaspora Croats for their financial and political support, which had the effect of encouraging cronyism at the highest levels.

Aside from sundry accusations and rumours concerning the personal histories or politics of Toronto Croat elites and the sincerity of their newly found allegiance to Croatia, vociferous criticism of the new regime itself was regularly expressed. When asked about their opinions of the new Croatian state, most interviewees began with an endorsement of the Croatian government (HDZ), but went on to argue that Croatian politicians were robbing Croatia of 'its true heritage'.

Toronto Croats were generally grateful for Tuđman's efforts to bring independence to Croatia but frustrated by the accusations of his supporters that disapproval of his leadership and party policies were akin to some sort of treason. They often countered with the claim that the government was stacked with communists from the old regime, a charge that continued to be made regarding the post-Tuđman coalition government (2000–3), specifically with regard to President Stjepan Mesić and Prime Minister Ivica Račan.

### Discontent with the Croatian Democratic Union, Discontent with Croatia

It is fair to say that the discontent of many with the Croatian Democratic Union (HDZ) government in Croatia was directed not only at its corruption and its economic policies. Increasing dissatisfaction has had to do with the failure of the Croatian government to satisfy the hopes and desires of the diaspora, exemplified by a number of decisions that were seen to have powerful symbolic implications in terms of how their interests were being represented. Among the HDZ's poor policy decisions that most deeply distressed some Toronto Croats was the plan, in the early 1990s, to eliminate Croatian regional names (e.g., Dalmatia was to be called 'Southern Croatia'). This offended mainly older, first-generation Toronto Croats for whom regional identities have been central reference points for memories and attachments and key sources of their social networks.[18] But regionalism (evidenced in the establishment of several regionally based political parties such as the Istrian Democratic Party and the Rijeka Democratic Alliance) was seen as a potential threat to the central authority of the Croatian state after Tuđman came to power. The renaming plan, seen by many as absurd, was reventually abandoned.

Nevertheless, changes to the historic Croatian coat of arms (the *šahovnica*) on the national flag incensed some Toronto Croats, who saw it as tampering with the authenticity of traditional symbols. The addition of a crown made up of five shields representing Croatia,

Dubrovnik, Dalmatia, Istria, and Slavonia inspired some Toronto Croats to refer to the flag as the 'zoo flag' because of the introduction of animals in the crest (five crowning shields, three of which sport animals – leopards, a goat, and a marten). The traditional insignia of lands now under Croatia's control have always signified Croatia's regional character. The sequence of colours in the 'chessboard' coat of arms (twenty-five alternating squares of red and white) also touched a raw nerve for those who felt that the official flag should accurately reflect the original (i.e., the earliest archaeological) version. Some expressed concerns about the symbolism of the colour of the top left hand square. This would appear to be a minor issue were if not for the fact that the only time that this square was white (versus red) was when the Ustaša were in power from 1941 to 1945. Most of the younger Croats with whom I spoke, some of them avid collectors of Croatian sports memorabilia, national soccer t-shirts, and baseball caps, were not overly concerned about questions regarding the 'authenticity' of the flag's design.

The seemingly ubiquitous corruption that characterized the Tuđman regime is perceived to have had an impact on how elections were run in diaspora communities. Diaspora Croats have been allowed to vote in Croatia's national elections. This has had the effect of strengthening diaspora Croats' political interest, commitment, and stake in the new state, at least for some. More than 2,500 Croats cast their votes in August 1992 at twenty-one polling stations across Canada. The sentiment among some was that the individuals and groups most tenaciously solicited to vote by Croatian government representatives and their diaspora supporters likely were supporters of Tuđman's HDZ. Toronto Croats, like diaspora Croats elsewhere, have overwhelmingly voted for the HDZ since 1992. Perhaps not surprisingly then, most if not all diaspora representatives elected to the Croatian Sabor were members of the HDZ. The political role of Toronto Croats, according to a dental assistant I interviewed, was thus reduced to that of 'pep team for the HDZ' (17 March 1995).[19]

The introduction in 1994 of the Kuna as Croatia's official currency, which incidentally, has the same name as the money used by Croatia's Ustaša collaborationist government during the Second World War, and the resurrection of other symbols of Croatia's Ustaša past as contemporary national symbols, has caused some consternation, particularly among those concerned about Croatia's Nazi taint, and the rehabilitated status Tuđman accorded the Ustaša. Comments made repeatedly by Tuđman, in both his speeches and in his publications, in essence relativized the genocidal aspects of the Ustaša, as part of the normal progress of war and of the process of ethno-national homogenization, and thereby freed Croatia it of its unique onus of responsibility (Tuđman 1996). Shortly after his 1990 electoral victory, Tuđman told supporters that he was grateful that he was married neither to a Serb nor a Jew (Greene, 6 January 2000). The Croatian-American writer Anto Knežević's book, *An Analysis of Serbian Propaganda* (1992), laments anti-Croatian bias and chastises critics (such as Robert Kaplan and writers for the *Jerusalem Post)* who have accused Tuđman of anti-Semitism.

Additional examples of the promotion of controversial historical figures and symbols includes the central position accorded to the political theory of the nineteenth-century founder of the Croatian right-of-centre Party of Right (HSP), Anté Starčević. Some have argued that his theory is the mirror image of the expansionist and racist Greater Serbia to which ultra-nationalist Serbs adhere. Others worry about the relationship of his ideas to the ideological foundations of both the Second World War fascist Ustaša government *and* to those of the HDZ-led Croatian government of 1991 to 1999. An enduring symbol of Croatia's struggle for statehood, Starčević believed that 'there could be no Slovene or Serb peoples in Croatia because their existence could only be expressed in a right to a separate territory' (Banac 1984:16).

The public relations nightmare brought about by some of the HDZ government's policy decisions – later to be followed by lack of cooperation with the U.N. International Criminal Tribunal for the former Yugoslavia – exacerbated the difficulties many Toronto Croats have felt in trying to convey a more enlightened image of their ethnic past and present. It is not surprising that some Toronto Croats have found some of the new state's image management strategies problematic and that they feel these are a direct assault on the images and symbols that have held such importance for them over the years.

Some argue that the hastily orchestrated efforts towards nation-building symbolism are simply symptomatic of growing pains in the fledgling democracy. But others have not been so forgiving. Regardless of their political points of view, Toronto Croats have made it very clear to me that they do not want their newly found national identity to be associated with fascism, especially given the efforts of Serbs both in the former Yugoslavia and in the diaspora to link present-day Croats to a Ustaša past. One man, a house painter, remarked: 'Too many people still believe we are Nazis' (14 December 1995). A computer technician

Figure 3.1. Ustaša symbols and accusations of Nazism. Top: Reprinted with permission of Sun Media Corporation. Bottom: Reprinted with permission of Torstar Syndication Services.

stated: 'Lately Croatian people identified with Ustašas, which is a terrible injustice to the Croatian people, as only 5% supported the Pavelić government' (age 51, 18 November 1993). Reports in Toronto newspapers during the Homeland War, with such titles as 'Neo-Nazis deface church' (*Toronto Sun*, 26 December 1995, 7), referring to Ustaša symbols and slogans ('*U Cro Knin*') spray-painted on a Serbian Orthodox church in downtown Toronto, contributed to the frustration and anger over the persistence of these images. The Our Lady Queen of Croatia church in downtown Toronto was also vandalized with spray-painted swastikas on 26 April 1992.

## The Political Career(s) of John Šola

The preoccupation of many diaspora Croats with their image and the role of elites during the Homeland War is exemplified in the political career of John Šola. This Ontario provincial politician of Croatian descent provides an interesting example of the impact of homeland events on both local Croatian politics and the management of Croatians' public image in Toronto. In 1987, John Šola was elected as a Liberal member of the provincial parliament in Ontario. He was well known for his vocal support for a free and independent Croatia – so much so that a reporter for a local Mississauga weekly newspaper stated that 'voters in Mississauga East have elected a man who seems to think he's gone to Queen's Park [the Ontario legislature] to free his Croatian homeland' (*Mississauga News*, 13 September 1987, cited in Bubrin 1994:71). Šola enjoyed the financial and political support of Croats in both his Mississauga East constituency (which has a large Croat population) and the Toronto area at large. Šola was not the only Croatian politician in the area, but he did stand out. Vladimir Bubrin, in his analysis of Croatian involvement in Canadian politics, states: 'In most cases, a candidate's Croatian ethnicity was an incidental biographical detail that did not play a role in his or her candidacy' (1994: 73).[20]

When I interviewed him in his office at the Ontario legislature, in 1993, Šola was emphatic that his political position and duties as a Liberal MPP were separate from his activities and views regarding the war in Croatia. However, during the war, Šola was involved and highly visible in Toronto Croats' efforts for the homeland. He was present at many Croatian functions and fundraisers in his capacity not only as provincial legislative representative for his Ontario constituency but also as a Croatian nationalist. At one of the rallies at the Norval Croatian Centre that I attended in late 1992, Šola was seated at the head table with several prominent members of the newly elected HDZ government.

Šola first ran into trouble in December 1991 for his comments about the war in Croatia when he stated, on the Canadian Broadcasting Corporation's current affairs television program *The Fifth Estate*: 'I don't think I'd be able to live next door to a Serb.' This remark provoked outrage from the Serb community, some of whose members were living in his riding. Crowds of Serbs shouting 'Šola resign' were heard at the provincial legislature. He was subsequently ousted from the Ontario Liberal caucus because of such remarks and what some critics called crude nationalist invective. But Šola was undeterred. He continued to make controversial statements, including those in a videotaped speech to Croatian students at York University in 1993, where he asserted that Serbian Canadians had shown that 'they support ethnic cleansing, that they support mass rape, that they support mass murder.'

Šola sat out as an independent until 1995, but lost his nomination bid for re-election. A headline in the *Toronto Star* read: 'Ethnic Loyalties Taint Election' (DiManno 1995:A6). A supporter of another candidate in the 1995 provincial election was quoted as saying: 'You can't get anywhere near the [Liberal] association executive [in Mississauga East] unless you are Croatian.' After his defeat, Šola left provincial politics and was appointed Consul General of the Republic of Croatia in Chicago. He now goes by his Croatian name, Domagoj Sladojević Šola, has returned to Toronto, and continues to be involved in the political and social life of the Croatian diaspora.

Toronto Croats I spoke to about these incidents have mixed reactions to Šola's displays of ethno-national partisanship. This reflects both their concerns with the role of elites in shaping public representations of the Croatian diaspora and their ambivalent relationship to Serbs in both Croatia and Canada. On the one hand, they believe that Šola did not exercise good judgment in making his feelings about Serbs public, particularly given his political position. On the other, almost all of them were pleased that he had been 'courageous' enough to put his opinion on public record. Šola's derogatory comments about Serbs gave voice to some fundamental emotions experienced by diaspora Croats during this difficult period. To simply interpret negativity towards Serbs as a reflection of deeply held anti-Serb sentiments would be not only an oversimplification of Croat–Serb relations but also underestimation of the effects of the war in the homeland on these diasporas.

Toronto Croat elites have played a major role in homeland affairs, specifically in helping to shape politics in Croatia in the 1990s. Observers of their participation placed particular emphasis on the more extreme interventions of these elites, and consequently this perspective acquired a great deal of media attention as well. The banal nationalism (Billig 1995) of other Toronto Croats seldom makes the news.

Of significance are Toronto Croats' engagements with and largely negative reactions to the efforts of self-selected Croat elites to direct discourses around patriotism and Croatness (*Hrvatstvo*), and the cozy relationships of particular Toronto elites to Tuđman and the HDZ. The complexities of leadership among Toronto Croats have made many Toronto Croats ambivalent towards involvement in the politics of the homeland and towards the activities of Croatian politicians in their own constituencies in Toronto: witness the career of John Šola. That many feel they have been silenced by these elites speaks to the difficulties of essentializing diasporic histories, identifications, and multiple forms and expressions of experience and connectivity. It also speaks strongly to the politics of representation and recognition for Croats in Canada – an ongoing (historical) process of negotiation. I have tried to present a balanced picture of the involvement of Toronto Croats in their efforts and often silent, albeit steadfast, support for the new homeland.

A seldom broached yet increasingly important dimension of this process is the significance of negotiating identifications beyond local diasporic spaces. In the next chapter, I turn my attention to how relations between diaspora and homeland have changed over the course of the decade since Croatia achieved independence. The standards for gauging Toronto Croat identities are debated and worked through largely in the context of the diaspora within which they live, but diaspora and homeland Croats are directly implicated in one another's lives and imaginaries, and these are constituted in ways that reveal their interdependence, for better or for worse.

*Chapter 4*

# Ten Years Later: Siting Croatness and Home

'The romanticism of becoming a state is accomplished – now what?' This comment was made to me in 2002 by a Toronto Croat, and it exemplifies the mood and tone of many of the Croats with whom I spoke a decade after Croatia became an independent country. The urgency and anxiety felt by Toronto Croats was palpable during the early 1990s. But now Croats are experiencing the best and the worst that admission to the ranks of statehood offers, not least among which is coming to terms with the changes in their legal, political, economic, and social status and circumstances. Amid these new Croatian realities hover issues of identity and questions of representation, of Croatness (*Hrvatstvo*). For generations, the centrepoint of most Croatian discourse was suffering and oppression, often paired with the dream of a Croatian state. Now that independence has been realized, has this changed, and if it has – how and for whom?

A central finding of this book is that tension and ambivalence continue to characterize relations not only among and between Toronto Croats but also between Toronto and homeland Croats. Since independence, Croats both at home and abroad have witnessed or participated in Croatian nation-building efforts and their impact on the conditions of everyday life in Croatia and on the, increasingly intense, relationships between diaspora and homeland Croats. My focus on diaspora–homeland relations stems from the observation that debates about the standards for assessing Croatian identity (Croatness) are informed by the realities of life for Croats where they live and by the connections between these realities. The principles and practices that guide everyday life for Croats, be that in Toronto, Croatia, Bosnia and Hercegovina, or elsewhere, both nourish and impinge on each other.

In understanding this interdependence we should note the sheer number of homeland Croats who have relatives living and working abroad: there are 4.5 million diaspora, which is about half the number of all Croats worldwide, and a multiplicity of entanglements character- ize their relations with the homeland. As already demonstrated, Tor- onto Croats were very actively involved in the cause of Croatia's independence in the early 1990s. Through fundraising and lobbying, volunteering for both the military and rebuilding efforts, Croats' social and symbolic sensibilities about themselves as a nation and as individ- uals were reinvigorated. Variously attuned to homeland affairs, Tor- onto Croats have had to adjust to the changed reality of an independent Crotia and the effects of this change on their life in Tor- onto. There has been a significant gearing down of wartime relief and fundraising initiatives directed at the homeland, and the direction and mandates of Toronto's Croatian organizations have changed somewhat to reflect major shifts in post-independence Croatia's priorities. The Canadian-Croatian Congress, founded in 1993, has incorporated some of the smaller Croatian organizations. Its original goals were to work towards Croatian independence through relief efforts and aid to Croats displaced by the Homeland War; its mandate now is mainly to help Croats displaced in Croatia and Bosnia and Hercegovina to get back to their homes.[1] Some organizations have disbanded, but many offers still exist and are even thriving, particularly those involved with aspects of Croatian culture and heritage.

A most significant finding is the persistence and, in some cases, rein- vigoration of the extent to which ties are based on region of origin.[2] Associations still are named after specific regions in Croatia, for exam- ple, Klub Bosiljevo, Grupa Livno (Bosnia and Hercegovina), Klub Kar- lovac, Klub Medjimurje, and Klub Zagorje. These clubs focus primarily on charity work and social events; nevertheless, their names under- score the continued relevance of ties to locality and the reterritorializa- tion of identity that occurs in diaspora (Levitt, 2001; Appadurai, 1996c).

The reactions of Toronto Croats to the prevalence of regional affilia- tions stand out as a defining feature of Croatian societal arrangements, especially when compared with the perceived state of relations among Toronto Croats before 1990. One of my interviewees asserted that 'before we were all together, we were all Croatians. Now they separate each other; we have so many clubs, Hercegovci, Karlovčani, Livnjači, etc., where they meet each other. They don't want to work together' (homemaker, age 24, 21 September 2000). Another said: 'Before independence, the Croatian community was closer. But now we are divided by political parties and are also regionally separated. Today we are not Croatians but people from Bosnia-Hercegovina, from the heart of Croatia. All of them have different clubs, their own churches and parks and other meeting places' (mechanic, age 27, 7 December 2000). In a similar vein, one young man observed: 'We have so many different parties, and now we are not Croatian but Dalmatinci, Bosanci, Hercegovci, Istrijanci, and Zagorci' (construction worker, age 30, 16 September 2000).

This prevalence of regionalism that Toronto Croats identify is not necessarily looked upon favourably by them. Some see the irony in perpetuating regional ties, which often separate Croats, even after Croatian independence, which should have fostered Croatian unity. Others expressly lament what they claim was but the temporarily unifying effect of the Homeland War and independence on Toronto Croats. One young man said: 'There is also a difference in defining Croatians. During and after the war we were all the same – people from Croatia – but now again we differentiate between regions ... I mean people from Istra, like me, see ourselves as separate from the rest of Croats – we don't really belong to Croatia and we also don't belong to Italy' (dental assistant, age 35, 17 September 2000).

Although smaller in number than before independence, there are at present branches of four of Croatia's political parties; three of these were represented in Croatia's coalition government of 2000–3. Some interviewees mentioned the informal existence of up to an additional fifteen political parties, including one called 'United Canadian Croats.' Diaspora Croats have access to several political publications (*Oluja*, and until December 2004, *Iskra*), church bulletins (*Župni vjesnik*), radio programs including 'Sounds of Croatia' (*Zvuči Hrvatske*), and a wide variety of cultural and folklore organizations, as well as business and-professional associations. The vitality of these can be attributed to factors that reflect changes in homeland circumstances, in Toronto Croats, and in diaspora-homeland relations.

The ubiquitous nature of the Internet has had the effect of intensifying the frequency and quality of contact among Croats everywhere. This includes a digital communications system that allows worldwide reception of Croatia's television and radio programs, which is particularly attractive to older, often first-generation Croats. Internet sites, ranging from electronic bulletin billboards to chat rooms and groups to

Croatian online media are used extensively by younger Croats. Large numbers of diverse interactive and non-interactive Internet websites have been aimed at and or generated by diaspora Croats.[3] The prevalence and accessibility of electronic technologies permit diaspora Croats to relatively easily develop and maintain continuous contact with other Croats and to access information of interest to Croats. The Croatian World Congress (CWC), established in 1993, has endorses use of the Internet as an important communication and lobbying tool for diaspora Croats: 'The CWC firmly believes that the Internet is a solid base for lobbying and public relations.'

The significance of computer-mediated diaspora spaces can be seen in the politicized interpolation of homeland across geographical boundaries. In his analysis of Internet use by people living in Indian diasporas, Amit Rai remains sceptical of the 'liberatory practices of the Self' promised by these virtual spaces (1995:42). Rai examines their potential for not only democratization but also the propagation of reactionary politics. One important dimension of the enhanced communications capabilities is use of the Internet for disseminating the conservative politics of the Croatian homeland. Aside from numerous Croatian government-sponsored sites, there are radical right-wing websites and web logs that, while claiming only a small number of members, nevertheless record large numbers of visitors.[4]

The Internet reveals the entire range of Croats' opinions and positions, from right wing, nationalist (and often ethnic absolutist) to those of Croats working for peace and for human rights in Croatia (see Stubbs 1999). There are issue-oriented websites, some of them quite short-lived, such as one that was generated in Australia in response to President Tudman's efforts in 1996 to shut down the independent Radio 101 station in Zagreb because of its critical stance towards the HDZ (Croatian Democratic Union). There are cultural and historical websites, and many others that have links to the personal homepages of Croats internationally. Most of the websites that sprang up during the Homeland War are now unavailable, but many endure.

## Siting Croats

Croatia continues to be significant in the day-to-day lives and sensibilities of Toronto Croats. Most of those I interviewed maintained contact with and visit friends and family in Croatia and Bosnia and Hercegovina; they communicate regularly by phone and email, and they continue to send packages and remittances.[5] But, although networks fostered through the church, family, and community continue to be relevant, their attitudes concerning Croatia have changed since 1990. Enthusiasm for Croatia and all things Croatian peaked during and immediately after the Homeland War, but the past decade has seen a significant decline in involvement with and interest in the political fortunes of Croatia. Nonetheless, regardless of how well informed or interested they are in contemporary Croatian homeland affairs, diaspora Croats continue to have strong opinions about the newly independent Croatia and, most significantly, their relationship to it.

Criticism of the socialist-era Yugoslav political system, a diaspora pastime for decades, has now in its place criticism over the nature and pace of the transition from communism. Most, particularly first-generation, diaspora Croats, express disappointment with and/or dismay by what they see as political corruption and continued lack of effective democratic processes in Croatia. They are also concerned about what they interpret to be Croatia's 'poor image' internationally. John Peter Kraljić, president of the National Federation of Croatian Americans, has said that Croatia's negative image is jeopardizing its chances of gaining entry into NATO and the European Union: 'For example, Croatia's flag continues to be defined as based on the Ustasha's flag – indeed I have found four such references which have appeared in 2001 alone, including in such publications as the *Economist*' (2002:81). Croatia's government, in the eyes of its diaspora critics, has been inadequate in dealing with these issues.

What also emerged during the past decade and more is discord among diaspora Croats themselves, particularly as there are those who feel that key diaspora players have hijacked the political process in Croatia and in the diaspora, as well. The International Club of Croatian Emigrants, Returnees, and Investors from the Diaspora (since renamed the Croatian World Assembly, HSSD), founded in 2000 by Niko Šoljak, an engineer and businessman based in Poreč, Croatia, represents one such group of critics. Although some of its members belong to the Croatian World Congress, long seen as an arm of the HDZ, there is the feeling that these political connections have undermined the position of the Congress and alienated it from other diaspora constituencies, and from Croatia's coalition government of 2000–3. Šoljak maintains that 'the unscrupulous robberies of Croatian people has split the diaspora in two: those who stood up for the tajkuns [sic] and were a part of them and those who felt cheated' (2002:17). The group's Proposal 18 (May 2002), which was directed to the Croatian government, 'requests an accounting of all spent money that the Diaspora gave during the creation of the Republic of Croatia' (ibid.).

I met Mr Šoljak in Zagreb in October 2003, where he was making numerous public appearances and giving interviews to the press prior to the national election that November. The mandate of the HSSD, according to Šoljak, is to rebuild confidence in Croatia internationally, rehabilitate the image of diaspora Croats, and rejuvenate the relationship they have with the post-Tuđman Croatian homeland. HSSD membership is comprised primarily of diaspora Croats from Europe (i.e., Germany, Italy, and Switzerland) and returnees to Croatia. The grievances listed by the HSSD and its supporters include the corrupt process of privatization (facilitated in part by those diaspora Croats close to Tuđman), the collapse of Croatia's banking system, the perceived neglect of the political and economic health of the country, and the abandonment of diaspora Croats by the coalition government of Ivica Račan (which fell with the 2003 election). While advocating for a stronger relationship between diaspora Croats and Croatia itself – 'Diaspora belongs to Croatia, Croatia belongs to Diaspora' (2002:19) – the HSSD is also critical of diaspora involvement in homeland politics. 'We are explicitly against every party's activity in Diaspora because those are [sic] just a damage for Croatia and the Croatian people as a whole' (2002:20). Among the changes advocated by HSSD is the establishment of a ministry for the diaspora. The HSSD has a news magazine, entitled *Korijeni* (*Roots*). While the focus of this organization is squarely on the rapprochement of diaspora and homeland Croats – specifically through Croatian government initiatives – it can be seen that broad-based diaspora organizations are, at some level, at cross-purposes regarding their constituencies, priorities, and loyalties.

In their interviews with me, Toronto Croats have been emphatic in their criticism of homeland Croats. They are critical not only of the former Yugoslav political system and every one of the administrations post-independence, but also of homeland Croats *themselves*. The tenor of such criticism often reflects disappointment with what is frequently asserted to be the abrogation of responsibility for self-improvement as citizens of the new democratic state, explained by many as the product of years of living under socialist rule.

The prevalence of this attitude of reprobation deserves closer attention because homeland Croats have been uniquely positioned in the politics of Croatian identity by virtue of their newly found status as

members of the new Croatian nation state. Increased and more immediate contact between diaspora and homeland Croats meant, among
other things, opportunities to assess and re-evaluate not only Croats'
conceptions of one another, but also of their lives in relation to one
another's. Greater contact during this period of profound changes in
Croatia has meant more opportunities for homeland Croats to re-
examine their lives in the context of the possibilities afforded by the
collapse of communism. Appreciable numbers of homeland Croats
have emigrated since independence, or they are planning to emigrate,
to North America or Europe; these Croats are almost invariably unin-
terested in linking up with Croats already in the diaspora. Diaspora
Croats are seen in less than favourable terms by homeland Croats. Said
one, a mechanical engineer: 'They have nothing to offer me. I don't
want to get stuck with the old ideas. They don't know anything about
life in Croatia now' (Split, 10 October 2003). Croats emigrating from
Croatia are not inclined to seek the support or guidance of their settled
diaspora compatriots. Most new immigrants to Toronto that I spoke
with did not want to have much to do with Toronto Croats.

Like their predecessors in the early twentieth century, most of those
who leave Croatia these days do so because of poor economic prospects, and they are interested in seeking prosperity, security, and stability but devoid of any political involvement in the homeland – or in the
diaspora. The continuous stream of new immigrants from Croatia
often disrupts representations of Croatness that have been nurtured by
Toronto Croats over the generations, and the the views of homeland
Croats regarding diaspora Croats range from ambivalence to frustration and even disdain. To understand what sets these sentiments in
motion it is important to consider the contexts within which they
develop and are cultivated.

## Politics and Post-independence Croatia

Commenting on Croatian politics after independence, Christopher
Cviić (1996) has argued that Croatia amassed a large democratic defi-
cit, evidenced in violations of human rights, the suppression of freedom of the press, the expansion and, at times, abuse of constitutional
powers for the ruling HDZ, and Croatia's interventionist, and some
even say, imperialist policy regarding Bosnia and Hercegovina. Croatian government efforts to imagine the new Croatian nation have also,
of course, been influenced by the process and products of the Home-

land War. Franjo Tuđman fashioned himself as the father of Croatian independence and hoped that, despite the worsening economic conditions and the growing isolationist response of the West, he could sustain the fledgling state on an ethno-nationalist vision.[6]

The vision for the new Republic of Croatia under the HDZ blended ethno-nationalist rhetoric with principles of social authoritarianism centred around the discourse of traditional (Catholic) morality and the preservation of the Croatian nation from the dangers of cultural decline (see Uzelak 1998). The essence of Croatness was constructed as ethnically 'pure,' systematically eliminating references to the complex historical, sociocultural, and political conditions that, over the years, have marked the physical and conceptual terrain of Croatian identifications. Metaphors of nation, Catholicism, family, and the 'Croatian way' became the centrepieces of Croatian political and religious programs.[7] These and other exclusivist notions also invoked pathologized versions of all that was non-Croatian, constructing anyone falling outside these parameters as the Other. These positions are not the product of recent political incarnations but have a long historical legacy, for the role of the past in fashioning Croatia's present remains fundamental to discussions of Croatian nation-building. The place of the past in determining what is Croatness, and what is a Croat, is central to the Croatian politics of representation worldwide.

## The Past in Croatia's Present

'Like many present-day West European states, Croatia arose from the ruins of the Western Roman Empire' (Bilandčić 1991:16). So begin many contemporary renditions of Croatia's history – its territory, people, and language. The past defined in this way sets the terms and conditions for Croatian nationhood. Far from being sidelined by victorious testimonies of Croatia's long-awaited statehood, the tropes of suffering, repression, and victimization are reinvigorated in the service of political expediency and the rewriting of Croatian history as one of fighting incomprehensible odds to achieve independence and statehood. Independence has become the point from which historians can trace Croatian events back in time, all of them leading to the breakup of Yugoslavia and Croatia's freedom. Since independence, the issue of Croatian history has been in the sights of all those eager to present a definitively Croatian version of their own narrative, meaning one not tainted by a Yugoslav perspective. The results to date have been telling of more than just a concern with 'getting the story right.'

The past as a social and political force has been theorized by a multitude of scholars including historians, philosophers, and theologians (see, e.g., Maier 1988; Verdery 1991, 1999; Hobsbawm and Ranger 1983). Raymond Williams has argued that the past is 'an intentional selective version of a shaping past and a pre-shaped present' (1977:115), wherein the passage of time smooths out the wrinkles (Rushdie 1991:15). The perspective that resonates best with the Croatian (national) experience is one that focuses on the construction of the past in memory, fantasy, narrative, and myth.[8] Mythical, heroic, and uncritical, these histories convey particular images of Croatian history. Their targets are not only homeland Croats but diaspora Croats as well.

The new official version of the Croatian past demonstrates that the process of remembering also involves the politics of forgetting, or more to the point, of omission (Boyarin and Boyarin 1992; Drakulić 1992). Dark periods in Croatia's past, such as Croatia's role in the Axis regime during the Second World War, are scarcely mentioned by Croatian historians, and where they are discussed, the locus of responsibility for the period between 1941 and 1945 is often set elsewhere (see Bilandžić et al. 1991).[9]

The past, however it is represented, is an essential element in the negotiation of identities, both personal and political, and it is therefore a potential site of conflict and contestation. Among the many challenges that Croats are faced with is the process of coming to terms with their past, and a great deal of effort has been devoted to that end. Shortly after Croatian independence, state resources were targeted for projects celebrating Croatia's history through its folklore, language, and culture. The government of Croatia busily resurrected and renovated selected Croatian historical, political, and cultural events and traditions. This led to a plethora of government-sponsored publications, television programming, and other initiatives geared to commemorating selected aspects of Croatia's past. State-run Croatian television and radio also regularly broadcast programs featuring regional folklore, customs, and (Catholic) celebrations.

Croatia's history has insinuated itself into the service of the new Croatian state-building project, involving what Charles Maier has called the 'usable past' (1988). The combination of lachrymosity, heroism, and images of suffering, as depicted under the guises of tragedy and melodrama, have become part of the present in the dramatic presentation of history. Vlado Jaram's *Povijest Hrvata* (*A History of Croats*, 2004) is a typical example of this kind of history in its rendering of the Croatian national narrative. School textbooks present particular renditions of Croatia's past (Leček et al. 1999). In her content analysis of contemporary Croatian university textbooks, Maja Brkljačić identifies the grand narrative of Croatian history as 'one of the continuous fight for a nation state,' where 'all events are appraised as beneficial or harmful for the creation of the state' (2003:42).

The process of historical nation-building has been greeted with mixed reviews by Croats and non-Croats alike, both within and outside of Croatia. The controversial revitalization of Croatian national symbols, for example, some of them emblematic not only of the medieval Croatian state but also of the fascist Ustaša period have caused some consternation. The importation of hard-line nationalist sentiments replete with symbols and slogans of the NDH (Independent State of Croatia) serve only to further polarize Croatian Serbs and Croats. The state has been actively engaged in collective processes of amnesia that seek to erase both the history of Croatia's Ustaša as well as its history as part of Yugoslavia (see Rihtman-Auguštin 2004; Mirković 2000). One of the most telling examples of this is the continuing dispute between Croats and Serbs over estimates of how many perished at the Jasenovac concentration camp. During a speech at the Jasenovac site on 24 April 2005, Croatian Prime Minister Ivo Sanader called attention to the controversial nature of this issue: 'Attempts to bend the truth, both by reducing and exaggerating the number of victims, were and still are being used to serve solely political ends ... And therefore we need the complete truth about the number of victims – Serbs, Jews, Roma, Croatians, and others that were killed in Jasenovac. On behalf of the Croatian government, on this occasion also, and precisely in this place, I wish to express our determination to permanently promote and assist expert and scientifically based research on the committed crimes and the number of victims in the Jasenovac Ustasha camp' (http://www.vlada.hr).

One symptom of Croatian efforts to do what is necessary in the 'march towards modernity' (Hall 1993:356 ) includes what Pusić has called 'the revolution of the symbols' (1992: 256; see also Banac 1993). The iconography of the new Croatia reveals a heavy preoccupation with the resurrection and renaming of monuments and public places. Several main city squares in Zagreb have been renamed: Republic Square is now Trg Bana Jelačića,[10] and the Square of Victims of Fascism

(Trg Žrtava Fašizma) was renamed the Square of Great Croats (Trg Hrvatskih Velikana), the latter a move that, to some, indicated efforts to rehabilitate rather than to condemn the memory of the fascist Ustaša state (cf. Roksandić 1995:271).[11] The original name of the latter square was reinstated in February 2001 as a result of protests by many Croatians, including members of the small but active Jewish community in Zagreb (see Hoffman 2001; Ruth Bettelheim, Zagreb, personal communication, May 1999).

Efforts to commemorate certain and, in some cases, controversial figures in Croatian history continue. In June 2000, for example, a monument dedicated to an Ustaša commander, Jure Frančetić, was erected by Croatian Second World War veterans in the town of Slunj, near the city of Karlovac. When I visited Slunj in 2003, there were bouquets of flowers at the foot of the plague. Some Croats, however, fear that the iconography of the new Croatia communicates an image of Croatia as a dangerously nationalist or proto-fascist state. In 2004, in response to pressure to distance the HDZ from its past, the memorial plaque along with several others was removed by the authorities.

Adorno (1974 [1951]) warned that 'bad tradition' must be dealt with carefully. The question in the Croatian case is: What if 'bad traditions' (e.g., relics of Croatia's Ustaša past) are important in forging an ethnonational identity? This question quickly became a focus of debate among Croats both in and outside of Croatia. The motives of the Croatia's government were clear to many familiar with the history of the Balkans. Measures to reconfigure the state along singularly Croatian national lines were initially conceived to unequivocally dissociate Croatian identity politically, nationally, and culturally from the former, politically Serb-dominated Yugoslavia, and to establish a distinctly Croatian identity. They were also accompanied by initiatives aimed at shedding the Balkan image of Croats, for example, the vexatious sense of poverty, backwardness, and violence often conjured up by (Western) imagery associated with the term 'Balkan' – an image reinforced over the years by many Western scholars, politicians, journalists, and writers (Todorova 1997; see also Kaplan (1994) and West (1982) [1941]).

The transformation of the geographical appellation of Balkan into 'one of the most powerful pejorative designations in history' (Todorova 1997:7) has become the subject of intense scholarly debate (Bakić-Hayden 1995; Bakić-Hayden and Hayden 1992; Todorova 1997; Wolff 1994). It has been argued that strong parallels can be found between Said's notion of Orientalism (1978), where in colonial Africa the primitive Other is contrasted with the white Western Self,[12] and 'Balkanism' where the Balkans constitute the Other of (Western) Europe. According to Bulgarian historian Maria Todorova, the East–West dichotomy is cultural, not geographical: 'The Balkans have served as a repository of negative characteristics against which a positive and self-congratulatory image of the 'European' and the 'West' has been constructed' (1997:188; see also Glenny 1992; Bjelić and Savić 2002).

Croatian geopolitical rhetoric holds that Croatia is not a Balkan country but a Western, middle European (*Mitteleuropa*) one. Croatia's membership in Europe is consistently linked not only to the stewardship (or more accurately, domination) of the Austro-Hungarian Empire but to Croatia's role as a bulwark against Eastern Ottoman influences. Catholic religiosity, also associated with Western Europe, serves as a national identifier. Any suggestion to include Croatia in the cultural space of the Balkans is commonly received as an insult by Croats. Croatian nationalist leaders, who vehemently denounce any association with the appellation Balkan, have vigorously promoted an image of a new/old democratic, Western European, and Catholic state. What underlies this response is that there is 'always the lurking danger that the rest of Europe may forget about them – or worse – confuse them with the people to the east and south' (Tanner 1996:xi). The phrase, 'Croatia is a southeastern European country' (Čuvalo et al. 1991:20) is heard often in Croatia. According to many Croatian historians and chroniclers of Croatian heritage, including various diaspora associations such as the Croatian World Congress, Croats aligned themselves with Western European civilization centuries ago.[13]

Tremendous energies have been devoted (primarily on the part of the government, commercial sectors, and some intellectual circles) to represent Croatia as a Western European country in every sense of word:[14] 'Pick up any recent publication by the Croatian authorities, even a tourist brochure, and count the number of times such words as 'Western,' 'Catholic,' 'Central Europe' or even civilization appear. Or try dropping the word Balkan into a conversation with a Croat and wait for the inevitable protest: Croatia is not part of the Balkans, but part of the West' (Tanner 1996:xi). The process by which this national image-making project has been carried out reproduces, however, the same tendency to essentialize that has been used in the West to disparage or marginalize Croats as a Balkan people. Since 1990, these binaries have emerged as Serb or Bosnian/Croat, Serbian Orthodox or Moslem/Catholic, East/West, or uncivilized/civilized. Discussions in

Croatia concerning where Croatia stands in relation to the West are phrased by some in terms of who will remain inside or outside the developed Western world. Therefore, Huntington's controversial work, *The Clash of Civilizations and the Remaking of World Order* (1996) was received favourably by Croatian politicians and some scholars, including several of my Croatian colleagues, because Huntington places Croatia in the Western sphere of his civilizational hemispheric map.[15] Specifically, it has been cited as evidence that Croatia belongs in the Western European religious and cultural sphere.

Jockeying for position in the West is not just a Croatian fixation but also a regional one that predates the Homeland War. According to Slavoj Žižek (1991), Slovenes see themselves as part of Mitteleuropa, while they view Croats as Balkan people who involve themselves in irrational ethnic feuds. Bakić-Hayden (1995) refers to this Balkan differentiation as a symptom of 'nesting orientalisms.' So, for Croats, the crucial frontier is Serbia and Serbs – the difference between Serbian Orthodox collective spirit and Catholic 'civilization,' where the former cannot grasp the values of Western individualism. This assessment oversimplifies what is clearly a complex and ever-changing reality. Nevertheless, it resonates with some prevailing Croatian rhetorical tropes. For example, Croatian government rhetoric routinely suggests that Croatia is the last bastion of European civilization in the face of 'Oriental barbarism,' most recently configured as Islamic fundamentalism in the context of the 'War on Terror.'

Tourism, a burgeoning industry in Croatia, is a major site for the dissemination of this discourse. Croatia has been heavily marketed as a Mediterranean destination.[16] Tourist brochures map these emerging sensibilities, and also the strategies framing Croatia's past, present and future. One such publication (in both the Croatian and the English versions),[17] put out by the Croatian National Tourist Office, includes a fold-out map displaying the coastline of Croatia. In the background (horizon) of the left-hand leaf of this map (in the northerly direction of Western Europe) are the names of major cities in Western and Central Europe in relation to Croatia (Salzburg, Munich, Vienna, Venice), placing Croatia firmly in the cultural space of Western Europe; however, the right-hand leaf of the map (showing the southern region of Europe) displays no names of major Southeastern or Eastern European urban centres. This brochure, and others like it in Croatia, reinforces Benedict Anderson's (1991) three indices of 'imagined community,' one of which is the map. The desire to emulate the perceived essence of modern Europe (as the embodiment of 'civilization'[18]) is evidenced in constant references to the cosmopolitanism of Croatia's urban centres and lifestyles, its cultural and artistic heritage, and in the valorization of everything Western European. The push to (re)define Croatness invariably leads to the drive to specify the parameters of Croatian national character.

## What Is a Good Croat?

The space created by war and independence has meant, among other things, the infusion of a new vitality and creativity into the exploration of the new Croatia and the new Croat, and this is reflected in ubiquitous cultural displays and artistic performances, some avant garde and subversive,[19] and others, celebratory and traditionalist. The atmosphere has also generated efforts by some to articulate more strident and exclusivist pronouncements of Croatness, as evidenced in the frequent invocation of the highly charged question: What is a 'good Croat' or what are *pravi Hrvati* (real Croats)? Although in Croatia several key indicators are proffered, for example, by political and church leaders (e.g., patriotism, Catholic religiosity), the majority of Croatian opinions that I encountered point to a preoccupation with those characteristics that disqualified someone from being a 'good' Croat. Croats are not alone in this regard.

In her analysis of Basque nationalism, Heiberg argues that it is not sufficient to be a Basque but rather one must be a good Basque (1989). Croats who were not solidly behind efforts to re-imagine the new Croatian state in ways that valorized the Croatian past, as defined by the new state and the Homeland War, risk being variously referred to as 'unpatriotic,' 'un-Croatian,' 'Yugonostalgic,' 'Yugophiles,' 'Yugo-zombies,' or even as 'enemies of the state.' The most common public targets of these accusations are intellectuals and journalists (e.g., Ugrešić 1998; Drakulić 1993); however, this issue is on the minds of some of the Croats I interviewed in Croatia, if only in as much as they are personally affected. Most often this is expressed as having to think about the consequences of publicly or, in some cases, even privately, condemning nationalist discourses, particularly before 2000 (when the HDZ was voted out of office). A woman bank clerk in Dubrovnik recalled: 'A few months ago, I was having lunch with a few friends, and we were talking about the banks collapsing. My boss, who was passing by, snapped at us for criticizing the financial management of the country and being unpatriotic. Can you imagine!' (May 1998). A woman who has been teaching mathematics in the high school system in Zagreb, for more than twenty years, complained that the new principal of her school, whom she and her colleagues were convinced got her appointment through political connections, had been pressuring staff to emphasize Croatian cultural (read as nationalist) themes in the classroom. 'I wanted to tell her that my job is to teach them mathematics, not politics' (May 2000).[20]

The frustration voiced on numerous occasions concerns the collapsing of nationalism and patriotism and the problems this introduces for those who are patriotic (expressed in positive valuations, for example, love of the Croatian homeland), but not necessarily nationalistic (the belief in the superiority of Croats over their former Yugoslav neighbours).[21] The distinction between patriotism and nationalism, first pointed out by George Orwell in his 1945 essay 'Notes on Nationalism' (1968), and still the subject of scholarly debate, is an important one in the case of Croats and the former Yugoslavia more generally. As Walker Connor points out, 'events within what, until recently, was known as the Federal Republic of Yugoslavia certify that Albanian, Bosnian, Croatian, and Slovene nationalism has each proven itself far more potent than a Yugoslav patriotism' (1994:197). The same can be said of the republics that together constituted the former Soviet Union. But, while Connor focuses his attention on the power of nationalist over patriotic sentiments, positive valuation is invariably attributed to the latter, as reflected in qualities of tolerance, freedom, dignity, stability, and citizen rights. A Croat businessman interviewed in Zagreb said: 'I love Croatia, but not in the way Tuđman and his boys love the country' (age 48, 21 May 1998).

Despite efforts to re-imagine and reshape the new Croatian state, the ethno-national vision of Croatia is not universally shared by Croat's citizens, as had been anticipated. In Croatia, a lot of intellectual production and public attention has been focused on the emergence of the new post-socialist democratic state and efforts to create the conditions for civil society (Basom 1995–96; Cviić 1996; Grdešić 1996; Mojzes 1997; Pleština 1995). During and after the Homeland War, there was a massive presence of civil society organizations and non-governmental organizations (NGOs.) Massey et al. suggest that ethnic national sentiments, while prevalent in Croatia, have increasingly been coupled with views that are distinctly liberal; their overall findings point to the fact that 'the core of political liberalism ... is widespread and may grow, not at the expense but alongside current nationalist sentiments' (2003:76). President Sanader's frequent allusions to Croatia's commitment to membership in the European Union 'at all costs' is also symptomatic of the general, although not universal, consensus in Croatia around moving outside the orbit of traditional affiliations and political culture.

While since independence political discourses on Croatian identity have often valorized Croatian culture and heritage in the interest of promoting a distinctively Croatian national identity, there has also been a large body of vocal commentary, as well as research, from both within and outside the country criticizing the direction of political, economic, and social processes in Croatia.[22] This criticism focuses largely on the national policies and practices of Tuđman's autocratic, and according to most, corrupt political regime (Pusić 1992, 1997a, 1997b; Banac 1993; Uzelak 1998; Mežnarić 1992, 1996; Drakulić 1992, 1993; Kearns 1996; Katunarić 1996, 1999). Broad-based disapproval of the direction of Tuđman's vision and policies resulted in the demise of the HDZ regime in 2000, only for it to re-emerge in late 2003. Croats have been struggling not only to come to terms with the day-to-day uncertainties and difficulties that have become more commonplace in post-independence Croatia, but also with how to accommodate to the discursive power and practices of the new state.

Alongside the government-controlled media, there is a popular and often critical independent press running the political spectrum: *Jutarnji List* and *Globus*, both considered to be centre-left, are owned by Europa Press Holding (EPH, which is 50% owned by the German media company WAZ). *Feral Tribune* is in a class by itself as a feisty and satirical weekly magazine that has been consistently critical of Croatia's government, and harassed as a result by government authorities, particularly during the first decade of independence, while *Hrvatsko Slovo* is decidedly right wing in orientation.[23] There is a wide range of political and public opinion in Croatia that is telling of, among other things, Croats' efforts to find a place in a changing social, political, and cultural landscape.

## The Cultural Politics of the Everyday

Quite apart from the plethora of measurable macro-level indicators of attitudes in Croatia, which typically appear in most political and economic analyses, are the cultural politics of everyday life for Croats in the homeland. Identity debates are based not only on the most heavily cited criteria of ethnicity/nationality (i.e., self-identification as a Croat) but also on a combination of factors reflecting largely worsening economic conditions and shifts in class boundaries and relations, the changing significance of regionalism and locality, and the continuing and ubiquitous presence, involvement, and/or scrutiny of numerous external interests (e.g., international economic, political, and humanitarian/aid interests, personnel, and agencies, and the like). These, combined with the devastating and disruptive effects of war, have had a tremendous impact on the politics of representation for Croats in the new state.

Almost immediately after Tuđman's death in December 1999, and the subsequent replacement of the ruling HDZ with a left-of-centre coalition in January 2000 pledging greater commitment to the development of virtues based on civil society and democratic values, efforts were undertaken to make a definitive move away from an ethno-nationally based vision of Croatia. Although since then Croats have witnessed major strides in providing greater civic freedoms, transparency, and representative government, the supporters of principles (and parties) that have, among other political platforms, not rejected an ethno-national vision, remain undeterred in their commitment. While moving forward in liberalizing legislation, reducing the powers of the presidency, and clamping down on political influence, corruption, and interference in the judiciary, media, and human rights, the coalition (replaced by the HDZ in 2003) had to remain sensitive to the efforts of its right-wing member parties such as the HDZ, HSLS (Croatian Social Liberal Party), and to nationalist forces, such as veterans' associations, to capitalize on or create opportunities to weaken the governing coalition.[24] Ethno-nationalism, the dominant rubric through which Croatian identity was configured by the nationalist HDZ in the 1990s thus remains, despite the strenuous efforts of some to purge it from political discourse.

As in many Central and Eastern European states, the process of transition in Croatia from communism has delivered few of the eagerly anticipated rewards of independence. The governing coalition of 2000–3 faced numerous pressures: corruption, extensive privatization of key sectors such as banking and the media, a steady fall in the standard of living, high unemployment, and greater uncertainty. Right-wing nationalist coalition partners, intent on preserving an ethno-nationalist focus, used Croatia's troubles to their advantage. The combined efforts of small right-wing opposition parties, hard-liners, and veterans' associations in resisting Prime Minister Ivica Račan's efforts (due to pressure from the Prosecutor Carla del Ponte, of the U.N. International Criminal Tribunal for the Former Yugoslavia, the ICTY) to extradite suspected war criminals to The Hague tribunal (e.g., Generals Mirko Norac and Ante Gotovina) placed considerable strain on the coalition. Their anti-government protests were framed in the language of patriotism for the 'heroes' of the Homeland War, evoking images and memories that resonate strongly with those for whom the wounds of war were still fresh. They also spoke indirectly to the growing frustration of Croats with the slow progress of democratic and market reforms. In addition to the troubled economy, ambitious yet harsh economic reforms – specifically drastic reductions in social spending – have resulted in greater hardship, and this provides more fodder for critics of the government. Appeals to patriotism, most frequently made by right-wing detractors, Croatian claims of victimization by the international community – specifically The Hague – and pride in Croatian identity appeal to those Croats who have been experiencing the greatest hardships.

Despite continued upheavals in the lives of Croats, both individually and collectively, the continuities that provide the foundations for their identification as Croats that are based on region and locality, remain. As the late Croat anthropologist Dunja Rihtman-Auguštin stated, 'although nationalism stimulates the search for identity, identity does not expend itself in the national consciousness. It is contained in ... *sub* national categories, i.e., in the culture of a community, and region and local traditions' (1995:110; original emphasis). Locality and memory, and their contingent sociocultural manifestations and expressions, always were and continue to be central to Croats' configurations of identity. Comments from Croats in urban centres, such as Zagreb or Split (on the Dalmatian coast), concerning their views on Croats and Croatness consistently make reference to regional affiliations that are defined in cultural (e.g., customary traditions, dialect) and sociohistorical (class, education, etc.) terms. The distinguishing feature of their assessments is that, whether positively or negatively viewed, these regionally based differences are seen as innate and impervious to change regardless of contemporary political circumstances.[25] The depth and richness of detail concerning regional characteristics and practices, products of familiar cultural spaces and continuities built up over years of shared experiences and memories, in some cases outweighed the generalities proffered in response to my questions concerning a distinctively national Croatian identity. Thus, being a Trogirani, Dalmatinci, or even a 'snob from Zagreb' can have as much or even greater everyday significance for Croats than the often strident, albeit often ignored, nationalist pronouncements of politicians and others.

Although the war in Croatia and the former Yugoslavia irrevocably changed the demographic characteristics of many (particularly the rural) communities and inevitably fomented and/or exacerbated the Serb–Croat axis of hate,[26] I found that the rhetoric of ethnic homogeneity was not as widely accepted as Croatian nationalist ideology would suggest.[27] This is reflected in Croats' opinions and attitudes concerning intra-ethnic relations. Some of the most negative ethnically based comments concern *not* Serbs but Croats from Bosnia and Hercegovina and (overseas) diaspora Croats, the two groups most valorized by Croatian nationalist elites, particularly in the early 1990s. Croats have generally responded negatively to the huge influx of Hercegovinian Croats into Croatia and to what is widely regarded, particularly in urban centres, as their corrupting influence on Croatia's politics and economy. Hercegovinian Croats have been a major presence in Croatia since the Homeland War, not just as refugees but also as new members of the political and business elite. Croats complain not only about sociocultural differences but also about subsidies and perceived taxation inequities that benefited Hercegovinian Croats, as well as about widespread irregularities and corruption. In an article in the *Feral Tribune* in 24 April 1997, the journalist Toni Gabrić referred to Hercegovinian Croats as 'Croatia's New Serbs.' Hercegovinian Croats in Bosnia and Hercegovina are allowed to hold Croatian passports and other identification and to vote in Croatia's elections. Many interviewees attributed their meteoric political and economic rise in Croatia to the influence of hard-line Hercegovinians, such as Gojko Šušak, in key positions in Tuđman's government.[28] Many Hercegovinian Croats, upon relocating in Croatia, have taken up residence in the cities and built homes, often without obtaining building permits. The family across the alley from where I lived in Zagreb, in 2003, owned a goat and a rooster, much to the chagrin of the neighbours. Although tied up in the backyard, the goat was clearly traumatized by the constant din of cars and horns blaring. This family was ostensibly 'off the map' for Croatian Croats, having not originated in the Croatian homeland and because of controversial and sometimes aggressive military acts of Croats in Bosnia and Hercegovina.

Thus, although the focus has been squarely on the derogatory effects of labels such as 'Balkan' presuming mainly national and religious identifications, it is important to remember the centrality of regionalism. It has been a potent source of differentiation among Croats for generations. While the disdain felt for Hercegovinian Croats is easily explained, given the large numbers who entered Croatia as refugees during the Homeland War (and, among other things, put a strain on local resources), their cultural and other differences, high profile, and often hard-line politics in government, and the new and sometimes corrupt Hercegovinian business elite, the reasons homeland for Croats' disdain of the overseas diaspora Croats deserve closer attention.

## Stretching the Boundaries – Diaspora Croats and Homeland Politics

The 'people production' (Balibar 1991) needs and efforts of the new state have meant that, to a certain degree, diaspora Croats have been implicated in the new Croatian state-building program. Diaspora Croats have self-identified as the 'third pillar of the Croatian national budget.'[29] In a speech given to the Croatian Fraternal Union in Pittsburgh, on 26 September 2004, Croatian Prime Minister Ivo Sanader referred to the Croatian emigrants as 'not only the second lung of our nation, but they were and they should be the motor of the future prosperity and promotion of Croatian interests and the Croatian nation in general.' In a more recent speech at Johns Hopkins University, on 18 October 2006, Sanader reaffirmed his appreciation for diaspora Croats and invited those who can to vote for him in his upcoming re-election bid.

In their quest to reshape the contours of what constitutes Croatness, nationalist elites have reached beyond their borders to the diaspora. An integral component of the Croatian state-building program, and one that draws further attention to the ethno-nationalist emphasis of Tuđman's regime, has been an active campaign to attract diaspora Croats to the homeland. Croatia has always been a nation of emigration, but soon after independence it set out to be a nation of immigration, with efforts to that end primarily geared at diaspora Croats.[30] A deputy minister of immigration with whom I spoke remarked on the parallels in the Croatian government's policy with Israeli efforts to repatriate its diaspora.

Most diaspora Croats enthusiastically embraced homeland efforts to involve them in Croatian national affairs. Since the January 2000 elections, however, the influence of diaspora Croats on homeland political and economic affairs has diminished considerably, particularly given the resounding defeat of the HDZ – which received more than 60 per cent of the diaspora vote. Government measures taken to accomplish this include closing the Ministry of Return and Immigration (see Chapter 5), delaying the tabling of a Bill of Returnees (modelled on the Israeli Law of Return), closing some consulate offices in the United States and Australia,[31] and parliamentary review of the 'special diaspora ticket,' introduced by the HDZ into Croatia's Constitution in 1995, that reserved twelve seats in the Croatian parliament for diaspora representatives.

The perceived need of the new coalition to distance itself from the legacy of the HDZ has been expedited in part through the marginalization of diaspora Croats, many of whom have directly or indirectly supported the HDZ. By way of comparison, it is interesting to note the discrepancy in political representation between ethnic minorities in the homeland and diaspora Croats. While the number of seats in the Sabor reserved for diaspora Croats is twelve (out of 120; 398,000 eligible diaspora voters represent roughly 10 per cent of Croatia's total voting population), for ethnic minorities in Croatia – including Serbs – it was seven. This was changed recently to reflect a small increase in seats available to minorities.[32] But, although many states have provisions that enable expatriates to participate in national elections, diaspora Croats have specifically designated parliamentary seats. But the implications of this provision are more symbolic than instrumental in terms of the electoral impact, as the number of seats allotted to diaspora (a maximum of twelve based on the percentage of eligible diaspora Croats relative to homeland Croats) is calculated on the number of votes (usually small) *registered* outside of Croatia.

In November 2001, Mato Arlović, then president of the Croatian Constitution Committee, announced the enactment of a revised electoral law which came into effect at the end of 2001. In it the number of members of parliament was reduced from 150 to 120 (ethnic minorities now have between five and nine seats), and the special diaspora ticket came under review. Now, diaspora Croats can have a claim upon their right to vote only if they do so in Croatia. These changes towards proportional representation have been welcomed by the centre-left coalition partners and by many homeland Croats, frustrated by the amount of influence on parliamentary affairs wielded by the diaspora. But diaspora groups and returnees, and their political supporters in Croatia (specifically members of the HDZ), have been engaged in public relations campaigns and lobbying to introduce, for example, a revised election law for the diaspora (through a mail-in vote), changes to rules concerning diploma equivalency, diplomatic initiatives, educational opportunities, and military service for diaspora Croats.

These initiatives to reduce the influence of diaspora Croats in electoral politics sparked outrage on the part of diaspora Croat organizations such as the Croatian World Congress. In an interview given in April 2001, Croatia's President Stipe Mesić made his position clear on the influence of diaspora Croats in Croatia's affairs: 'There are a number of Croats who come from Croatia, whose grandfathers and great-grandfathers were Croatians, but who are now citizens of other countries. They may be Croatian patriots, but they are, first and foremost, residents of other countries, like the U.S.A. or Chile.' This position is motivated in part by the efforts of the Croatian government to move away from nationalist concerns and to concentrate on gaining inclusion into the European Union. To this end, the ruling coalition began a major overhaul of its minority and immigration policies, speeding up the process of privatization, proclaiming greater government accountability, and gradually liberalizing the media. To nationalist forces (supported by many Croats in the diaspora), these measures compromise the national integrity and sovereignty of the Croatian state. Increasingly, indications of resurgent ultra-nationalist sentiments at home and abroad have included vehement reactions to the Croatian government's willingness to cooperate with the ICTY. This resentment is compounded by the fact that many see the Homeland War as one fought without Western political or military support.

Numerous indictments and highly publicized domestic trials of Croatian military leaders, some of whom have developed a cult of popularity as Homeland War heroes, for example, General Ante Gotovina, have resulted in protests organized by right-wing Croatian organizations such as veterans' associations, Croatian Invalids of the National War (HVIDRA), and several opposition political parties.[33] This is because Croats see the 1991–95 war as an act of legitimate defence against Serbian aggression. Some view the question of war crimes committed by Croats as an affront to the integrity of the Homeland War and as an attack on the dignity of those who defended their country. The case against General Ante Gotovina, wanted by the ICTY and at large until his arrest in the Canary Islands on 7 December 2005, became a flash point for homeland and diaspora Croats frustrated over international opinion on Gotovina's wartime activities. Croatian language newspapers regularly carry stories about him, and there is a website dedicated to advocating for Gotovina's exoneration from accusations of war crimes, sponsored and administered by the Croatian-American Association. The subheading of that website reads: 'Let us continue to make sacrifices - for the freedom and honor of our homeland!' under a banner headline – 'Ante Gotovina – Heroj!' (Hero). An open letter to Canadian Prime Minister Stephen Harper, entitled 'Close the ICTY,' was posted on the Voice of Croatia website in March 2006.

Although the Croatian population in general has been supportive of these measures (i.e., those of the ICTY), right-wing opponents have been aggressively pursuing opportunities to impugn the actions of the coalition government of 2000–03. These issues, combined with a troubled economy, unemployment, and political uncertainty, have created the conditions for the emergence of new and often competing discourses around the meaning of Croatian nation and Croatian peoplehood. The reopening of these sometimes troubling discursive spaces in Croatia is reminiscent of the imbrication of the rhetorics of patriotism and freedom and of suffering and sacrifice during the Homeland War. Whereas during the war the main aggressors were seen to be Serbs, the new antagonists are the leaders of the European Union.

The controversial removal in 2000 of the executive director of the Croatian state-supported diaspora organization, the Croatian Homeland Foundation (HMI), Ante Beljo, who is a prominent returnee from Canada, further illustrates the implications of these changes for diaspora Croats. His removal enraged diaspora Croats. The intensity of the response from diaspora Croats is expressed in an article published by the Homeland Office of the Croatian World Congress, condemning the removal in the following manner: 'The way in which Ante Beljo was replaced reminds us of the ways and methods of Serbian extremists when they practiced expelling the non-Serbian population from occupied territories during the Homeland War ... That is why we consider the change at HMI to be a direct attack against the Croatian Diaspora. Naturally, we will continue cooperating with and contacting HMI regardless of who is Director because that is our institution, an institution for us and established because of us that live abroad.'[34]

Several members of the revamped administrative board of the HMI – including Boris Maruna, a member of the largest of the coalition parties, the SDP (Social Democrats), and a returnee from the United States, as well as Jakša Kušan, a returnee from the United Kingdom – sent a message in 2000 to delegates of the fourth convention of the Croatian World Congress, in Zagreb, justifying the decision to oust Beljo: 'In the most recent period, HMI has been limiting its contacts to like-minded people, whether the society or individuals happened to be in question, that blindly followed the politics of the Croatian Democratic Union (HDZ).' Diaspora links with the legacy of Tuđman's HDZ were confirmed once more.

Yet, such condemnation has not been universal. The vociferous reactions of diaspora individuals and associations are not universally mirrored in the perspectives of the many Toronto Croats that I interviewed. Although most feel that they have been virtually eliminated from state decision-making structures and direct involvement in Croatian homeland politics, there are those who do not mind this change, so long as they feel that they may continue to recast their involvements and connections to the homeland through visits to Croatia and homeland commemorations. In other words, while there are many Toronto Croats who are unhappy with the situation in Croatia, they did not feel that they should have a more direct role in voicing their opinions to influence change. 'If the population supports the new government, who are we to judge?' (homemaker, age 53, 17 June 2003). 'I don't think that we have an important impact on Croatia's future. People in Canada live their lives, and people in Croatia have nothing to do with us' (administrative assistant, age 24, 14 August 2003).

Diaspora Croats, as a whole, do continue to support initiatives that will increase their profile in the homeland. In November 2001, the Croatian National University Library featured an exhibition entitled 'A Century of Croatian Books in Emigration.' It featured Croatian authors from all over the diaspora, including Rudi Tomić and Vinko Grubišić, both from southern Ontario. The University of Zagreb Alumni Association, Alma Matris, holds meetings and reunions in Croatia. The Croatian American Association, which lobbies American politicians, has made numerous submissions to U.S. officials on behalf of the political interests of Croatia. It has expressed support for John Bolton, until recently, the American ambassador to the United Nations, an institution for which many diaspora Croats have contempt. The association also lobbies politicians to encourage bilateral trade and to remove investment restrictions for Croatian American entrepreneurs who to do business with Croatia.

Croatian politicians still actively lobby diaspora Croats and make visits to Toronto. Prime Minister Ivo Sanader has personally worked to restore diaspora Croats' interest in and commitment to the homeland by travelling to North America and Europe to meet with diaspora Croats. Major events involving the collaboration of diaspora Croatian organizations and homeland associations, towns, and communities are continuously being organized, a recent example being the launching of the 'Olympic Games of All Croatians' or 'Crolympics.' The games were hosted in the resort town of Zaton near Zadar, between 15 and 21 July 2006, and were supported by the Croatian World Congress. Nonetheless, the overtures and rhetoric aimed at a rapprochement between homeland and diaspora Croats belie a different set of realities on the ground.

## Homeland Croats and Disdain for the Diaspora

At no time in Croatian history has the relationship between homeland and diaspora Croats been more intense than it is now. Homeland Croats have been drawn into the identity politics of diaspora Croats as a result of the Homeland War and Croatia's independence. Diaspora Croats had high hopes for the new Croatian states, and many participated enthusiastically in its emergence. Their ambitions for Croatia were motivated by desires that reflect a need for recognition, vindication, and/or reconciliation. Croatia's independence set the stage for an intensification of personal and political interactions between diaspora and homeland Croats, and the reactions to these rang from exhilaration and euphoria to ambivalence and contempt.

Although many homeland Croats embrace Western practices, ideals, and imaginaries, diaspora Croats are not generally looked to for guidance in formulating and/or achieving their goals. Rather, diaspora Croats are often portrayed in an unfavourable light by some Croatian media and in public opinion as either political/economic opportunists or high-minded idealists out of touch with contemporary realities in Croatia. Moreover, most homeland Croats I interviewed do not share diaspora Croats' views on the direction and the future of the Croatian state.

Before the change of government in January 2000, homeland Croats frequently remarked negatively on comments made by public officials and politicians praising the contributions of diaspora Croats to Croatia's fight for independence and their contributions to the homeland. They further expressed frustration with the view that they – the homeland lot – were somehow suspect for having remained in Croatia. They felt that they were seen as either 'stupid' for not taking advantage of economic opportunities outside Croatia or somehow lacking initiative and Croatian political or national consciousness: 'as if nothing has happened to us in Croatia over the past fifty, never mind the past six years!' said a high school teacher in Zagreb (18 April 1997). The perceived implication of this view, for some, is that homeland Croats had tacitly accepted the socialist regime of Tito and/or that they were/are ignorant. Some interviewees commented on the irony in the frequent depiction of diaspora Croats by HDZ officials as political émigrés – that those who left the homeland did so because they were denied employment or faced other forms of persecution in the former Yugoslavia because of their nationalist or political views. My research with Toronto Croats reveals that while this was the case for some, it certainly was not the main explanation for emigration from the homeland. The majority of Croats who arrived in Canada after the Second World War fled because they feared retribution by the post-1945 socialist regime for their suspected involvement or association with the Ustaša; many other Croats, however, went to Canada and the United States (see Kraljich 1978) during the early decades of the twentieth century as economic immigrants, well before Croatia became a socialist state, and later, between 1967 and 1971 (the largest wave of Croatian immigration to Canada), when Tito liberalized Yugoslavia's emigration laws.[35] These sympathetic and often laudatory impressions, which were fostered by the first elected Croatian government and its supporters (and echoed by diaspora elites), resulted in the valorization of the diaspora, but they also had the effect of contributing to negative feelings about diaspora Croats for those in the homeland.

Most homeland Croats I interviewed stated that diaspora Croats received preferential treatment by government authorities when they returned to the homeland (e.g., subsidies and housing allowances). Several claimed that Croatian students from the diaspora can enrol in Croatian schools or universities with less stringent entry requirements than for Croatian nationals and further, that they receive scholarships more easily than Croatian nationals.[36] 'My daughter has to write very difficult entrance exams to get into university unlike kids from Canada or Australia' (21 May 1998).

The most vociferous reactions, by far, were reserved for the extensive diaspora involvement in Croatia's politics. My questions to homeland Croats concerning such involvement were often greeted with scowls. Interviewees criticized the often right-wing nationalistic views of diaspora Croats as anachronistic, jingoistic, and damaging to Croatia's image abroad. One interviewee in Zagreb stated: 'They are a bunch of romantic idealists living in the past' (house renovator, Zagreb, 19 October 2000). Another asserted: 'They are nationalists from the last century' (NGO worker, 18 November 2002). Interestingly, the career of Gojko Šušak was cited as an example of diaspora involvement. To Croats in Croatia, Šušak epitomizes what is wrong with the relationship between Croatia and the diaspora. He has often been criticized in the Croatian media for financing and essentially running the Croat region of Bosnia and Hercegovina, profiteering from black market arms' dealing, subverting the Dayton Peace Accords, and hiding indicted war criminals. Ironically, while Croatia's political leaders (from the HDZ in particular, but also from other right-of-centre parties) and elites have endlessly praised and commended the contributions and commitment of diaspora Croats and Bosnian Croats to Croatia's freedom and prosperity (not to mention the frequent references to their presumed ethnic 'purity'), Croats in the homeland often regard them with disdain.

Comments by interviewees in Croatia about diaspora Croats reflect sentiments ranging from ambivalence to outright scorn. A retired Zagreb factory worker said: 'I don't understand why they feel they have a right to say anything about what goes on here!' (18 November 2002). Most expressed resentment at what they argue is not only the often preachy and, some said, generally superior attitude of diaspora Croats towards them but also the high regard with which they have been held by Croatia's politicians. The underlying reasons for these attitudes towards diaspora Croats reflect concerns, some of which are quite common among homeland peoples in general, such as what is viewed as the retention of a vulgarized ethnic culture and obsolete political ideals, capitalizing on investment opportunities of questionable benefit to the homeland, and meddling in the homeland's internal political affairs (see, e.g., Sheffer 1986; Connor 1986).

Attention to homeland attitudes towards diaspora ways of being Croat are as important as are political differences of opinion because of the imbrication of Croatian culture with politics, especially in the nationalist vision of the first post-independence regime and its supporters. Many of the Croats I interviewed remarked on the anachronistic and romanticized view of Croatia and, by extension, of diaspora Croats, who are often seen to be peasants (*seljaštvo*) – ill-mannered and uneducated. Although homeland Croats admire – sometimes grudg-ingly – the financial success of diaspora Croats, they have little positive to say about their political acumen or their Croatness. Rather, they find their cultural idioms, references, and practices outmoded and some-times vulgar. Diaspora Croats, often represented as unsophisticated, provide a critical reference point for those homeland Croats who are eager to distance themselves from aspects of their collective past (exemplified in the preoccupations of diaspora Croats with tradition) and to reinforce their self-image as modern Croats/Europeans.

The level of diaspora Croats' involvement and material support for relatives increased exponentially during the Homeland War, although it subsided once the war ended. But, while familial contacts and rela-tionships have, on the whole, intensified since independence, home-land Croats' opinions concerning changes in the nature of their relationships with diaspora Croats remain mixed. Although, 'the nation-state as an "imagined community" needs diasporas to remind it of what the idea of the homeland is' (Mishra 1996:424), these images are contested and often rejected by its citizens. Nonetheless, diasporas want and, in the case of many Toronto Croats, *need* to be needed.

## The Honeymoon Is Over

Croatia's independence provided the opportunity to publicly celebrate Croatian identity in Canada, thanks in part to the initially favourable media attention generated by the Homeland War.[37] It both galvanized Toronto Croats and gave them a legitimacy and visibility that they never had before. Independence and the war resulted in a flood of information and new avenues for transnational communication between homeland and diaspora Croats, including among other things, the establishment of news services, newspapers (e.g., *Hrvastka Novine, Iskra*), the proliferation of amateur videos, documentaries, and publications on the war and on Croatian history, among them national-ist treatises and medical journals chronicling the human toll of war, and websites on the Internet, many of which have come and gone.

Independence and the promise of a future free of socialism gave Toronto Croats occasion for articulating nationalistic sentiments and renewed ethnic pride, and also occasion for renegotiating the terms of their sense of belonging in Canada. By promoting the Croatian state's efforts to establish a pluralist society modelled on Western liberal-democratic traditions, Croats have not only been affirming their loy-

alty to the new Croatian state but also demonstrating their commitment to and stake in the traditions and values of Canadian political
culture. International recognition of Croatia as a sovereign and democratic country has provided Croats in Canada with a new sense of
pride and pedigree as members of the new Croatia and not as just
another ethno-national group officially lumped together with all the
other nationalities from the former Yugoslavia. The language of citizenship also provides a new vocabulary for diaspora Croats leaders by
constituting the ground for identity formation in Canada. Nonetheless,
Croats have to continue to negotiate their identities as Canadians and /
or Croats (or both) on terms dictated by a state – Canada – that dis-
courages explicitly nationalist affiliations with homelands.[38]

These processes are compounded by internal tensions that characterize life for diaspora Croats in Canada. While ideological divisions
have, at least publicly, diminished substantially (evidenced in the disappearance of diaspora branches of homeland political parties, with
the exception of some, e.g., the HDZ and HSS, the Croatian Peasant
Party), the processes that have unfolded after independence in many
ways have served to reinforce rather than to minimize the heterogeneous character of Toronto Croats. Efforts at presenting the illusion of
cohesion for experiences and formations that are far from homogeneous underscore the complexity of Croatian self-identifications since
independence. As Chapter 3 demonstrates, diaspora elites – self-
selected interlocutors for Toronto Croats – have endeavoured to exert
control over Croatian identity narratives through the nationalist rhetoric promulgated mainly by those with strong ties to the HDZ. This has
resulted in a largely negative reaction on the part of many Croats, who
feel they are being silenced by these discursive strategies, which has
only served to exacerbate existing tensions and contradictions based
on, for example, class, regionalism, and generation.

In addition, the domestic politics of families have been, in some
cases, significantly affected by independence. While the bases of loyalty, affiliation, and identity among first-generation Croats often reside
in the localized spaces of the Croatian or Bosnian villages or regions of
origin that they share, having grown up in Canada has meant that
ways of being Croat in Canada have been disciplined through the cultural logics of citizenship and belonging in Canada. Janko Perić, who
until June 2004 was a Liberal member of Canada's parliament (and of
the political party that introduced the federal Multiculturalism Act in
1971), made a point of foregrounding the cultural dimension of his
Croatian ancestry (born, raised, and educated in Croatia, he emigrated

to Canada in 1968), for example, as the 'first Croatian federal MP in Canada.'[39] Current expressions of Croatian identity for many young Toronto Croats are often entrenched in the essentializing of a distinctively Croatian culture.[40] Even so, many second- and third-generation diaspora Croats are ambivalent and/or conflicted over the issue of identities and allegiances. Since 1990, the increased awareness, exposure, and involvement of many young diaspora Croats has added new dimensions of complexity and, in some cases, urgency to these questions. Toronto Croats in general occupy a 'double space' wherein they grapple with their commitment to their identifications as Canadians and/or Croats, as nationalists or not, and to often competing ideals, visions, expectations, and/or practices of membership and belonging. But the analysis does not end here.

A crucial dimension of diaspora efforts to navigate the space(s) opened up by the creation of the new Croatian state lies, at some level, in their relationships to the homeland. The inevitable changes in the roles, expectations, and overall significance of diaspora and homeland peoples for each other have had a number of important consequences for the configuration of their post-independence identities. The most important of these has been an expansion of ties from the personal, kin-based links to include more broadly based political and economic ties. While the opportunities for increased contact and communication have had their benefits (particularly in the area of transnational family connections), they have also injected a degree of tension previously not experienced.

Tensions in the relationship between the diaspora and the focus of their desire – a free Croatian state where its citizens are participating in the production or 'recovery' of the historic Croatian state – often manifest themselves in criticisms of the attitudes and actions of their compatriots in the homeland. Typical comments from diaspora Croats include: 'People I know back home are used to having had everything done for them under the communists. Now they constantly complain that things aren't what they expected. They're lazy, to tell you the truth' (dental hygienist, age 37, 21 September 2003). Another interviewee said: 'The mentality of Croatians back home is stuck in Yugoslavia' (artist, age 42, 15 May 2002). One of the students I interviewed stated: 'I couldn't believe how they treated me when I visited ... like I don't belong. They either ignored my opinions or argued with me about Croatia's future. It's not like it's not my future too!' (age 23, 17 July 2004).

Diaspora Croats generally assert that Croats in the new state should be left to chart their own national course; however, some feel that homeland Croats should look to *them* for inspiration and guidance in their 'transition to democracy.' This attitude asserts not only their commitment as Croats to the future of Croatia (as they imagine it) but also a view of themselves as the exemplars of a democratic – in this case, Canadian – political culture.[41] One Toronto Croat observed: that 'Croatians at home don't know the meaning of democracy. They have been under the communists for so long. They have a lot to learn.'[42] The contradictions in these two political positions (democratic pluralism versus ethnic nationalism) can be seen in a feature article in the Split-based *Slobodna Dalmacija* newspaper that focused on diaspora Croats: 'Used to the democratic political criteria of the developed countries in which they live, they simply cannot swallow all the servility and *mindless sacrificing of vital national interests* which they notice all too often' (quoted in Čelan 2000, emphasis mine).[43]

Homeland Croats are not living up to the nostalgic imaginings or expectations of diaspora Croats. Their opinions of homeland Croats reflect not only frustration with the lack of progress towards the goals that diaspora Croats envision for Croatia but also more importantly, resentment about their indifference to or rejection of diaspora involvements in the new homeland. In a similar vein, Rubinstein and Rubenstein (1991) argue that the efforts of Australian Jews to define the right and proper Jew are made not only for the diaspora, but also for Israel, and resented there. The political scientist Yossi Shain has observed that 'the tacit assumption of many Jewish-Americans who engage in the debates that have swept Israel, as it grapples with its identity, is that the diaspora has much to teach its benighted Israeli cousins. Living in a heterogeneous environment, American Jews – so the argument runs – have learned the blessings of diversity and accept the legitimacy of many different forms of religious Jewish expressions ... In short, American Jews and American Judaism have flourished in an atmosphere of pluralism and tolerance, and Israeli Jews would do well to learn from their example (2000:193).

By comparison, discourses on the Republic of Croatia continue to be filled with references to Croatia's glorious past, rich cultural heritage, and beautiful landscape. Many of the romanticized images projected by diaspora Croats onto the homeland convey the desire for a familiar territory infused with symbolic sentiments and collective memories, powerful enough to generate a sense of a common community and loyalty. These images are easily accessible and desirable to diaspora Croats regardless of their personal connections to the homeland. Furthermore, these efforts to generate a sense of homeland, through a connection with geography and an idealized past, present fewer obstacles to conjuring up positive images than do the efforts of homeland Croats.

Diaspora Croats have always looked to the homeland for images and meanings that resonate with or reaffirm their ideas of what being a Croat is or should be. However, by spurning the desiring gaze of the diaspora, Croats in the homeland, in effect, blunt diaspora Croats' efforts to positively identify with and/or participate in the (re)invention of the homeland. Therefore, while Croatia, like the rest of Eastern Europe (with the possible exception of the Czech Republic), may be returning to the West 'the repressed truth of its democratic desire' (Žižek 1990:58), in all its nasty populist and xenophobic forms (especially in the early 1990s), diaspora Croats struggle to define their tenuous, yet increasingly intimate relationship with the homeland. As in the case of homeland Israelis and Jewish Americans, diaspora Croats persist in locating Croatia not only as the source of their personal and collective identities but also as 'the legitimate and crucial target of their influence' (Shain 2000:165). The reinscription of diaspora identities (actualized through socialization and participation) and desires onto the homeland has therefore, to all intents and purposes, been thwarted.

Relations between Croats in the diaspora and those in the homeland are characterized by increased and often unavoidable contact – both homeland and diaspora Croats can and do participate in each other's lives in ways that were never before possible. But these are modulated by a variety of factors such as the domestic constraints of the politics of representation within the countries they live in, as well as internal differences and ambivalences that are the product of contradiction, uncertainty, and often overlapping and fractured loyalties. Given that an estimated half of all Croats live outside the homeland, Croatian identitifications will increasingly be negotiated locally, nationally, and transnationally.

In the next and final chapter, I investigate the phenomenon of return migration to Croatia since 1990. Diaspora returnees to Croatia have been implicated in post-independence processes in ways that are similar to but differ from their diaspora or homeland Croatian counterparts. Their experiences reveal a great deal about the collision of ideals and imaginaries nurtured in the diaspora with the realities of everyday life in the homeland. A discussion of diaspora Croat return is a natural and necessary extension of questions concerning diaspora-homeland relations and issues of home/land.

# Chapter 5

# 'Going Home': From Longing to Belonging

Every morning when I wake up I say to God: 'How can I thank you for bringing me back to Croatia?'

My case is the best proof that what politicians have been promising to Croatians in Canada since 1990 is untrue. I can't wait to go back home to Canada.

Very different in tone, these two comments, obtained during interviews conducted in 2003 with returnees living in Zagreb – the first from a 43-year-old woman who returned to Croatia after twenty years in Canada and the second from a 33-year-old Canadian-born man who resettled in Croatia in 1995 – hint at the complexity of the sentiments and conditions that contribute to the decision to return to the homeland and, most importantly, what follows upon such return. Concepts and practices of 'home' and 'return' continue to be significant for establishing, reinforcing, or disrupting Croatian perceptions and experiences of belonging. Since 1990, diaspora Croats have been speaking in earnest about returning to the Croatian homeland but in ways that reflect the new reality of an independent country. The possibility of return has had an enormous impact, both symbolically and practically, for Croats who, for generations, have regarded homeland return as essentially impossible.

A crucial first step in examining Croatian returnee migration is to examine the contexts that help shape the decision to 'go home.' Are references by diaspora Croats to home/homeland and return simply rhetorical strategies symptomatic of revitalized Croatian national sentiments? Given their knowledge of the continuing political and economic instability in Croatia, which has caused many (particularly young) homeland Croats to emigrate, why do diaspora Croats decided to move to Croatia? What kinds of hopes, joys, aspirations, disillusionments, and frustrations do returnees experience, and how do these influence their ability to call Croatia home? How have homeland Croats reacted to the arrival of diaspora Croats? Finally, what contributes to the decision either to remain in Croatia or to abandon plans to (re)settle in Croatia and go back to the diaspora?

Much of what has been written on return, both academic and biographical (with the exception of that on Jewish return – *aliyah* – to Israel) focuses on the return from exile of those displaced by turmoil in the homeland (Ilcan 2002; Long and Oxfeld 2004, Malkki 1995; Hill and Tiit 2000). According to Brian Axel, 'homeland is now a necessary part of diasporic processes of identification' (2001:199), even though literal return is only relevant in those cases where emigrants *from* a homeland, return *to* it.[1] But the term 'return,' as it is most often used by Croats, does not differentiate between individuals who are returning to the country of their birth and those Croats who move to Croatia but were born and raised elsewhere. What made this particular issue interesting were the differences between opinions on return held by many first-generation Toronto Croats and those of their children. Many of these parents associate the homeland with hardship and at times, suffering but those of their children who are interested in returning or have actually done so, do not. I found that, regardless of their symbolic, patriotic feelings towards the homeland, parents routinely try to dissuade their children from returning to Croatia for the long term.

The conditions of life in exile or emigration have an enormous impact on those who live in exile or a diaspora, so much so that, as Said has stated, 'it is what one remembers of the past that determines how one sees the future' (2000:xxxv). For first-generation diaspora Croats return involves the idea of reconnection with the space of the homeland and with a time before emigrating or fleeing from it, but a reconnection that is seldom realized. Second- and third-generation diaspora Croats, come to the experience of return from a perspective informed less by the kinds of experiences, remembrances, and longings typical of first-generation diaspora Croats than by the desire for the imaginary to become real. Sentiments of patriotism and belonging to the homeland resonate differently for them than for those who themselves emigrated from the homeland. Interestingly, many of the returnees I interviewed stated that their decision to return to Croatia was not met with enthusiasm by their parents. Their experiences provide compelling insights into return from the diaspora.

Integral to the Croatian returnee experience, regardless of the conditions of return, is the use of 'home' and/or 'homeland' as a conceptual space of identification (discussed in Chapter 1). Over the course of this research, Toronto Croats often spoke of returning home to Croatia, regardless of their own place of birth or their citizenship status. When the homeland was inaccessible under communist rule, it provided a powerful symbolic referent for diaspora Croats, a moral geography and explanation for what made Croats different from non-Croats, while also similar and connected to Croats.

Croatia stood for the immemorial past. Diaspora encounters with the homeland since independence have brought this space into the present. The impact of this change is acutely felt by returnees. They are both the products of and the participants in post-independence processes, and their return to Croatia reflects the culmination of diverse and complex interpolations of the idea of a unified, imagined, homeland and the realities of everyday life in the diaspora and in Croatia. Return to Croatia has also been a central political platform and nation-building tool of the Croatian state, particularly during the first ten years of independence. What are the contexts within which return migration of diaspora Croats has been made appealing and possible?

**Who Are the Returnees (Povratnici)?**

Since 1990, the term 'returnee' has become central not only to Croatia's nation-building rhetoric but also to Croats' sense of their place in the world. To sort out the descriptive and discursive elements of the use of return presents a formidable challenge. Therefore, I begin with a definition that delineates the origins of returnees and their destinations. 'Returnee' refers to those Croats who were born in Croatia or Bosnia and Hercegovina, emigrated, and subsequently returned and also to individuals of Croatian descent who were born outside of Croatia or Bosnia and Hercegovina and choose to emigrate to Croatia, to the 'homeland.'[2] Croatian citizenship status, beyond the existence of official documentation, is difficult to determine, as many who return to Croatia are not accounted for because the majority have dual citizenship and need not formally register with the Croatian authorities.

The Croatian Ministry of Internal Affairs reported in 1998 that, between 1990 and 1997, a total of 30,429 individuals had registered as returnees, but no data are provided that discriminate between diaspora returnees and those who were displaced by the Homeland War and returned from Bosnia and Hercegovina or elsewhere. Most returnees cannot be found at their registered addresses, which suggests that they are living and working elsewhere for at least part of the year or simply retain an address in Croatia. Some returnees who have registered as permanent residents in Croatia live abroad for part of the year. Of the forty-four interviews that I conducted with diaspora returnees, in Zagreb and Zadar, approximately one-half were with Croats who had left Croatia at an early age, and the rest were typically second-and third-generation Croats who were born in countries like Australia, Canada, Germany, and the United States. It became necessary to limit my parameters to include only those who have stayed in Croatia for a minimum of one year and profess their intentions to resettle permanently.[3]

Returnees include high-profile and sometimes wealthy Croats who received plum government appointments or profited financially under the Tuđman regime. Some returnees are Croatian-born nationals who left Croatia for various personal, professional, or political reasons in years past and now live in Croatia after having spent extended periods overseas. I also focus on second- and third-generation returnees who were born outside of Croatia, many of whom are the children or grandchildren of native-born Croats who left Yugoslavia after 1945. There is a complex array of transnational movements that must be considered in contemplating the meaning of return. This includes, retirees who split their year between Canada (and other diaspora homes) and Croatia, university students, and entrepreneurs who, by virtue of their commercial activities, travel extensively and have several home bases; all in all, their length of stay in Croatia is contingent on the demands of their professions and/or personal circumstances.

For the above-mentioned reasons, it is difficult to get either a definitive estimate of the average stay for returnees or of the number of returnees who remain in Croatia for at least one year. Nevertheless, older returnees appear to be more likely to resettle for the long term, albeit with frequent forays back and forth to the diaspora countries from which they returned (mostly as retirees), while younger returnees vary widely in their commitments. Their decisions are most often influenced by employment opportunities, personal relationships, and their ability to adjust to life in Croatia. Restitution of property lost during the socialist era or the war was not cited as a reason for return for ethnic Croats. Furthermore, the conditions of return are voluntary, and therefore the sorts of obstacles that characterized the experiences of their parents and grandparents (e.g., as displaced persons) are vastly different.

Among the first returnees I met on my initial visit to Croatia, in 1997, were members of the now-disbanded Diaspora–Homeland Association, who had returned to Croatia after having lived in various European countries for extended periods. Their stated purpose is to help Croatia through the transition from communism by providing advice based on their knowledge and experience living in Western countries. They are highly critical of the Tuđman regime, although they are strongly nationalist. These returnees complain bitterly about what they claim has been a process of marginalization and condemnation of their efforts by the HDZ government. Some of their comments included the following: 'We were called 'enemies of the state' by Tuđman' and 'they [the HDZ] sold their souls to the devil.' The frustration of these returnees stem partially from the fact that their advice was not sought, nor considered salient, but more often than not was dismissed by officials in the new government.

As a group, perhaps the most interesting were the young returnees, that is those who were either born outside of Croatia or had emigrated with their parents when they were but young children. While their reasons for returning to Croatia vary greatly, their experiences reflect the frequent collision of their imaginaries, expectations, and goals with the realities of their life in the new Croatia.

## Croatian Emigrés and Croatia's Government

A key place to start thinking about returnees is the role of the Croatian government in facilitating the process of return, as reflected in changes in policies and the treatment of returnees. Milan Kundera, the Czech writer, reminds us that communist countries hurled anathema at emigration, deemed to be the most odious treason (2003). Yugoslavia was no exception. The assumption that only those affiliated with the demonized Ustaša left Yugoslavia, while Partisans remained, was nurtured by the Yugoslav government for a long time. Those who left had diverse reasons and political sympathies. But Croatian emigrants, once vilified by the Yugoslav government, were aggressively courted to return by Tuđman's regime. In his inaugural address to the Sabor (parliament), in May 1990, the new president made his intentions on this issue clear: 'The new Croatian government should undertake effective steps in order to facilitate the return of the largest possible number of Croat men from around the world to the homeland as soon as possible.' Tuđman's program of repatriation (*Iseljena Hrvastska*) offered diaspora Croats tax incentives and subsidies, most of which never transpired for the vast majority of returnees. However, the homecoming of key diaspora figures had a significant impact on the balance of power and on Croatia's economic and political arrangements.

It is important to note that the position of the Croatian government on returnees has gone through several changes since 1990. Initially, there was interest in developing a law of return, modelled on that of Israel. Several prominent diaspora figures in Toronto, as well as in Croatia, mentioned to me that this had been their goal. Given the efforts of the Tuđman government to expedite a Croatian nation-building project based on ethno-national principles, the implementation of a process that encouraged the return of ethnic Croats was to be expected.

Because of its appeal to Croatia's legislators and even to diaspora Croats during this early period, a discussion of the Israeli Law of Return is instructive in understanding the role of return in nation-building. The Israeli law, established in 1950, began as an open-door immigration policy for Jews that, among other things, provided extensive support benefits for immigrants. According to this law, 'Jews have a 'natural right' to return to their historic homeland' (Shuval 1998:4), and they therefore automatically acquire Israeli citizenship upon arrival: 'Ius Sanguinis – the law of the blood – determines eligibility for citizenship by means of an ascriptive, ethnic-religious criterion based on identification which includes Jews, children and grandchildren of Jews and their nuclear families, even if the latter are not Jewish. These criteria are established by means of written, documentary evidence or legal testimony,' (DellaPergola 1998, cited in Shuval 1998:4). The inspiration for the Israeli law stems from the Jewish religious ideology of return from exile and, as such, carries tremendous symbolic meaning (see, e.g., Levine 1986). The phrase 'next year in Jerusalem' is heard both in prayer and in song. The positive valuation of the process is reflected in the terminology as well. The process of returning to Israel is referred to in Hebrew as *aliyah* (to go up) while to leave is *yerida* (to go down) – the former a positive act, the latter, a source of derision for Jews.[4]

The parallels, both symbolic and procedural, with Croatia's efforts to institute a law of return are striking. Although a law of return has not been formally implemented, key sections of Croatia's Constitution are devoted to returnees. Article 16 of the Law on Citizenship (part of the constitution) guarantees automatic citizenship to any Croat who 'issues a written statement that he or she considers himself or herself to be a Croatian citizen.' Tudman set up special government offices and the Ministry for Return and Immigration to represent the Croatian population abroad. The ministry published *Bilten*, a magazine detailing government programs and returnee experiences. The mandate of the ministry was adjusted several times to reflect the changing priorities of the state, and it was soon renamed the Ministry for Development, Emigration, and Reconstruction. While actively pursued by the first Croatian government, the coalition government of 2000–03 was not as supportive of diaspora returnees. Eventually, the ministry was absorbed into the Foreign Ministry to become the Office for Croatian Minorities, Emigration, and Immigration.[5] A government press release circulated in 2000 stated:

> There will no longer be a specialized administration or department dealing only in issues relating to emigrants or returnees. During recent changes to the organisation of state bodies, the new government did not adopt the proposal of the Sabor Committee for Emigration that business relating to emigrants and returnees be taken over by the Ministry for Reconstruction, Construction and Public Enterprise. The Committee believes that a special administration in the above ministry would be more appropriate as experience in the field shows that emigrants and returnees encounter the most problems in those areas ... As a special ministry or department no longer exists, returnees and emigrants will have to adapt to the new system ... We hope that these will be more understanding and helpful and that the procedure is a simpler one.

As may have been expected, many diaspora Croats were infuriated by the implementation of these measures and voiced their concerns through the Croatian World Congress and other diaspora organizations, as well as to the Croatian government itself. They argued that these changes were symptomatic of the increasingly hostile attitude of the coalition government towards diaspora Croats in general. Furthermore, many feel that they are being punished because diaspora voters overwhelmingly (63%) supported the HDZ in the 2000 elections. All six members elected to the Sabor that year by the diaspora belonged to the HDZ.

Diaspora Croats' grievances date back to the first years of the new state. Aside from major administrative changes, benefits for returnees have been adjusted at least four times since 1990, and each time, their number and range has diminished. Initially, returnees could take all their assets with them. Now (2006) there are limits on what returnees can take into Croatia, and for everything new that they bring with them, they have to pay taxes and custom fees that are often prohibitively high. An absorption centre, Velika Gorica, on the outskirts of Zagreb, which was set up to house approximately thirty returnee families (particularly those who needed financial support), has been closed. During its existence, responsibility for it was shifted from the Ministry for Return and Immigration to the Ministry of Labour and Social Welfare. In commenting on the experience of returnees, Niko Šoljak (see chapter 4) dramatically emphasized the cost of return for some who had lost their life savings in Croatia: 'Many people committed suicide because they could not deal with the tragedy of it all. They were too embarrassed to return to the countries from where they had come to Croatia' (2002:17). Elsewhere he states that 'it was only a small number of Croatians who actually managed to return to the homeland. Those who did come back and started working and earning money in Croatia soon went bankrupt.'

The government of Croatia tried to reassure diaspora Croats that they were not being neglected, but the perception of diaspora Croats was that the government's actions clearly indicated otherwise. On 12 December 2001, the Ministry of Foreign Affairs, concerned over criticism from diaspora Croats, circulated a press release stating that it had not intended to marginalize returnees. The ministry announced that it would create new and more favourable conditions to incorporate emigrants into the economic life of Croatia and that it would offer them assistance in enterprises and investment and in educating the younger returnees through state support and similar aid. 'Our attitude towards Croatian emigrants and immigrants has remained unaltered since 1999.' One of the government's main concerns though has been the exodus of young Croats anxious to pursue opportunities outside the homeland, because the state of Croatia's economy is grim (Golub 1996). Estimates from the Ministry of Foreign Affairs show that 140,000 young Croats emigrated from Croatia in the 1990s.

Diaspora organizations remain unconvinced of the sincerity of

Figure 5.1. Cartoons depicting diaspora grievances. Source: Internacionalni Klub Hrvat-Skih Iseljenika, Povratnika I Investora Iz Dijaspore 2002, Zbornik – Prvog Sabora Hrvatske Dijaspore. Reprinted with permission, Niko Šoljak.

Croatia's efforts to embrace diaspora returnees. Enhancing the status and role of returnees is a key goal of the International Club of the Croatian Emigrants, Returnees and Investors from Diaspora (renamed the Croatian World Assembly and discussed in Chapter 4). One of the organization's mandates as stated in the founding assembly in May 2002 is to 'encourage the return of Croatian emigrants, to help the returnees solve their legal problems and issues and to understand and adapt to Croatian Legislature, and to help the returnees who have invested their money in the Croatian banks that have gone bankrupt.' Editorials and commentaries have appeared regularly in diaspora publications and on websites regarding the difficulties encountered by diaspora returnees. Toronto Croat journalist Rudi Tomić (1998) reflects on the problem of return to the homeland, in his *Nema Povratka u Mirnu Hrvastsku* (*There Is No Return to a Peaceful Croatia*) and *Kako Stimulirati Povratak Iseljenika u Domovinu* (*How to Stimulate the Return Home of Emigrants*), underscoring the concerns and anxieties of diaspora Croats over the question and their reception by Croats in the homeland.

## Diaspora Attitudes towards Return

I began this chapter by asking what motivates some diaspora Croats to return to the homeland. What leads some to make the move to Croatia and others not to do so? Almost immediately it became clear to me that Toronto Croat's attitudes and relationships with the new homeland are mediated by the current conditions of life in the diaspora. Now that the possibility for a return to Croatia exists, most older first-generation Toronto Croats acknowledge that they have no plans to do so. As expected, the reason most often given, is that they are now established in Canada and things have changed too much for them to be able to readjust comfortably in Croatia. Some spoke of their traumatic memories of Croatia. One retired Toronto Croat said: 'I won't go back to Croatia because of my memories there. My mother was imprisoned by the Nazis in the Second World War because her father was a Partisan. What she went through was terrible, and it pains me too much to think of returning to the place she was tortured' (age 73, 18 November 1997). Statements on the preferred social, political, and material conditions of life in Canada for some have the added effect of vindicating their views on the 'evils' of communism and the vestiges of a 'communist mentality' in Croatia. Even the staunchest supporters of the nationalist Croatian government, who regularly proclaim the virtues of the new Croatia, acknowledge that the continued presence of Communist Party elements in the government, and the presumed 'ingrained attitudes of Croatian society,' make it impossible for them to confidently entertain the idea of themselves returning.[6]

The majority of diaspora Croats prefer to 'stay put,' enjoying the benefits of their status as permanent moral gatekeepers while remaining in the diaspora. Remembrances of the homeland do not necessarily signal a desire to return (Fortier 2000:161; see also Malkki 1995b). When asked what they think of those who have returned to Croatia, some are cynical, particularly with regard to returnees who profited from their association with the Tuđman regime. Most, though, say that returnees are an inspiration and that return is a laudable goal to be worked towards by diaspora Croats, much like *aliyah* for diaspora Jews.

For first-generation Toronto Croats who have chosen to remain in Toronto, memories of the homeland are piqued by the sights, smells, and sounds of life in Croatia. But memory is not always coterminous with nostalgia and longing. According to Rapport and Dawson, 'home ... is 'where one best knows oneself' where 'best' means 'most' although not always 'happiest' (1998a:9). This was the case for those diaspora Croats who left Yugoslavia under difficult circumstances.

Nonetheless, older first-generation Toronto Croats convey strong sentimental and romantic imaginaries of the Croatian homeland.

Those who have been separated from the homeland the longest, rely heavily on their memories of the towns and villages from where they originated. What these experiences with memory underscore is its effects, for as Michel de Certeau states, 'memory responds more than it records' (1984:88). Similarly Svetlana Boym argues that the stronger the nostalgia, the emptier of recollections memory becomes (2001:42–3). Emphasis on the recollection of memories notwithstanding, the real significance of memories lies in the role they play in the present.

The positive valuation of homeland by diaspora Croats is often typical among those who have lived outside Croatia for a long time. Those who emigrated to Canada after 1990 though have relatively few positive recollections of Croatia. But the conditions of life for diaspora Croats when they did live in the homeland, as well as the circumstances of their departure from Croatia, have yielded a range of sentiments concerning Croatia as home. As the previous chapters demonstrate, tropes of home and homeland inflected with narratives of longing have been central to the language of diaspora Croats across the generations. These findings about diaspora Croats are corroborated in Slobin's analysis of Russian émigrés: 'The émigré sense of its "sacred" mission, now combined with post-communist nostalgia, appeared to inspire longing for an impossible return to some version of a "misty" pre-revolutionary Russia, with the "originary tradition" still intact' (2001:523). But feelings of longing and the like coexist with tropes of suffering and loss or with memories of hardship and dissatisfaction. These are all part of a wider repertoire of discourses around the history of Croatia under various and sometimes oppressive regimes. They have become part of the collective memory, albeit contested, of Croatian history. Thus, for Croats, 'homeland' and 'home' (*domovina*) are terms imbued with various, sometimes conflicted and ambiguous meanings. The views and experiences of second- and third-generation young Toronto Croats are interesting for their discursive power with regard to home and homeland, and particularly when viewed in relation to the views of their parents. Most young Croats in considering the idea of return focus on long-term career plans and the prohibitive logistics of a move to Croatia. Surprisingly, quite a few say that they have seriously entertained the idea of either temporarily or permanently relocating to Croatia. Those who are actively pursuing the goal of return through contacts with Croatian consular authorities, family in Croatia, educational institutions, and prospective employers, or who are investigating business and/or investment opportunities, provide unique insights into the appeal that return has for individuals who have had but little direct experience of the homeland.

What is striking is how these young people use the language of 'return' or 'going home.' While home refers to 'a place of origin returned to' (Hollander 1993:34; Weil 1978), this is obviously not the case for prospective returnees whose only physical contact with Croatia has been through occasional vacations there. But the idea of return nevertheless, carries a heavy freight of symbolic meaning and emotion, exemplified during the euphoria experienced by many diaspora Croats after Croatia's independence. The reasons most often cited for the desire to return to Croatia, reflect the pull of romantic nationalist imaginaries nurtured from childhood onwards and reinforced after independence.

It is significant that the term 'return,' as it is used by diaspora Croats, does not differentiate between return to the country of their birth and return by those who were born and raised elsewhere. For most young returnees, and particularly those who had neither lived in Croatia nor have any memory of their early childhood in Croatia, the Croatian homeland is something less experienced than imagined through a series of symbolic mediations and representations developed in the diaspora. Many of these young diaspora Croats were children or adolescents when Croatia became an independent state. They were therefore exposed primarily to the exhilaration shared by Toronto Croats in the early 1990s, many of whom enthusiastically participated in the lead up to independence and the celebrations that followed.

## Why 'Go Home'?

The motivations and experiences of returnees are, in many ways, as diverse as the individuals who choose to return. While the nature and intensity of returnee experiences vary considerably depending on demographic and other factors such as age, class, region of origin, and gender, the continuities are remarkably consistent. Reactions coalesce around several themes, including but not only, nationalism, belonging, and a sense of home. It was in the context of the question of Croatian identity and belonging for Toronto Croats that the most compelling insights into motivations for return revealed themselves. In this regard, the ways in which ideas of home and belonging are made explicit and narrativized, is striking, reflecting a wide range of impressions and experiences, shifting interpretations, and contrasting expectations of life in the diaspora and in Croatia. Return is at once a deeply personal *and* political process regardless of one's commitment to or disregard for explicitly political-ideological positions on the Croatian state.

Of central importance for many returnees is not only *how*, but *where* one can be truly Croat. This was made apparent in their responses to questions about this issue. One interviewee, an engineer by profession, said: 'To be Croatian in Croatia is the most important thing to me' (age 53, Zagreb, 7 November 2003). A homemaker I interviewed, who was much younger than the engineer, explained: 'Although I used to feel first and foremost a Canadian, my feelings changed the more I stayed here. I feel more Croatian now than anything' (age 33, Zagreb, 28 October 2003). Another returnee said: 'It was in Canada that I felt that Croatia would always be my home' (mechanic, age 52, Zadar, 2 May 2003). One woman, who had lived in Canada for eighteen years and returned in 1999, put it this way: 'I felt horrible abroad. I couldn't forget that I was living in a foreign country. I had a feeling that I had been torn off from the place where I belonged' (Zagreb, 31 May 2003). A medical researcher revealed what was of central importance to her in returning: 'I don't want to talk about problems, and there will probably be many more problems, but Croatia is here for us! The most important thing is that we are here and not abroad' (Split, 14 April 2002). This 44-year-old woman used the Croatian word *tudjina* in her description of living outside of Croatia, a term that can have pejorative connotations, meaning 'strange' or 'foreign.'

Sentiments based on ethnic and national considerations are particularly evident in the comments of returnees who have strong political opinions. Although, in spite of the ubiquitous Croatian nationalist rhetoric in both the diaspora and homeland, such returnees are a minority among those I interviewed. Inspired by the promise of a reinvigorated national homeland, they say that they are back in Croatia to stay and that it is the duty of all Croats to help forge a national identity in the homeland. In the words of one such nationalist: 'We are full of enthusiasm and can be very helpful. This the only way for us to become real Croatians – helping our homeland' (contractor, age 34, Zagreb, 16 October 2003). Another young returnee said: 'I came home to help my country and make it a better place for all Croatians' (construction worker, age 26, Zagreb, 26 October 2003). Other returnees, however, were quick to dissociate themselves from returnees with nationalist leanings and to assert that their own decisions to emigrate to Croatia were based on their unique personal circumstances, rather than on romanticized notions of an ancestral Croatian homeland. They are also aware of the oft-heard claims by homeland Croats that diaspora returnees are misguided idealists and 'right- wing zealots.'

Some personal reasons for returning included the following: to marry a Croatian national, find a good job, or just simply for the adventure. A returnee, who lived in Croatia for seven years and then went back to live in Toronto, said 'I didn't go there because I was like, patriotic or nationalistic or anything like that. I went because there was a job opportunity that sounded exciting' (sales associate age 28, 20 May 2002). Another told me 'I came here in the summer of 1989 and met my husband. I've been here ever since and would never think of moving back. My family is here now' (researcher, age 33, Zadar, 17 April 2002). These and other considerations are not mutually exclusive and do, of course, overlap at times. Their relative importance varies depending not only on immediate and/or contextual factors but on nationalist/ideological sentiments, making it difficult to generalize with regard to the motivation to return.

## When Worlds Collide: Returnee Expectations and Reception in Croatia

What happens when the imagined homeland becomes the site of everyday life, and the returnee does not find what had been hoped for (see, e.g., Rapport and Dawson 1998)? Encounters with the homeland and, more significantly, expectations about return, provide a prism through which to investigate the relationship between the realities of everyday life in Croatia and the values, ideals, and priorities that influence returnees' decisions to stay.

Expectations of life in the new homeland varied based on a multitude of factors. First-generation returnees, who left Croatia under whatever circumstances, return with a cache of memories – vague or vivid – of the homeland as it was and, more significantly, as it *should* be. However, they themselves have changed as a result of their experiences of emigration, their lives in the diaspora, and their absence from the homeland. Aisha Khan observes that: 'the place to which one returns is not necessarily the place from which one came' (1995:96). James Clifford and George Marcus suggest that 'perhaps there is no return for anyone to a native land' (1986:173). There is no 'home' to go back to (Hall 1990; see also Said 1999). What stands out in the responses of first-generation returnees is the consistency of their views on the meaning of return.

Regardless of their personal histories of emigration from and re-migration to Croatia, return is marked by feelings of longing that rarely have strong nationalist underpinnings. Their motivation to return is most often expressed as the fulfilment of a personal dream but one that, in some cases, has not been adequately realized.

Plans to return to the homeland for a 64-year-old returnee interviewed in Zagreb (originally from Zagorje, he had lived in Canada for twenty-five years) began 'as soon as the Homeland War broke out,' although he waited until 1997 to 'come home' (26 August 2002). He said that he now detects certain differences between himself and other homeland Croats. He attributes this in part to the fact that he did not fight in the Homeland War, something for which he feels he will never be able to forgive himself.[7] He firmly believes this to be the main reason why Croats will always treat him and other returnees differently. That he had not fought for his country, at times turned into 'a great difficulty' for, this returnee although he was reluctant to explain how.

A 53-year-old woman, who returned after twenty years in Canada stated: 'I plan to stay in Croatia forever because, at my age, one should return to the place of one's origin.' (Zadar, 7 May 2003).[8] Her voice represents that of many older returnees who see return as the fulfilment of their goal to come back to their place of origin. Regardless of her actual circumstances – divorce, loss of employment in Canada, and the need to care for her elderly mother in Zadar – for this returnee, the homeland presented less an option than a destiny.

Apart from the more general difficulties in making the transition from life in the diaspora to life in the new Croatia, some first-generation returnees wonder whether they can fully adjust both socially and psychologically to the changes brought about by independence and the attitudes of homeland Croats towards them. The expectations of younger, mostly second- and third-generation, returnees were not influenced by having previously lived in Croatia, but rather by family experiences, visits to Croatia, and imaginaries fostered in a diaspora Croat environment through their involvement in and/or exposure to Croatian culture, language, customs, and sometimes, politics. What stands out for them is the sometimes stark contrast between life as Croats in the diaspora and life in Croatia. Returnees expect to feel 'at home' in their homelands. However, the symbolic, emotional, and ideological weight of the idea of return does not provide any space for reflecting on the possibility of encountering problems or tensions. These are neither anticipated nor desired.

The realities of living in the new Croatia present challenges that, if they did not surprise, then certainly they did frustrate many returnees. Most returnees complaints revolve around inconveniences and irritations with Croatian bureaucracy, taxation, the high cost of living, the ongoing political instability, perceptions of unfair employment practices, and significantly, homeland Croats' reception of them. Some returnees cited troubling stories circulated in the media about returnees' experiences. As early as May 1993, a letter appeared in Vjesnik, a Zagreb daily, describing returnees' attitudes. It was written by twelve individuals who had returned to Croatia and it tells of their disappointment with the Croatian media and government, who they claim regard them as 'enemies of the state' because of their criticism of Croatia. They assert that they were denied employment opportunities with the explanation that they do not have 'relevant Croatian experience,' although most returnees have a functional command of the language and a disproportionate percentage are university-educated (although this was not the case for those I interviewed.) Occasional editorial pieces in *Slobodna Dalmacija*, another daily newspaper, on the problems faced by returnees, feature articles spotlighting these issues. The June 2001 issue of the right-of-centre Croatian magazine *Fokus* contained an article on the obstacles – bureaucratic and otherwise – that returnees face upon return.

Diaspora lobby groups such as the Croatian World Congress have been quick to respond to what they have claimed is the dismal role that Croatia's government has played in facilitating return and welcoming diaspora returnees. The assumption conveyed in the tone of their protests is that the government is responsible for creating a climate favourable to return and resettlement. But what comes through most in the comments of returnees, both those who remained in Croatia and those who went back to Canada, is the general dissatisfaction with their reception by homeland Croats. One, a 47-year-old mechanic in Zagreb, said: 'They treat us like second-class citizens' (31 October 2003).

The reception of returnees by homeland Croats emerges as a key barometer of the quality of returnee experiences. The issue of returnee reception is most interesting given that it speaks to the relationship between national imaginaries and realities encountered upon arrival and resettlement in Croatia. Only five of the thirty-eight returnees with whom I spoke about this issue have found the homeland welcoming to them. This observation applies to both Croatian-born returnees and those who are living in Croatia for the first time. Many feel that Croats in Croatia treat them differently, that they are resentful or simply ambivalent towards them. Frequently this is expressed in the form of attitudes or comments directed at them, for example, that returnees are 'rich,' 'flaunting their wealth,' 'complainers,' or 'failures' in the diaspora who have come to Croatia to try their luck. One returnee said: 'Some of the hostility surprises me' (service employee, age 32, Zagreb, 21 October 2003). Another, a 34-year-old who had lived in Canada for ten years, said that Croatian nationals treat him as 'one of them' but that they have the wrong idea about returnees.[9]

'All the émigrés have already come home or at least put in an appearance.[10]

Mílan Kundera, *Ignorance*

The return of diaspora Croats evokes a variety of opinions from homeland Croats. According to Nicholas Van Hear; 'among the reactions to returnees may be welcome, toleration, grudging acceptance, rejection, antagonism or conflict' (1998:56). On a train to Gospic in central Croatia in 1999, I met a young Canadian Croat, who told me that he had come to Croatia the previous year with plans to reignite Croatian commitment to Catholicism. He explained that years of socialist rule had weakened the Catholic faith in the country. He then proceeded to recite verses from his Bible, at which point an old woman sitting across from us yelled obscenities at him and several young people sitting across from him fixed him a disdainful stare. When we disembarked, a man who was also in our train compartment told me: '*Just* what we need!' Each time I told this story to friends and colleagues in Croatia, the response was the same – returnees do not represent the 'best' and 'brightest.' Indeed, other homeland Croats with whom I raised the issue of returnees routinely displayed a general lack of interest in them and in their experiences or difficulties. Their comments, as a whole, confirm the concerns and experiences of returnees around the issue of their reception. Among them: 'What do they expect from us here?' (contractor, age 34, Zagreb, 14 October 2003). 'They come here with ideas about how we should run things. They should keep their ideas to themselves' (salesperson, age 27, Zagreb, 20 October 2003). 'I work with one who came here in '99. She is really nice but still hasn't got a clue about things here' (bookkeeper, age 32, Zagreb, 17 November 2003). One of the more humorous responses I heard was: 'I tell you what. I'll go to Canada and he can stay here' (salesperson, age 36, Zagreb, 10 November 2003).

One response of returnees to the challenges of acceptance in Croatia has been their consistent efforts to find other returnees to associate with. Many said that developing new networks with homeland Croats outside of family relations is difficult, and that therefore they seek out other returnees, frequent the same cafes and restaurants, and often work with each other. One young returnee, who works in retail sales, said: 'We all tend to hang out. My best friends are Canadian but if you are Australian, Canadian, or American, we all go through the same kind of stuff so we tend to be each other's support system' (age 33, Zagreb, 26 October 2003). Another told me: 'I think most of my friends were actually outsiders or classified as outsiders' (electrician, age 37, Zagreb, 1 November 2003). Rather than melt into the Croatian body politic, returnees can rarely escape their 'outing' as diaspora, as immigrants, as Other by homeland Croats. While lamenting their conditional acceptance or outright rejection, returnees also participate in the reproduction of the conditions of difference, wherever and however they have been fostered. Some of this comes as a result of their own resentments born of the rejection and/or disdain of their reluctant co-nationals in Croatia.

On the whole, returnee motivations, goals, and representations, and the landscapes that they construct as they traverse transnational circuits between diaspora country and homeland, vary significantly. The countries from where returnees originate (e.g., Canada, Australia, or the United States) are all marked by context-specific dynamics of class, gender, ethnic, and other forms of differentiation to which they were accustomed. These invariably frame and influence their encounters in Croatia. The opinions of returnees' often reflect a tendency to compare their experiences growing up and living elsewhere with those of the homeland. Most of the young women from Canada I interviewed were struck by what they found to be particularly overt sexism in Croatia. Returnee experiences with, and perceptions of the Canadian political system also have an impact on their assessments of the progress of post-independence Croatia's political affairs now that they themselves are living in the homeland. Many mentioned their frustration with the negative vestiges of what they called the 'communist mentality' of their homeland compatriots concerning efficiency, political culture, and personal ambition. This was a refrain I heard from Croats continually in Toronto. Homeland Croats are aware of these sentiments and do little to endear themselves to their new arrived neighbours.

The enthusiasm and commitment of many returnees has been tempered by the realities of return. When viewed together, the experiences of returnees dispel romantic notions of an ingathering of peoples or a sense of collectivity. For most, this is revealed in the disjunctures between the imagined and the real, and the difficulties in transforming longing into belonging. The difficulties articulated by returnees consist largely of the day-to-day challenges of living in Croatia, but as a whole, their reflections undergird the ambivalences inherent in the process of negotiating their sense of *how* to be Croatian in the homeland. In this returnees have had little direction or support from homeland Croats, or at least so that is how they feel. For some, this has led to the decision to abandon their plans to live in Croatia and to return to Toronto.

**Failed Return**

The story of diaspora return, whether inspired by political vision, romantic imaginings, and/or pragmatic considerations does not always end in a happily-ever-after. Although their numbers are difficult to determine, there are returnees who have abandoned their new lives in Croatia and gone back to Canada, disappointed and disillusioned. This disillusionment stems from a variety of factors – personal, professional, and others. In combination, their overall experiences reflect a disconnect between their expectations before they arrived in Croatia and their experiences afterwards. By far, the most common theme was profound disappointment. Almost all of the ex-returnees I interviewed commented on their difficulties in adjusting to life in Croatia, and they regularly complained about problems that are similar to those identified by the returnees who have remained: these include excessive bureaucracy, the attitudes of homeland Croats concerning work, customs, and habits, and the reception of returnees by homeland Croats. I spoke to young, primarily second- and third-generation diaspora Croats on the basis of what I learned in Croatia and to assess the impact that formative homeland imaginaries constructed through family, community, and other influences accumulated in the diaspora had had their expectations and experiences in Croatia.[10]

The admission that their return to Canada was attributable to the unrealistic expectations they had taken with them to Croatia was as much a statement about conditions in Croatia as it was about their own symbolic investment in a Croatia that was nurtured in the diaspora.

These young people had returned to a country that they were only partially familiar with. For some, the motivation was pure idealism. Three ex-returnees remarked that they moved to Croatia because they wanted to make a contribution to the new state. One young woman said: 'I really thought I could make a difference' (salon employee, age 31, 16 June 2004). While this sentiment provided some with the impetus to emigrate to Croatia, for others it was the source of dissatisfaction. Another young ex-returnee explained: 'In the beginning I was patriotic as well. I was always Croatia, Croatia, Croatia. And I still love Croatia but the one thing I realized, they don't care about us, so why care about them ... I was raised to be really patriotic, and Croatia was the centre of our lives' (salesperson, age 26, 27 July 2004). A young teacher commented: 'When I got back to Croatia after the war, after Croatia was finally independent, people didn't care if it was called Croatia or not. That surprised me' (age 28, 12 August 2004).

The symbolic power of the homeland, as experienced in an upbringing heavily influenced by immersion in Croatian culture and customs common to many young returnees, is reflected in their views on the varied meanings of Croatness. Being Croat for second-and third-generation Croats entails a performative dimension, given their exposure to Croatian cultural activities while growing up in Toronto. Furthermore, it frequently becomes the basis upon which assessments and evaluations of Croatness are made. Views on what constitutes Croatian identity are often expressed through family and community rituals and formalized practices, as evidenced in the following statement from a 35-year-old ex-returnee, who spent five years in Croatia: 'When you were growing up here [in Canada] you were socialized to be very Croatian, so to speak. And very patriotic. The Croatian park and the Croatian church and the Croatian school, *tambouritza* ... and you go to Croatia and realize that wow, some things they don't even know about. I was shocked, I thought everyone knew how to do Croatian dancing. I got there and ended up teaching *them*!' (sales manager, 17 August 2004).

Another interviewee, who returned to Canada in 1999, made a comment that, at first glance, seems absurd but reveals an interesting perspective on perceptions of the true or real essence of Croatness: 'It's sad that the Croatians there don't nurture or relate to their culture as much as we do here in Canada' (retail sales manager, age 32, 28 July 2004). A young office manager gave this assessments: 'I think that we are more Croatian than they are. Here we go to church. I mean that's something for us. That's what tied us together, the Croatian school and the church. And over there, nobody was really into that. Well after the war, everyone started going, but I think that it's winding down again now' (age 31, 31 March 2004). These views can be partly attributed to the efforts of their parents and communities to instill cultural Croatian values and practices in their children. The influence of multicultural discourse on young Canadian exreturnees which officially valorizes and promotes the cultural dimensions of group identities, is also detectable in their assessments of their experiences. But more importantly, these ex-returnees' experiences speak to the anxieties of [not] belonging, organized around and expressed in the language of cultural and historical tradition.

For most, return to the homeland was motivated by the desire to connect with something conceived as familiar. One young woman, who lived in Croatia for three years said: 'It was so cool to sit in a café and hear everyone speaking Croatian' (bank clerk, age 26, 20 June 2004). Yet, when she spoke Croatian to friends and co-workers in Zagreb, they invariably commented on her accent and scoffed at the regional dialect she had learned from her parents in Toronto. Similar experiences were described frequently by other ex-returnees. Just as their parents who had emigrated to Canada had to deal with the limitations of poor and accented English, so too, these exreturnees had to cope, not only with reactions to their accented Croatian, but with the stigma of their parents' often regional Croatian dialects. Ex-returnees' impressions and recollections of their time in Croatia are greatly influenced by the degree to which they felt accepted by homeland Croats. One told me: 'They thought we came on a free ride, that we were getting everything we wanted from the government. That is the total opposite of what happened' (contractor, age 35, Toronto, 15 May 2004). A returnee who came back to Canada with her Croatian husband stated: 'The natives think that the returnees are crazy. Why on earth would you want to live here when the majority of people just want to get out. And then we say, 'Oh ya, I just returned here from Canada,' and they just sort of look at you.' Another young ex-returnee said: 'I don't think I'll ever fit in. I'll always be 'the Canadian' (accountant, age 28, 10 August 2004). A Canadian-born Croat who returned from Croatia to Toronto after living in Zagreb from 1992 to 1994 stated: 'They fought for Croatia but we helped too. I mean how many hours that we spent putting up posters all over, the food drives, having clothes drives. It was unbelievable how much outpouring, I think especially from the younger generation here.

We formed clubs. We formed organizations. We sponsored the soldiers. And our kids from Croatian school wrote letters and sent toys to their children. So we did a lot. I think a lot of it was unsaid, unnoticed, and unappreciated' (20 April 2004).

There was, however, a recognition on the part of these ex-returnees of the often disparate renderings of the homeland based on generational, class, and other differences. Whatever their initial impressions they experienced a different Croatia from that of their parents' generation. One said: 'The picture my parents had of Croatia is very different from the reality. Croatians at home are not stuck back at the turn of the century. People have heating in their homes and telephones, things that my parents' generation didn't have. So their experiences of hardship are not the same as people's now' (dental assistant, age 28, 27 July 2004).

These intensely personal, lived experiences of separation and belonging reflect the complex struggles between the personal and the political and between the ideal/imagined and the real. Contrary to the expectations of most of these ex-returnees, there were few resources available to help make returnees feel welcome in Croatia. Even though many had relatives in Croatia, they still felt disconnected. When questioned on their expectations in this regard, few had specific suggestions other than general efforts that homeland Croats might make to ease the transition for returnees. Although their experiences did not, have the desired result, that is, permanent resettement in Croatia, few ex-returnees expressed feeling like failures for returning to Canada. Most often, their explanations for coming back are phrased in terms that reflect personal or professional decisions rather than in terms of being forced to abandon their plans to remain in Croatia. But, while several stated that they would perhaps eventually return to Croatia, most plan to remain in Canada. It is striking is that approximately half of the ex-returnees interviewed confessed that they have less to do socially with Croats in Toronto now than they did before they left for to Croatia. Together, these experiences lay bare the paradox of the dream of return, of return itself.

Returning home has tremendous appeal for diaspora Croats who are looking for a renewed or revitalized sense of belonging. The impact of access to the homeland since independence, in the sense of ethno-national community and collectivity, is fundamental in their struggle to belong in Croatia. However, coming together in the very location where they expect to find commonalities and a natural ethnicity, instead, often generates an experience of difference and disjuncture. The irredentist overtones of so much diaspora discourse have had the cumulative effect of blurring the lines between the teleology of return and its realization. Although many diasporas sustain an ideology of return, there is little research that chronicles the process, specifically voluntary return (versus, e.g., state-and/or NGO-sponsored repatriation programs), when it does occur. Diaspora Croats' experiences of return, successful or not, seldom merely reflect the 'burning desire' to return to the homeland (Naficy 1991, 1993) or its 'haunting' effects (Matsuoka and Sorenson 2001), as described in the case of other diasporas. For diaspora Croats, return signifies much more and, in some cases, much less.

Following Nigel Rapport and Andrew Dawson (1998), it is through distilling the essence of their past diaspora selves that new migrants – or returnees in the Croatian case – to the homeland begin to be at home and to imagine futures for themselves there. In his examination of returnees to Israel, Rapport argues that former diaspora discourses around the homeland are resurrected as immigrant discourses by returnees, which then shape the routinized lives they develop in the new homeland environment (1998b). But for Croats, the official and unofficial reception of returnees in the homeland remains problematic at best. Returnees to Croatia are the benefactors and/or the pawns of a deliberate process of nation-building, perpetuated transnationally through the diasporas that have spawned them (the returnees), the homeland peoples who spurn them, and Croatia's political/economic interests that hope to benefit from them.

Unlike many other diaspora groups for whom return has been a dream and/or an option, diaspora Croats have, over the past century, been on a roller coaster of rejection (disdain) and courtship (desire) by successive regimes – seen as treasonous and corrupt by some regimes, and by others as 'true' Croats, patriots, and individuals deserving of financial and political support for their return. These sentiments have sometimes even been expressed by the same regime, as in the Tudman years. Homeland Croats have displayed various levels of ambivalence, distrust, tolerance, and acceptance towards returnees. These factors leave many returnees feeling unsure, confused, and sometimes hostile towards the homeland and/or its people.

All the discourses, entreaties, and considerations – practical, political, and sentimental – that contribute to the decision to return to

Croatia have consequences for the discussion of diaspora in relation to expressions of belonging and to the contingency of identifications. The experience of return compels returnees from the diaspora to reflect on or rethink issues of citizenship and nationality, religious, ethnic, personal, and even, at times, professional identifications. For returnees who went back to Canada, such discontinuities compounded their difficulties in adjusting to life in Croatia and disrupted their ability to find for themselves a place of relational identification and cultural attachment. Irrespective of outcomes, the experience of return speaks to the contingency of Croatian subjectivities and the multiple contexts within which the politics of desire and disdain are played out.

# Conclusion: Croats at a Crossroads

We see the straight highway before us, but we cannot take it because it is permanently closed.

Ludwig Wittgenstein, *Philosophical Investigations*

## The Personal as Political

When the Yom Kippur War broke out in 1973, I was fifteen years old and committed to enlisting in the Israeli Army, as my mother had done in the 1940s. My resolve was firm. My birthplace was Canada, but my homeland – Israel – was at war. Everything I had learned about my mother's family history, including her role in the struggle for the independence of Israel, destined me, I felt, for a defining role in Israel's future. What I had known, experienced, and felt seemed to culminate in the compelling, indeed intoxicating, prospect of not only making *aliyah*, but also of serving 'my country.' Few of my friends shared my desire to return. Nevertheless, the dream of – or the Zionist entreaty to – return to the homeland, to live and/or fight for it, which inspired me then, continues to be fundamental to Jewish identity in the diaspora. My mother's reaction to my plans – a resounding 'Absolutely not!' – was much the same as that of many of the diaspora Croat mothers I interviewed over the course of this research. Although I did 'return' to Israel, my stay as a university student wound up being shorter than I had anticipated, my politics shifted dramatically, and I never fought in any war. But unlike me, young diaspora Croats did go to Croatia to fight, in the Homeland War of 1991–95. This they did with or without their parents' blessing, and some were casualties of that war.

Here I come back to the questions that initially piqued my interest when I witnessed clashes between Serb and Croat students in the university student centre in the spring of 1992. At that time, I was intrigued by their passion for the homeland and all things Croatian (or Serbian, in the case of the Serb students). This led me to more general inquiry regarding the historical precedents and consequences for representations and practices of identity, belonging, and place. An exploration of these themes became the basis for my initial investigation. Yet, as I delved deeper into the nature of identity for Croats in Toronto, I was increasingly drawn into Croatian transnational circuits of contact and meaning. This research led me in turn in an ethnographic direction that I had not initially intended to pursue, specifically to Croatia, yet I have argued that this was inevitable. The Croatian case presented here exemplifies the difficulties – ethnographic and conceptual – of presuming the discreteness of diaspora and homeland peoples, as well as the processes and the possibilities afforded by a consideration of their interdependence.

## Transnationalism and the Transition to Democracy in Croatia

Post-communist societies have been increasingly drawn into an ever-expanding and often perplexing array of networks and linkages, a fact recognized and addressed by scholars, but only partially. While a great deal of attention has focused on the impacts of globalization on post-communist Europe, little of it has been directed at transnationalism and its role in producing distinctive cultural practices, differentiated identities, nostalgia, memory, and trauma.

Throughout this book, I have sought to avoid a presentation of transnationalism that suggests a dichotomous relationship between the diaspora and the population of a locality and 'people remaining in familiar and ancestral places' (Gupta and Ferguson 1997a:7), but rather one that avoids the dual axes of migration between discrete territorial entities and where the nature of histories and ancestors is an ongoing matter of discussion, debate, and at times, conflict. The complexity of revived, imagined, or emergent bases of differentiation and/or compatibility, agreement, or disagreement among and between Croats provides a context for thinking differently about the issue of transnational identifications. As noted earlier, it is possible to move beyond the conventional juxtaposition of transnational sites and their inhabitants and the usual preoccupation with how the 'there' is articulated 'here.' The statuses and/or identitifications of diaspora Croats, returnees, and homeland Croats are fixed neither in time nor place. The Croatian case demonstrates how diaspora processes can be directly related to the experience of difference in homelands. Croats everywhere have always been implicated in each other's lives, memories, and imaginaries. But this is not to suggest that the discursive strategies, and ways of remembering, forgetting, or place-making are absent – far from it. I have been concerned with teasing out the many overlapping processes temporal and spatial, that factor into making sense(s) of *Hrvatstvo* – Croatness. Significantly, these processes are reflected, in part, in the history of relationships between diaspora Croats and the homeland, relationships that span everyday social practices in the local and transnational fields of family and kinship, peer group, workplace, and particularly, in politically charged affiliations and involvements in both the diaspora country and the homeland.

While the increased traffic in images, goods, and people to-ing and fro-ing between the Croatian homeland and diaspora sites has accelerated considerably since the collapse of the former Yugoslavia, this has not necessarily translated into greater affinities among Croats. Efforts to map the conceptual terrain of a new pan-Croatian identity are at odds because what Croats envision has been formulated in contextual, historical, and relational terms that invariably mitigate against consensus or unanimity. Indeed, this has been the history of Croatian identity politics for generations. I have discussed various ways in which home and homeland have played a role as discursive spaces of identification, a metaphor for being, becoming, and belonging, as well as a source of tensions and/or unity and pride, a place to remember, to forget or to return to. Significantly, the culmination of diaspora dreams for an independent homeland has opened up new spaces of contestation and ambivalence, rather than resolution and closure.

The creation of a sovereign and independent Croatian homeland has been fundamental, albeit to varying degrees, to Croatian dreams and goals, frustrations, identifications, and imaginaries, both in the diaspora and the homeland for decades and even centuries. The promise of the new post-socialist Croatia was one of purpose and pride, stability, and certainty as reflected in ubiquitous pronouncements on the strength and resilience of Croatian national character and the culmination of a history marked by suffering and sacrifice. However, when the moment of possibility finally arrived, in 1991, it did not produce the clarity of vision and purpose that had been the rallying cry for all

Croats who had fought for and/or waited the day when Croatia would be free of Socialist rule. Soon after the initial euphoria of independence, the contradictions and ambiguities that are Croatia and remain present among Croats everywhere, re-emerged and/or intensified. Thus, the question of identity and representation remains as complex as ever, Croatian sovereignty, notwithstanding.

For Croats, identities have been influenced by centuries of wars, invasions, and empires, as well as by shifting borders and balances of power involving competing visions of peoplehood. These have included the imperial identifications of Austro-Hungarian, pan-Slavic unity, fascism, and Yugoslavism, in its various forms. This historical context, defined by social and political turmoil, has shaped the sensibilities with which Croats have come to experience the contemporary reality of Croatian statehood. While the former socialist Yugoslav state demanded loyalties based on the ideology of 'brotherhood and unity,' changes during the past decade and a half have put the question of loyalties – national, ethnic, or otherwise – to the test. Pre-existing bases of differentiation among homeland Croats have been amplified by the emergence of pressures and paradoxes brought on by the need and the desire to respond to new social, political, and economic realities. Since independence many Croats, particularly those who are younger, have turned their backs on government entreaties to rebuild Croatia and on traditional (e.g., ethno-national, regional) forms of identification. Many see their future in a life outside the homeland and have emigrated from Croatia in large numbers in pursuit of opportunities abroad. Thus, many recent Croatian immigrants report finding little in common with most Toronto Croats, particularly those who identify with nostalgic renderings of the homeland.

The context of Croatia's independence and Homeland War set in motion the conditions for the emergence and/or exacerbation of a politics of desire and disdain among and between diaspora and homeland Croats, as revealed in contestation over the essence and meanings of Croatness. The circulation of identifications – some old and some new, but most comprising elements of each such as real Croats (*pravi Hrvati*) and Croatness – has been complicated by Croatian efforts to project an image of unity. Although Croatia's independence was occasion for boisterous displays of unity for Croats worldwide, the public face of a destiny fulfilled belies commonality and consensus.

Enthusiasm for the collapse of socialism is evidenced in the ubiquitous rhetoric of freedom from 'communist tyranny.' Events of the past fifteen years in countries in what used to be called the Eastern Bloc, and the former Yugoslavia specifically, might lead one to think that Croats are firmly united in their rejection of communist Yugoslavia, however, the presumption of unanimity even on this issue is problematic. To be sure, the goal of independence has, to varying degrees, dominated Croatian discourse throughout these years. But, while the historic occasion of independence has succeeded in bringing about the long-awaited goal of autonomy and sovereignty, it has also revealed disjunctures along with convergences for Croats anxious to assert newly found bases of commonality. Where convergences do occur, they are conditional and reflect specific circumstances and sensibilities as evidenced, for example, in comparisons between diaspora and homeland Croats.

For homeland Croats, sentiments concerning socialist rule in Yugoslavia remain varied and mixed. Most regard their years under socialism in complex ways – as a system that deprived them of elemental freedoms and one that institutionalized a system of finite expectations and few rewards. However, socialism also provided them with certain guaranteed, if minimal in many cases, social and economic supports and security, most of which have since disappeared. The historic idea of the Yugoslav nation, characterized by the equality of all its constituent groups, held appeal for many Croats (Sekulić 2004). Historically, Croats were at the forefront of the development of the ideal of pan-South Slavic unity; however, from the outset the reality of Serb political domination, and later, the entrenchment of socialist elites intent on preserving their power bases in their respective republics by whatever means, rendered the Yugoslav ideal politically unsustainable. But efforts to reduce all sentiments relating to the former Yugoslavia as simply nostalgia ignore the complicated reality that Croats lived during in the years between 1945 and 1990. Thus, despite efforts by the Tuđman government and Croatian nationalists to demonize the idea of Yugoslavia, and despite the nostalgia felt by some for the socialist era or aspects of it (see, e.g. Ugrešić 1998; Drakulić 1992, 1993, 1996), the ambivalence that underscores these views and experiences is not to be dismissed.

For diaspora Croats, equivocation over socialism is less common. Most Toronto Croats describe a history of hardship and brutal oppression under socialism – *whether or not* they personally were in Yugoslavia to experience it – punctuated by politicized remembrances including tales of suffering and catastrophe (e.g., the 1945 Bleiburg massacre features centrally). These have been ideologically constructed by diaspora Croats to explain not only their separation from the homeland but also what unites them as Croats. Primarily through the foregrounding of selected aspects of ways of being Croat, attempts to distill an essential Croatian identity are derived. As Angelika Bammer observes, the act of telling the story of the homeland (especially one under siege as during the Homeland War) has the benefit of creating the 'we' that belongs to it (1994a). 'The story does not express a practice ... It *makes* it' (de Certeau 1984:81). The story, narrativized and commemorated in these ways, provided the foundations upon which for decades many diaspora Croats imagined and (re)presented themselves.

Nonetheless, even Toronto Croats are not unanimous in their condemnation of Croatia under Tito. As noted in Chapter 1, some of the Toronto Croats I interviewed during the early 1990s, even those heavily involved in Croatian institutions or events, were ambivalent about life in the former Yugoslavia before Milošević took power. As time wore on though, they became less inclined to identify with the former socialist state or at least less inclined to publicly display anything but unequivocal support for Croatia.[1] Nevertheless, although Croats differ in their political and personal views and opinions of the new state, the Croatian homeland provides the primary constitutive bond that unites Croats globally.

### The Meaning(s) of Home/land

The terms 'home' and 'homeland' elicit myriad sentiments, meanings, and responses from Croats whether they be living in or outside of Croatia. Even for Croats who have lived in the territory of Croatia all their lives, the chequered political and social history of Croatia has had an impact on how they view themselves in relation to land, region, nation, and polity. The history of Croatian national, regional, and ethnic identifications is characterized by a wide range of visions and political philosophies. To presume unity of purpose and vision is to attribute an exclusivism and an essentialism not reflected in Croatian history.

In the years since independence, many Toronto Croats have had to refocus their energies on balancing the changes brought about in the homeland with those of living in Canada. This process is mitigated by the conditions of life and of representation in the Canadian nation state, where the state – while celebrating ethno-cultural diversity –

seeks to discipline and, in effect, neutralize the political significance of homeland ties through master narratives of multiculturalism (emphasizing equality and tolerance). Allegiance to nations and/or states other than Canada is discouraged in favour of principles and practices promoting social cohesion within the Canadian body politic. Linkages with homelands deemed to be acceptable by the Canadian state are thus decidedly non-political. Personal relationships with family in the home country, economic, and educational exchanges, and support for various Croatian historical and ethno-cultural events are therefore promoted. This has been especially so since the events of 11 September 2001 and resulting concerns over security and the surveillance of transnational political connections.

The celebration of distinctive ethno-cultural traditions is not, however, nor has it ever been, a benign process. In due course, pre-existing political loyalties and opinions on Croatia have resurfaced among diaspora Croats. Through time conflicting renderings of a shared vision for Croatia and Croats have emerged and/or have been exacerbated. That new players have come onto the Croatian political and economic scene, both from the diaspora and in the homeland, has added new tensions to an already volatile mix of political, social, and economic statuses and sentiments. Antagonisms over representational authority for Croats have become the rule rather than the exception. The implications of coming face to face with the self-evident nature of Croatian identity are revealed in the often sharpened sensibilities and discourses of sameness and difference (in terms of, e.g., hierarchical social categories of origins) and loyalties (regional, political, national, and the like).

These among many other indications draw attention to the relevance of competing yet complementary tensions of desire and disdain and their role in the process of Croatian subject formation. Most diaspora Croats are privy, but only partially, to the intricacies of Croatia's political processes and to the pragmatics of everyday life for homeland Croats. Their understanding of these processes is limited by the nature of their contacts with family and friends or their recreational and/or commercial activities in Croatia and in Bosnia and Hercegovina, expedited primarily through the technologies of communication and travel. More important are the logics, sensibilities, and expectations built up over years of living and coping with life in the diaspora that together shape the prism through which diaspora Croats see, understand, and evaluate conditions in the homeland. The conditions of existence for

Toronto Croats have, for many, served to reinforce the classic modernist logic of the Croatian state through transnational means, an outcome that is far different from that theorized by many who are enthusiastic about the subversive and liberating potential of diasporas. The experience of diaspora returnees to the homeland (discussed in Chapter 5) reveals the contradictions inherent in the idea of a unified, imagined homeland and the realities of everyday life in Croatia.

Many of the Toronto Croats I interviewed, although always ready to share their political views, are content to let Croats in the homeland steer their own future political course. Yet there are those diaspora Croats who, whatever their motivations, persist in providing mostly unsolicited 'expert advice' to homeland Croatian authorities, family, and friends, and who are otherwise attempting to insert themselves into Croatia's homeland affairs. They are confident in their assessments of life in Croatia and, more importantly, about what Croatia and Croatians need. Reception to these overtures in Croatia is invariably, and increasingly, chilly.

Although the political involvements of diaspora Croats (specifically those of right-wing diaspora Croats) in Croatia have garnered the most academic attention, antagonisms over imagery, history, customs, and other symbols or expressions of Croatness have also been the focus of diaspora efforts, but these have attracted less interest. The resulting tensions over such initiatives are evident not only between diaspora Croats and homeland Croats but also within diaspora Croat groups. Post-independence identifications for Toronto Croats have involved, as ever, more contestation than reconstitution. Thus, although Croatia's independence has been a dream come true for Toronto Croats, it has not, nor can it ever completely succeed in satisfying their desires for the homeland or for Croatness.

For their part, homeland Croats, by and large, reject and/or resist diaspora efforts to assume a role in the development of a vision for the new Croatia and the new Croat. Since independence, Croats in the homeland have encountered the best and the worst that the West has to offer, and they have consequently been able to re-evaluate their own lives, ambitions, and goals. Although generally speaking, Western social, cultural, and political influences are valued by many homeland Croats, they do not look to diaspora Croats living in the West as a source of inspiration or advice. The almost unanimously negative opinions voiced by homeland Croats on what many of them argue are the vulgar romanticism and anachronistic ideals of diaspora Croats, speak to a general desire to embrace change, shed their Balkan image, and promote distinctively modern European persona and politics.

Evidence of the desire of most homeland Croats to move Croatia away from its recent experience of post-independence nationalism (under Tuđman) and towards greater incorporation into the European body politic is seen in the efforts undertaken by the current Croatian prime minister, Ivo Sanader. He has endeavoured to change the hardline nationalist image of the previous HDZ regime. The goal of membership in the European Union is at the forefront of Sanader's political strategy (e.g. the Croatian Ministry of Foreign Affairs and European Integration), underscored by his stated willingness to work with the U.N. International Criminal Tribunal for the Former Yugoslavia (ICTY) in The Hague, which was a point of contention for the governments of Tuđman and Račan. Overtures to minority communities of Serbs and Italians (in Istria) have been among the most dramatic departures from the HDZ's traditionally ethno-nationalist platform. The Organization for Security and Cooperation in Europe (OSCE), the U.N. High Commissioner for Refugees (UNHCR), and Balkan Human Rights reports from the area acknowledge improvements, albeit limited, in the areas of minority treatment, repatriation of Serbs to the homes in Croatia that they fled during the Homeland War, and war crimes trials of Serbs in Croatia. Although it is still too soon to judge the outcomes of these policy shifts, the very fact of their introduction into HDZ political discourse is indicative of the new government's reading of the preferred goals and priorities of the majority of Croat voters *within* the borders of Croatia.

Diaspora Croats will no doubt have to adjust their often divergent sensibilities concerning Croatia and Croatness to contemporary changing homeland realities, for example, their vocal opposition to many of the International Criminal Tribunal for the Former Yugoslavia (ICTY) indictments of such military leaders as General Ante Gotovina. Essentially, Croats everywhere will continue to negotiate diverse sensibilities about what it means to be a Croat. As Stuart Hall argues: "instead of thinking of identity as an already accomplished fact, which the new cultural practices then represent, we should think, instead, of identity as a "production" that is never complete, always in process" (1990:222).

In keeping with my commitment to context-based complexity as *the* guiding principle of anthropological inquiry, I have presented an analysis of diaspora Croat identity politics that moves beyond typical preoccupations with the relationship between 'where you're from' and 'where you're at' (Gilroy 1991–92) to consider the role of homeland Croats themselves. I began this research with the intention of examining the impact of Croatia's independence on diaspora Croats only. Gradually the need to critically rethink the 'context of diaspora' (Axel 2004) in the Croatian case necessitated a consideration of the crucial role of homeland Croats (not just Croatia as in place of origin) and the phenomenon of diaspora return.

I have also endeavoured to unsettle ubiquitous and time-worn assumptions and perceptions about people and their politics and, more broadly, about diaspora as a totality. For a long time Croats as a whole have been portrayed unsympathetically as fascists, terrorists, and ultra-nationalist zealots. At times, homeland Croats have been complicit in this assessment of diaspora Croats as well. Scholars too have not all been immune from generalizations of this nature (see, e.g. Anderson 1994; Kaplan 1994; Clissold 1979). Upon learning that I was conducting research with Croats, a colleague who specializes in nationalism and ethnicity remarked: 'Why are you studying those fascists?'

Politically moderate or the broad middle of diaspora and/or homeland Croats who are often either marginal to or disengaged from Croatia's politics, are seldom the focus of discussions about Croats. The changing social and political sensibilities of Croats also seldom factor into analyses. The complexity that defines Croats – diaspora Croats in particular – is often lost, with the result that the tensions and ambiguities that have shaped their lives are ignored and/or dismissed in favour of a characteristically essentialist portrait of Croatian politics and practices. This inevitably leads to assumptions about the nature and composition of Croats as a group. The processes associated with the politics of desire and disdain, at the centre of the analysis presented here, demonstrate the weakness of these claims and assumptions. Disrupting the proclivity to oversimplify reveals the diverse expressions and sensibilities of Croatness.

These days, the Croatian Student Association's table, adorned with Croatian tourist pamphlets and flyers, flags, buttons, and souvenirs, is usually set up in the campus student centre during the annual university-wide multiculturalism week and other student-centred events. It attracts students interested in travelling to Croatia (e.g., annual summer *Task Force* excursions to Croatia), ski trips and sports clubs, barbeques, and other club events, and most importantly, Croatian students interested in meeting and hanging out with one other. The conversations of these students now focus less on homeland politics than on socializing and travel. The politically charged and sometimes vitriolic exchanges that characterized discussion during the early to mid-1990s are now rare. Yet, not long ago, I overheard a Serb student passing by the table mutter 'Ustaša,' a taunt that was quickly met with 'Četnik' from the Croat student to whom it was addressed. Some habits never die.

# Appendix A

# In the Field

Quite apart from the theoretical challenges introduced by transnational perspectives are the difficulties in developing methodological strategies that can respond to the global context of contemporary social and cultural conditions. Ethnographic frameworks developed around conventional, localized research methods are increasingly being challenged by the transnational character of social landscapes. Increasingly common in anthropological work, the subject of location has presented a series of problematics that require not just adjustments in fieldwork practice but also in thinking about 'the field.' Although a great deal of ink has been spilled over this issue in the past fifteen years, the contingencies of this research call attention to the relevance of these debates. Experiments with textual form and ethnographic practice are emerging across disciplines exemplified in such strategies as multi-sited ethnography (Marcus 1995), remapping memory (Boyarin 1994), and textual analysis and dialogical methods (Clifford 1988), all of which try to address a world where the 'mere movement of subjects' (Marcus 1995:106) is secondary. Numerous anthropologists have taken up this challenge, for example, Emily Martin (1994) who, through her work, has considered the question of social and cultural processes that are not well localized spatially through the community study.

While the concept of culture has also been vigorously critiqued in the past few years (Ortner 1999), as has the practice of writing anthropology (Clifford and Marcus 1986), the concept of 'the field' has only recently begun to enjoy the same sort of scrutiny (Ferguson and Gupta 1997). Culture, as a space carved out by anthropologists, has been largely left to common sense. While Gupta and Ferguson (1997) argue that we are willing to give up and/or interrogate ideas of territorially

fixed communities and stable, localized cultures, we are still committed to spending long periods in places far away in the field – firmly
insisting on the method of fieldwork as central to the construction of
anthropological knowledge. Appadurai too poses the problem of the
world described by anthropologists, as having changed immeasurably
without a corresponding shift in disciplinary practices (1991).

There is a growing consensus that the task is to emerge with less of a
sense of the field than a sense of a mode of study that cares about and
pays attention to the interlocking of multiple social-political sites and
locations (cf. Fog Olwig and Hastrup 1997). While anthropologists
studying the effects of globalization are engaged with this way of
thinking about fieldwork, this perspective has not yet been fully
embraced by anthropologists working in post-socialist societies, as
they are busily trying to cope with the tumultuous beginnings of emergent nation states and the fallout of the Second Great Transformation
(Verdery 1996; DeSoto and Dudwick 2000).

The research on which this book is based began in 1992, and consisted of several phases of fieldwork beginning in Toronto. The first
period of intensive fieldwork in Toronto spanned ten months from the
spring of 1992, the second entailed thirteen months in 1995-96, and the
last in 2003-04 for approximately eight months. The gaps during the
period 1992-96 were filled with less intensive although continuous
contact. The ethnographic methods most suitable to gaining an in-
depth view of Croats' lives included formal and informal interviews
with Toronto Croats; visits to people's homes; attending Croatian
events, church services and functions, speeches and lectures, rallies,
and fundraisers; and just plain 'hanging out.' I also conducted self-
administered surveys with a total of 215 Croats over a three-year
period. Decisions over whom and how many to interview had to be
carefully planned out for several reasons. First, according to current
estimates, the Croatian population of Metropolitan Toronto exceeds
120,000 (Croatian embassy estimates, Census Canada 'Dimension
series,' 1996); however, these figures were problematic in that, until
recently, not all Croats declared themselves as Croats in government
censuses. Although many claimed their Croatian ethnic status, some
referred to themselves as Yugoslav while others identified themselves
according to region of origin, such as Slavonia or Dalmatia. This is a
practice not unfamiliar to first-generation Croats who, in Yugoslavia,
first under Austro-Hungarian rule, then under Yugoslav rule had not
been accustomed to declaring themselves as Croats. This became glar-

ingly obvious when I compared the 1981, 1991, and 2001 censuses in Canada where many Croats had abandoned the designation Yugoslav in favour of Croat.

In addition, diaspora Croats in Toronto, not unlike most other diasporas or immigrant groups, are characterized by tremendous internal diversity based on factors such as region or republic of origin (e.g., Bosnia and Hercegovina, Dalmatia, Istria), dialect, and custom. I, therefore, spent a considerable amount of time first learning about Croats in Toronto to determine not only where, when, and how Croats self-identify and socialize, but the bases of their identification and the parameters of their association, for example, class, region of origin, generation, and length of stay in Canada. Over the course of this research, I have interviewed and surveyed hundreds of Croats both in Toronto and in Croatia, a fact that may seem to make any attempts at analysis unwieldy. However, I have also had the time to scrutinize and closely examine all of these data, given the fifteen-year time frame within which this material was collected. As part of my methodological strategy, I circulated two sets of surveys – one in 1993 to Croatian members of two churches and received 160 responses and the second to five Croatian university student associations across southern Ontario for which I received 57 responses. Much of the data were analysed during and immediately after each major phase of field research throughout this period, the results of which have been synthesized for the purposes of this book.

The snowball sampling method (which involves making use of informants' networks of friends and family to identify new interview subjects) was a valuable preliminary tool because during this time (early to mid-1990s), many Toronto Croats were quite suspicious of non-Croats. As has traditionally been the case for many anthropologists, my earliest encounters with Croats in Toronto were with prominent members of the community, that is, the gatekeepers. Some were initially suspicious of my motivations for doing research with Croats, and others were leery of how I would interpret, for example, Croatian history during the Second World War II – 'We have a bad rap here' – and the Croatian involvement in the war in Bosnia and Hercegovina. To partially mitigate the potentially negative consequences of these research conditions, I had business cards made up that were embossed with the logo of my university. The administrative staff in my department told me on numerous occasions that people had phoned to check on my faculty qualifications. I did though gradually gain the trust of many of the Toronto Croats I worked with, as evidenced in the numerous referrals I received and the ultimate emblem of trust, word of mouth.

While I focus primarily (and initially exclusively) on the effects of homeland independence on Croats in Canada, it became increasingly important to follow what Marcus refers to as 'connections, associations and putative relationships' (1995:97) among and between Croats both in Toronto and in Croatia and to investigate the circulation of cultural meanings, objects, and identities that are at the heart of Croats' struggles over the definition (or possibility) of a collective reality. This was made clear to me primarily by my Toronto Croat subjects who implored me to visit Croatia. Over the course of my research, most asked if I had visited Croatia and invariably urged me to go. The comments that provided the main motivation for doing fieldwork in Croatia are conveyed in the following statement by one first-generation Croat: 'If you really want to know what makes us tick then you must go and see my homeland.' Up to that point, my impressions of Croatia were framed by media reports; the then-burgeoning literature on Yugoslavia (authored primarily by political scientists, journalists, and historians) and the narrative constructions of my research subjects. It became clear that I had to visit the homeland that diaspora Croats spoke of so passionately, and from which many gained their inspiration and a renewed sense of peoplehood and hope. I, therefore, began a series of field trips to Croatia beginning in 1997, where I have since spent considerable periods of time primarily in and around Zagreb, but also in the Krajina region (Knin and Gospić), Zadar, and the southern Dalmatian coast cities of Split and Dubrovnik.

The contacts I have accumulated in Croatia over ten years consisted initially of contacts made through Toronto Croats, but then they changed to focus primarily on Croatian organizations and associations, academics, students, journalists, and activists and the locals in the neighbourhoods I was living in, as well as contacts made through a variety of other personal and professional routes. I was fortunate to be in Croatia during various municipal, regional, and national elections, during which I was privy to the political machinations of local elites and politicians, their supporters, and their critics. I have conducted archival research in both Toronto and Croatia examining Croatian consular and (now defunct) Croatian Ministry of Return Migration and Immigration and Foreign Ministry records from 1991 to 2001 on Croatian government initiatives to attract returnees in the form of promotional materials and programs such as settlement services and resources (e.g., taxation subsidies and housing allowances). I have also, over the years, analysed myriad documents both in Toronto and Croatia including newsletters and publications of various clubs, religious publishers (such as *Župni Vjesnik*), political organizations, and cultural and other associations.

This book also contains information on demographic patterns and rates of migration obtained from the Croatian Bureau of Statistics, beginning with 1991. The release of the 2001 Canadian census by Statistics Canada and the Croatian census database provided useful comparative data to build on; not so much for the purpose of statistical analysis (see, e.g. Asad 2002) but rather for how and in what ways Croats self-identify ten years after independence. For example, as already mentioned, the sociodemographic profile of Croats in Canada including data on self-identification have shifted since Croatia's independence, as indicated in the 1996 census, to reflect a marked decrease in identification as 'Yugoslav' in favour of 'Croatian' and in migration patterns. 'New forms of association, conversation and mobilization' (Appadurai 1996c:196) available through the Internet have also proved invaluable. Interactive Croatian website pages, news groups, chat rooms, and email discussion groups made computer-mediated communication central to this research. Weekly Croatian satellite television and radio programs in Toronto, produced and broadcast in both Canada and Croatia, also provided a steady and useful source of information and insights over the years.

My findings are not typical of the experiences or sentiments of all or even most Croats. Thus, I have not sought to present a portrait of Toronto Croats as a community writ large or a comprehensive account of life in selected locales in Croatia. With these caveats in mind, I have tried to capture and communicate the spirit of what Basch (et al.) have referred to as those 'moments and locations in which meanings/identifications are made or come undone' (1994:34). My goal has been is to present an ethnography of what Malkki refers to as the 'contingent socio-historical processes of making and unmaking categorical identities' (1995a:6) by chronicling a set of transnational processes that converged and unfolded over the 1990s and since – a momentous period in Croatian history.

The resources on Toronto Croats consist primarily of work by Croatian scholars such as Vinko Grubišić (1984), Ivan Čižmić (1994a,1994b), and Zlata Godler (1981), and documentation such as church and association bulletins and newsletters, commemorative publications, organizational histories, and academic theses as well as minutes of Croatian association meetings. These were supplemented with taped interviews, self-administered surveys, and oral histories conducted with long-established members of the Croatian community. In addition, my debt to the extensive and superb scholarship of the Canadian historian Anthony Rasporich (1978a, 1978b, 1982, 1994, 1999) will become apparent especially throughout Chapters 1 and 2.

## Appendix B

# Notes on the Croatian Language and Its Pronunciation

The Croatian language, its origins, and its uniqueness, has been a hotly contested issue for generations, if not centuries. In the past hundred years or so, and especially since Croatian independence in 1991, the relationship of Serbian and Croatian has been highly politicized. Throughout this book I refer to the language spoken by my research participants as Croatian and not Serbo-Croatian (as it was called in the Socialist Federal Republic of Yugoslavia). The choice to use the former is based solely on the fact that most Croats call the language Croatian. Although words are sometimes spelled in different ways by non-Croats (e.g., Tudjman vs the Croatian Tuđman) I endeavour to retain Croatian spellings of names and places. Thus, the more commonly seen English spelling of Herzegovina is rendered here as Hercegovina.

Croatian orthography is phonetic, consisting of thirty phonemes, one letter for each sound. Every one is relatively easy for English speakers to pronounce.

### Table of Pronunciation
A as the *a* in *architect*
B as the *b* in *boy*
C as the *ts* in *hats*
Č as the *ch* in *church*
Ć similar to Č but softer, as in the sound between *teach* and *time*
D as the *d* in *day*
Dj as in the sound between d in *duke* and dg in *fudge*
Dž as the *J* in *Jane*
Đ as *Dj*

E as the *e* in *bet*
F as the *f* in *fix*
G as the *g* in *get*
H as in the Scottish *ch* in *loch*
I as the *i* in *machine*
J as the *y* in *yes*
K as the *k* in *kiss*
L as the *l* in *letter*
M as the *m* in *mother*
N as the *n* in *note*
O as the *o* in *pot*
P as the *p* in *please*
R as the *r* in *race*, a rolled "r"
S as the *s* in *sit*
Š as the *sh* in *shower*
T as the *t* in *table*
U as the *u* in *rule*
V as the *v* in *violet*
Z as the *z* in *zoo*
Ž as the *s* in *measure*

This pronunciation table is based on Celia Hawkesworth, *Colloquial Croatian and Serbian* (London: Routledge Press 1998) (pp. 5–6), and Alex Bellamy, *The Formation of Croatian National Identity* (Manchester: Manchester University Press 2003).

# Notes

## Introduction

1 It is also important to point out the differences between the use of Croat and Croatian this book. Croatian is used as a descriptor, as in Croatian identity, Croatian history, or Croatian citizens (i.e., people who live in and are citizens of Croatia state). Croat(s) is used to designate ethno-national identification and affiliation, thus, reference is made to Bosnian or Herce-govinian Croats, Toronto Croats, homeland Croats, and individuals who claim Croatian ancestry.

2 This is the subject of my current research project, which is entitled 'Mujahe-din in Our Midst: Bosnian Croats after the Yugoslav Wars of Succession.'

3 This event has taken on tremendous symbolic significance for Croats worldwide. It stands as testimony to the crimes of the Tito regime, and the complicity of the world – here the British forces (occupying Austria) who turned back these refugees only to be slaughtered by the Partisan forces – in the suffering of the Croats. Many have chronicled this tragedy but emigre writers such as Ante Beljo, a Bosnian Croat from northern Ontario, have inflated the legacy of Bleiburg by claiming that it was a disaster unparal-lelled in human history (1995).

4 For the most recent round of debates on this issue, see the series of articles and rejoinders in the journal *Anthropological Theory*, issues 4(1) 2004 and 5(4) 2005.

5 A Croatian Studies program begun in September 1993 was offered at the University of Zagreb and is now the Centre for Croatian Studies (http://www.hrstud.hr, accessed 3 September 2006).

6 This is how it is usually presented in written documentation by Croats. The

Homeland War carries significant symbolic and historical weight for Croats everywhere.

7  However, Hockenos's book on exile patriotism among Croats, Serbs, and Albanians focuses exclusively on those right-wing diaspora Croats who catapulted Tuđman to power (2003).

8  All interviews took place in Toronto, except where stated otherwise.

9  For a discussion of the concept of 'peoplehood' consult Immanuel Wallerstein's 'The Construction of Peoplehood: Racism, Nationalism, Ethnicity,' in Balibar and Wallerstein, *Race, Nation, Class: Ambiguous Identities* (London: Verso Press, 1991), 71–85.

## 1: Locating Croatia in Diaspora

1  The Yugoslav government was also preoccupied with ensuring the steady flow of remittances from Croatian emigres to the homeland. According to the Croatian economist R. Bičanić (1938), of all the money that was sent back to Yugoslavia, over 60% came from Croatian immigrants.

2  The ethnic press played an important role in the political socialization of diaspora Croats and often served to enlarge the base of supporters for political movements (Godler 1981:39). Even those who were not informed and/ or involved in politics in Croatia became sensitized to and often politicized by reading Croatian newspapers (including the CPP *Hrvastki Glas* (Croatian Voice) and *Borba* (the Struggle). The influential *Zajedničar* (the Fraternalist) published since 1904, was an important vehicle through which Croats in North America were informed about political events in their homeland. *Hrvatska Matica Iseljenika* (Croatian [Emigrant] Heritage Foundation) began publishing diaspora almanacs in 1954 and continues to publish a regular edition of its magazine *Dom i Svijet* (*Home and World*). Despite its insistence that its focus is exclusively cultural, it remains a political institution, even a nation-building one.

3  Indeed, during the war, Croats in Hercegovina (in the western part of the republic) formed the short-lived Croatian Community of Herceg-Bosna (*Hrvatska Zajednica Herceg-Bosna*, 1991–94) under Mate Boban as a national supra-organization that aimed to protect their interests. It was declared illegal by the Constitutional Court of Bosnia and Hercegovina in 1994.

4  Despite its association with the Axis regime, the date the Ustaša took over, 10 April 1941, is listed in the 1984 edition of *Toronto and Its People* (1984:84). The symbolic significance of the date has changed, however, as do all commemorative occasions, to fit contemporary realities. While it continues to be a defining moment in the memories of many first-generation Toronto

Croats who fled Tito's Yugoslavia, Croatian independence from 1941 to 1945 has taken on more general significance as a symbol of the Croatian thirst for independence. Nonetheless, many Toronto Croats have reservations about the celebration of this controversial period in Croatian history. Toronto Croats, thus, are bound together as much by remembering as by forgetting.

5 The term 'communist' was not just a political accusation but a comment on one's character – as lazy, lacking moral fibre as well as national and religious commitment.

6 See, e.g., Dusenbery (1997) regarding the reactions of Sikhs to Canadian efforts to classify them as Indian. Macedonians, many of whom have come from Bulgaria, Greece, or Yugoslavia have also experienced similar difficulties (see, e.g. Danforth 1995:86; Vasiliadis 1984).

7 This position is exemplified in the influential social philosopher Charles Taylor's analysis of Canadian multiculturalism. In his widely read discussion of the 'politics of recognition' (couched in a liberal social ethos), diaspora is seen as problematic: 'societies ... are becoming more porous. Their porousness means that they are more open to multinational migration: more of their members live the life of diaspora, whose centre is elsewhere ... the awkwardness arises from the fact that there are substantial numbers of people who are citizens and also belong to the culture that calls into question *our* philosophical boundaries' (emphasis mine; 1994:63). According to Taylor, 'our identity is shaped by recognition or its absence' (1992:25). The demand for recognition comes in the form of political calls for rights, for example, feminism and, in the case here, the politics of multiculturalism.

8 The sociodemographic profile of Croats in Canada including data on self-identification have begun to shift since Croatian independence, as indicated in the 2001 Canadian census to reflect a marked decrease in identification as 'Yugoslav' in favour of 'Croatian.' However, classifications in the Canadian Census of 2001 still use the term 'Balkan origins.' Where Croatian is identified it falls under the 'other' category.

9 In 1971, two Croatian exiles assassinated the Yugoslav ambassador in Sweden, and in 1976, a group of Croatian exiles hijacked a TWA plane in order to raise awareness of the Yugoslav treatment of Croatians. This was accompanied by the detonation of a bomb set off at Kennedy Airport, which killed a policeman. Toronto Croats were also both the targets and the perpetrators of incendiary acts. 'The terrorists were usually members of emigrant associations that supported the unconditional creation of an independent Croatia' (Pusić 1997). However, there were also moderates,

such as Jakša Kušan, who headed the diaspora organization Hrvatska
Matica Iseljenika in Croatia and who started the moderate monthly *Nova
Hrvatska* in London. For about 30 years it remained the most widely read
paper in the diaspora.

10 After her release, Julie Bušić, the American-born (non-Croat) wife of one of
the hijackers, Zvonko Bušić, convicted of air piracy, was appointed to political posts by Tuđman including one as senior adviser. She published
*Ljubavnici i Ludjaci* (Lovers and Lunatics), which received a Croatian
national literary prize. The diaspora community continues to lobby for her
husband's release.

11 This refers to the river Drina that runs along the eastern border of Bosnia
and Hercegovina and was controlled by the Ustaša between 1941 and 1945.

12 *Otpor* has been associated with numerous acts of violence, all in the name of
Croatian independence. For example, in 1982, a trial was held in New York
City in which ten Croatian nationalists were convicted of being part of a
'nationwide criminal operation' to spread extortion, arson, bombing, and
murder across the country in the name of independence from Yugoslavia. A
Canadian of Croatian origin, Drago Sudar, age 50, of Etobicoke, Ontario,
was described as being a 'skilled bomb maker' who travelled widely in the
United States and Europe to teach his skills. Many of the explosive devices
used in the alleged acts were said to come from Toronto (see http://
www.pavelicpapers.com for information on the Ustaša). Indeed, the Ustaša
friendly newspaper *Nezavisna Država Hrvatska* (Independent State of
Croatia, also the same name as the fascist puppet state of 1941–45), began
publication in the United States in 1959, but moved to Toronto in 1960 and
remained in Toronto until 1998, when it was moved to Zagreb. According
to the editor-in-chief, Dr Psenicnik: 'Our paper will ... follow the ideas of
the HOP which was founded by Dr Ante Pavelić. It will be an ideological
paper based on the 10th April revolution [10 April 1941, the founding of the
NDH]; we will fight for a historical truth about NDH and Dr Ante Pavelić,
refuting numerous lies about the Ustashe movement which accumulated
and spread during the Communist rule.'

13 My credibility as a researcher was often queried by interviewees and survey participants, who, on occasion, contacted my university to verify my
credentials. Thereafter, I distributed business cards with the logo of my university to participants and attached them to letters of introduction.

14 Balkanization is unique as it takes a region's name and identifies a process
of continuous conflict and fragmentation. This is discussed at greater
length in Chapter 3.

15 Others focus on the often radical political activities of diaspora groups in

exiled national liberation movements which may draw followers from that segment of a diaspora (e.g., political refugees) forced to flee their nation state for political reasons (Shain 1989:55).

16 The Israeli government has repeatedly called upon Canadian Jewish leaders, who are increasingly politically conservative, to act as lobbyists for the promotion of pro-Israeli policies (Taras and Weinfeld 1993). Japanese, Greek, Chinese, Italian, Filipino, Indian, Ukrainian, and other diasporas in Canada have also been sought after by their homeland governments and economic interests.

17 Elsewhere, the interest of political scientists in particular in the role of diasporas in the rise of ethnic (versus civic) nationalism is in the seemingly inevitable connection between diaspora and nationalist sentiments. Although some discuss the actual and/or potential role of diasporas in advocating for civic principles of pluralism, democracy, and human rights in homelands, most have focused on how diasporas in effect reinforce ethnic nationalist goals.

18 We can see this in the evolution of Zionist ideologies among Jews since the beginning of the twentieth century. According to Cohen (1997), the dominant ideological construct for American Jews has shifted in the past 30 years from pro-Zionism to pro-Israelism. The goal of the eventual resettlement of all diaspora Jews in Israel (*aliyah*) has shifted (since the Second World War) to lobbying and financial support for the Jewish state.

## 2: 'The War Made Me Croatian'

1 Approximately 250 Canadian Croats joined the Croatian National Guard in 1991.

2 Alma Matris was formed in 25 March 1990 as a 'patriotic Croatian organization representing and defending Croatian interests' (*Gaudemas*, June 1998).

3 The historian, James Sadkovich (1996) criticized the media, particularly writers for *The Nation* and other news outlets for 'tarring all sides with the same genocidal brush,' as Serbs.

4 In 1994, the Croatian Anti-Calumny Project in New York City published a booklet entitled 'Croatia and Croats in "The New York Times"' where it faulted the *New York Times* for promoting an image of Croats as fascists. Former *New York Times* columnist Leslie Gelb wrote in 1991 that 'Croatia is known more for its fascists than for its democrats.'

5 Bedem Ljubavi (with four chapters in Canada) became the Canadian Croatian Women's Congress in 1993; it has published bulletins and offers counselling and information for newcomers to Canada.

6 Recently, the Library of Congress in the United States officially recognized Croatian as a distinct language.

7 In 1967, e.g., the 'Declaration Concerning the Name and the Position of the Croatian Literary Language' was published, which was a repudiation of the 1954 Novi Sad agreement on the unity of the Serbo-Croatian language.

8 The Albanian novelist Ismael Kadare (1978), was committed to removing the traces of Turkish and cultural influences from Albania. His perspective reflects the anxieties that obtain in territories of complex linguistic traditions and histories of conflict.

9 I was surprised to find non-Croat students taking both the Croatian and the Serbian courses in order, according to one student registered in the class, to get 'an easy extra credit for a course I've already taken in Serbian.'

10 For an analysis of political affiliation and social mobility in the former Yugoslavia, see Massey et al. (2003).

11 'Newfies' is an often pejorative term for Newfoundlanders. Newfoundland, on Canada's east coast, has a predominantly resource-based economy, with a traditionally high rate of unemployment.

12 Their office space was donated by a Croatian builder from Toronto, who is now an influential entrepreneur in Croatia.

13 One of the most uncomfortable moments for me was when one of the main organizers of the CCIC referred to Bosnians as 'Jihad.'

14 I was, however, recently pleased to learn that there is a 'Yugoslav Club' at my son's high school; its mandate is to promote harmony amongst the constituent groups of the former Yugoslavia, although their members are mainly Serbs.

15 These are the names of two rival soccer clubs, the first from Croatia and the second from Serbia.

### 3: 'We Are Not Fascists'

1 Mary Sopta, the Canadian-born wife of Marin Sopta, ran for public office in Ontario as a Liberal candidate and was subjected to a smear campaign by those who associated her politics with those of her husband.

2 According to Fra. Ljubo Krasić (1999), in Canada 2002 children studied Croatian,while only 492 studied Croatian in the United States.

3 'Slažem se, današnja je Hrvatska norvalska, po mjeri hrvatskih emigranata iz Kanade, ali neče dugo biti takva!' (Cited by Darko Hudelist, *Globus*, 2000, no. 471:72).

4 The Norval church complex approximately forty kilometres outside of Tor-

onto has been attended primarily by Hercegovinian Croats and is run by the Franciscan Order.

5  In contrast, in his brief treatment of diaspora Croats, Alex Bellamy makes a point of drawing a distinction between radical separatist diaspora groups, some with links to the Ustaša, and other moderate diaspora Croat organizations such as the National Federation of Croatian Americans (2003:92–5).

6  Even Vesna Pusić, the leader of liberal HNS stated that 'although generally fairly moderate, the émigrés always included in their ranks small but passionate and well-organized groups of extreme nationalists, some of whom were terrorists' (1997a).

7  Many émigrés to Canada came from the poor but strongly nationalist regions in the south of Bosnia and Hercegovina.

8  While in Zagreb on 3 October 2003, I watched a television documentary entitled 'Anton Kikaš: Ponovne Rođen' ('Anton Kikaš: Born Again'), produced by Hrvoje Habeković in 2003 and aired on HRT3, which presented a highly sympathetic portrait of Kikaš's efforts on behalf of the Croatian nation state.

9  On 8 November 1995, a small side-bar news item in the *Toronto Star* reported: 'Croatia-bound weapons, Ammo seized from farm in Proton township in Ontario. The materials were found in a rented, 12-metre shipping container.'

10  Although approximately 2,600 diaspora Croats in Toronto were eligible to vote in 1992, when I asked representatives of the Croatian government in both Toronto and Ottawa about the criteria for eligibility, they were either vague or unsure. As of this writing, the situation has changed somewhat in that the diaspora vote has diminished substantially because of the abolition of the Upper House of the Sabor and other constitutional changes since the new ruling coalition came to power – changes aimed in part at reducing the influence of a diaspora that is loyal primarily to the HDZ. Nonetheless, the Croatian government remains sensitive to the demands and sentiments of the diaspora in that recognition of the diaspora is still enshrined in the constitution. The Citizenship Law and electoral legislation grants citizenship, and thereby the franchise, on purely ethnic grounds to ethnic Croats abroad with no genuine link to the country. The Citizenship Law distinguishes between those who have a claim to Croatian ethnicity and those who do not. Ethnic Croats are eligible to become citizens, even if they were not citizens of the former Socialist Republic of Croatia, as long as 'he or she issues a written statement that he or she considers himself or herself to be a Croatian citizen.' (Law on Citizenship, Croatian Constitution, Article 16). Persons who are not ethnic Croats must satisfy more stringent requirements

through naturalization in order to obtain citizenship. Even those who previously were lawful residents of Croatia in the former Yugoslavia were
compelled to provide proof of previous residence and citizenship that was
not demanded of ethnic Croats. Non-government organizations assisting
ethnic Serbs with documentation issues continued to report local officials
applying this legal double standard (Balkan Human Rights Report, 2000,
available at www.balkanhr.com).

11 The popular satirical writer and journalist, Tanya Torbarina, dubbed him
'pizza man' in her column in the weekly *Globus*, and the name stuck. Many
mistakenly assumed that he was a wealthy Croatian-Canadian entrepreneur. This impression was based on his ability to access to large amounts of
money solicited from the Toronto. This misconception was also reproduced
by the European Community's special envoy to former Yugoslavia, Lord
David Owen, in his book *Balkan Odyssey*, where he claims that 'Šušak ran a
highly successful chain of pizza restaurants in Canada' (1996:138), and by
the former U.S. ambassador to Yugoslavia, Warren Zimmerman, when he
dubbed Šušak a 'pizza millionaire' (1996:154) .

12 For an English language analysis of the Hercegovinian Croats, see Goldstein (1999) and Tanner (1996). For Croatian sources check Cvitković (2006)
and Hadžiosmanović (2006).

13 The term 'intelligentsia' has been defined in numerous ways (Gella 1977). I
follow Martynowych's interpretation because it is developed in the context
of a similar diaspora population in Canada – Ukrainians. The intelligentsia
in this context are teachers, entrepreneurs, and those whose education sets
them apart from the immigrant masses. They constitute a 'self-conscious
social stratum that assumes for itself the role of social or political vanguard'
(1991:xxviii). The intelligentsia sets nationalist interests above class and
denominational concerns and calls for an independent state in the homeland.

14 The table of contents of one of these publications, *Croatia between War and
Independence* (Bilandžić et al. 1991), is noteworthy for its handling of the
contentious issues regarding the Second World War in Croatia. The heading
of the chapter covering this period reads: 'The Wartime Period: (a) "The
Antifascist Movement in Croatia and the Federal State of Croatia as Part of
the Allied Coalition" and (b) 'Casualties of War.' The collaborationist Independent State of Croatia – the NDH – is briefly discussed in the context of
how it was misrepresented by 'Serbian propaganda.' In this rendering of
Croatian complicity with fascists, the 'radical part' of the NDH is blamed
for atrocities, a blame that the authors argue is equally shared by all collaborators – Croatian, Serbian, Slovene, etc. See also Katich (1983).

15 Interestingly, the term 'holocaust' often comes up to describe the predicament of Croatians at war in the homeland. Just as the Jewish holocaust of
the Second World War made Israel a symbol of survival and a centre of Jewish identity, so too, does independent Croatia represent a symbol of triumph over persecution for Croats.

16 In the introduction to the 1990–91 edition of the *Croatian-Canadian Business
Directory*, the editors write: 'We are especially pleased with the news that
business people in Croatia as well as the newly elected Croatian government are interested in our *Business Directory* and want us to forward a
rather large number of copies.' The president of the Croatian-Canadian
Business and Professional Association was known to have had close ties to
Franjo Tuđman.

17 The most famous example is that of Androniko Lukšić, from Chile, who
invested in a large, and now highly successful, brewery in Karlovac.

18 Much to the dismay of many homeland Croats, the HDZ government
altered the division of regions in Croatia in 1993 to comprise 21 counties
(*županiji*), plus Zagreb, officially dismantling historic geographic entities.
(For the historical significance of *županija*, see Vrbošić 1992.)

19 According to Mirko Meheš, a Croatian historian in Canada, although
Croatian political activism was encouraged among Croatian emigrants by
Croats in the former state of Yugoslavia, it is clear that they now envisage
no political role for the diaspora (1993:23).

20 The two exceptions he cites, John Šola and Mary Sopta, are from Toronto.

## 4: Ten Years Later

1 Several exposés have appeared in Croatian media outlets, such as *Nacional*
(21 February 2001), reporting that the Croatian National Fund was a con-
duit for the illicit use and laundering of funds procured mostly from unsus-
pecting diaspora donors.

2 Interestingly, Michael Kenny has discussed the effects of political change in
Spain on Spaniards living in Mexico, finding that new forms of differentiation based on region of origin and political allegiances in the mother country have emerged among Spaniards in Mexico (1984).

3 Some examples include, http://www.crowc.org, http:// www.studiacroat-
ica.com, http://www.croatianworld.net, and http://www.croatia.ch.

4 The *Crna Legija* (Black Legion) site is one such case where the recorded
number of visits (hits) as at November 2005 was close to 700,000 (http://
crnalegija.com). Others include http://www.bogihruati.com, and http://
www.ustasa.net.

5 In 2001, Croatia placed fifteenth in the list of the top 15 countries with a per capita remittance figure of U.S. $167.90; Bosnia, with a large Croat population, placed tenth overall. International Monetary Fund 2003, *Balance of Payments Statistics Yearbook 2002* (Washington, DC: IMF 2002).

6 Tuđman remains very popular even though he died in 1999. Bus tours from Europe and Bosnia are brought to see Tuđman's grave, an enormous monument at the entrance to the Mirogoj cemetery in Zagreb. Most of these tourists have their picture taken in front of his grave and place small flags as well as candles embossed with the Croatian flag.

7 Among the desired qualities of the 'new Croatian' were traditional family values, exalting motherhood as a vocation, espousing pro-life values, fiercely attacking gay and lesbian lifestyles and relationships, and vilifying feminism (personal communication, Ela Grdinić, Judge, County Court, Zagreb, and Maja Mamula, Counsellor, LEGALINA Project, Zagreb, 1999). See also Bundalo (1997) and Mežnarić (1994).

8 According to Elie Kedourie, national historians are myth-making intellectuals (1993:14).

9 This may have something to do with the socialist period in Yugoslavia where historical analysis was constrained by political concerns.

10 The bronze monument of Baron Josip Jelačić (appointed by Kaiser Ferdinand V in 1848), in the centre of the square, has long been a symbol of Croatian continuity, co-opted by many for political purposes. Tuđman was the last in a series of political leaders to claim him as a national symbol. After having been removed from the square in 1947, the monument was reinstated in 1990 after independence.

11 On 9 May 1999, spectators threw stones at protesters who were demanding that the square's original name, Victims of Fascism Square, be reinstated. It, along with 3,000 other memorial sites from the Second World War in Croatia, were erased after Tuđman came to power (reported in *Feral Tribune*, 17 May 1999).

12 The creation of the European man as the universal subject in Western social and political thought was realized by defining 'him' against a plethora of 'Others.'

13 Croatian scholarship often links the Croatian nation to Europe. For example, Gulin Zrnić (1999) links Croatia to the Italian Renaissance via the Slavic artists and intellectuals in fifteenth- and sixteenth-century Dubrovnik.

14 The Croatian contestant for the televized 1997 Miss Universe pageant introduced herself as from the 'beautiful middle European country of Croatia.'

15 'This line ... then goes through Yugoslavia almost exactly along the line

now separating Croatia and Slovenia from the rest of Yugoslavia' (Huntington 1993: 24).

16 In a 17 July 2005 piece of the *New York Times'* Travel section entitled, 'In Croatia a New Riviera Beckons,' the writer Steve Dougherty observes: 'As the wounds of war heal, Croatia's beautiful and historic Dalmatian coast is being rediscovered by international trend setters.' Croatia has also been featured on numerous television shows on travel.

17 *Hrvatska – Mala Zemlja za Veliki Odmor*, Hrvatska Turistički Zajednica (Croatian National Tourism Office), Zagreb 1996.

18 The terms 'civilized' and 'civilization' have been used in Croatian publications when reference is made to the place of Croatia in modern Europe. 'Only those who live in this country will be aware of the great efforts made by its citizens to make this society a civilized, self-assertive and globally integrated society' (Švob-Đokić 1996:153).

19 Several of these include *Frakcija* (Fraction) magazine for the performing arts, *Hrvatski Institut za Pokret i Ples* (HIPP, Croatian Institute for Movement and Dance), and the *MAPAZ* project (Moving Academy for Performing Arts, Zagreb). The group *Not Your Bitch* focuses on the problems of identity of women and girls through a form of dance theatre.

20 See Bellamy (2003) on the influence of Tuđman's nationalist project on the education system in Croatia.

21 It is important to note that the Croats who commented on this facet of Croatian identity politics pointed out the distinction between the nationalist discourses and images promoted by the ruling HDZ and a more general sense of patriotism and pride. The Croatian national presence at World Cup soccer tournaments in both 1998 and 2002, and the rise in profile of Croatian athletes in, for example, tennis and the Olympics, has contributed to the pride, diaspora Croats feel for their compatriots.

22 This critique of essentialized Croatian imagery and experience is echoed in the work of several Croatian ethnologists at the Institute of Ethnology and Folklore Research in Zagreb, who have been working on a 'multi–voiced ethnography of war' (Jambrešić Kirin, 1999, Jambrešić Kirin and Povrzanović 1996) and in critiques of Western-based scholarly representations of 'nationalist' Croatian scholarship (Prica 1995; Feldman 1995; Rihtman-Auguštin 1997).

23 During the Tuđman era, many of the newspaper kiosks were owned or operated by those loyal to the HDZ, which reportedly had a negative effect on the distribution of newspapers or other publications critical of the current government.

24 The Istrian Democratic Union (IDS) left the coalition in June 2001, following a dispute over their desire for autonomous regional status as well as the ambivalence of the coalition regarding extreme right-wing forces.

25 The fascinating question of whether the demographic changes brought about by the exodus or expulsion of minorities -mainly Serbs – from Croatia during the Homeland War has had the effect of intensifying intra-national tensions among Croats based on, e.g., regionalisms, as opposed to international tensions (e.g., Serb-Croat) is beyond the scope of this book. It is important to note though that regionalisms have long been a factor in the politics of difference in Croatia (Goldstein 1999; Šantić 2000; for more detailed examinations of regionalism in Croatia consult the Croatian journal *Društvena Istraživanja*).

26 Nonetheless, as of the time of this writing, some hostility towards Serbs as a result of the war remains, especially in war-affected areas, as evidenced in the difficulties experienced by Serbs repatriating to Croatia. See, e.g., *World Refugee Survey*, U.S. Committee for Refugees Report (2002), 187–8). During 2002, 11,000 Croatian Serbs participated in organized return to Croatia from elsewhere in the former Yugoslavia and Bosnia (OSCE Reports, 2002, 2003, 2004). There have been instances of attacks on and harassment of Serbs. Despite the Croatian governments' stated commitments to repatriation, there have been numerous cases of (often local–level) bureaucratic obstacles for Serbs hoping to return to Croatia to reclaim property or procure employment. Nonetheless, the widespread violent backlash against Serbs anticipated after the war did not materialize.

27 The images I recall most from the train trips between Zagreb in the north and Split on the southern Dalmatian coast were of the odd look of towns and villages such as Knin and Gospić that were, between 1991 and 1995, under Serb control in what was called the Republic of Serb Krajina. The widespread looting and burning of, first, Croatian (in 1991) and then Serb property (when in August 1995, the Croatian army captured Serb-held Krajina territory in *Operacija Oluja* [Operation Storm]), have left a strange patchwork of destruction. Houses, some burned, strafed with bullets, or demolished, stood alongside others that were unblemished, occupied, and well maintained. Some of the damaged houses had the words 'Do not burn – Croatian house' painted on the outside. These images invariably speak to a recent (pre-war) past of coexistence or, at the very least, mutual tolerance, reflecting histories, memories, and locally specific logics that have been shaken but cannot be erased by the rhetoric of cultural or national homogeneity.

28 One example of the influence of the powerful Hercegovinian lobby in

Croatia came from the daily televised weather report on HRT1 (in 1997), which displayed a regional map demarcating each of the former Yugoslav republics with distinctive borders and colours, all with the exception of Bosnia and Hercegovina. Although the official Bosnia and Hercegovinian border (with Croatia) was displayed, western and northern sections of Bosnia were shaded in the same colour as the Republic of Croatia.

29 The author of this comment is Marin Sopta, a diaspora returnee from Toronto and the director of the Institute for Social Sciences Ivo Pilar (where many of the researchers and affiliates are supporters of HDZ). '2001. Cemo svim mladim Hrvatima iz Dijaspora Platiti Dolazak u Hrvasktu' *Jutarnji List*, 27 December 1998:8–9.

30 While Croatian statistical sources (e.g., Statističke Informacije 1998) report a large net increase of immigrants to Croatia over emigrants, most newcomers to Croatia since 1992 are from Bosnia and Hercegovina. The Croatian case demonstrates how the rhetoric of return is not reflected in numbers. According to Croatian Ministry of Return and Immigration (July 1998 figures), the number of returning Croatian Canadians was 974. Accurate statistics are difficult to obtain because most Croats who have emigrated to Croatia (either temporarily or permanently) have maintained their dual Croatian and Canadian citizenship, a factor that would not be apparent in immigration or other official government statistics in either country. The elimination of visa requirements for travellers to Croatia, in late 1997, also makes these numbers difficult to pin down. Furthermore, not all emigrants who leave Croatia with the intention of permanently settling abroad report their departure to the Croatian ministry registration office (Nejašmić 1993).

31 Strong resistance by Toronto Croats to Croatian government efforts to close the consulate in Mississauga was successful.

32 Under pressure from the Croatian opposition and the international community, the fixed quota system of diaspora representation introduced by the HDZ in 1995 was changed to a proportional system based on total number of diaspora votes cast.

33 General Ante Gotovina, formerly a member of the French Foreign Legion before the war in Croatia in 1990, became a commander in the Croatian Army. He advanced from brigadier in 1992 to major general in 1994. He was the commanding officer of the Split military district between 1992 and 1996, including the 1995 Operation Storm. In 1996, he became the Chief of the HV Inspectorate, but was dismissed from active service in 2000. Gotovina was indicted by the ICTY in 2001 for crimes against humanity and violations of the laws and customs of war; the court holds that troops under his command committed autrocities against the Serbs in

what the Serbs proclaimed as the Republic of Srpska Krajina during and after Operation Storm. Gotovina, however, fled and remained at large for some years. There were rumours that among the many places that he hid was the Norval complex in Mississauga, Ontario. The Washington-based organization Rewards for Justice (established by the 1984 Act to Combat International Terrorism, Public Law 98–533, U.S. Department of State's Bureau of Diplomatic Security) put forward a $5 million reward for information leading to Gotovina's capture and arrest. His fugitive status has been cited as the main reason why the Netherlands and the United Kingdom have not ratified the treaty initiating the Croatia's accession to the European Union.

34 'Hrvatski svjetski kongres i smjena u Hrvatskoj matici iseljenika' Croatian World Congress and Changes in the Croatian Heritage Foundation.

35 According to Ivana Djurić (2003:119) Canada is home to 'the largest percentage of post-Second World War [Croatian] immigrants (the "newcomers").'

36 University tuition in Croatia is expensive for most Croatians, a factor that has been exacerbated by rising unemployment and the high cost of living. Several Croatian contacts, one of whom teaches pedagogy at the University of Zagreb, confirmed this and explained that standards for diaspora students are lower, given that educational standards differ widely from country to country. She argued that students in Croatia receive more rigorous (and compulsory) training in mathematics than do students in North America. Since 1993, four students taking my courses have taken up Croatian scholarships and bursaries (including residence allowances) to study at the University of Zagreb. Once they meet entrance requirements, diaspora students are enrolled as full-time regular students whose enrolment and other student-related costs (like residence, food, and social insurance) are covered by the government, specifically the Ministry of Science, Education, and Sport. Other students pay for their study regularly without any special concessions.

37 While the initial effects of this increased profile were positive (as Croats were largely portrayed as the victims, particularly during the Serb assault on Croatia during the early stages of the war, in 1991–92), they later came under criticism particularly because of the interventionist and aggressive military policies of the new Croatian state in Krajina and (pre-Dayton Accords) Bosnia and Hercegovina.

38 The Canadian Standing Committee on Citizenship and Immigration of 1994 recommended that Canadians holding dual citizenship accord precedence to their Canadian citizenship.

39 He has since then been actively involved in promoting Croatian-Canadian business and cultural contacts in Croatia.

40 These findings are based on my analysis of Croatian university students at four universities in southern Ontario in 1996–97.

41 This view may also reflect long-held insecurities concerning their perception of the Canadian view of Croats as Balkan peoples (reinforced during the war through Canadian and international media reports of 'Balkan tribal hatreds,' etc.) and their desire to free themselves of association with socialist Eastern Europe and Yugoslavia.

42 Frustration with evidence of cronyism, corruption, and outmoded bureaucratic and professional practices in Croatia was often expressed.

43 *Slobodna Dalmacija* has been one casualty of post-socialism. Through a series of privatization moves (in 1993, it was taken over by Tuđman loyalist, Miroslav Kutle, forcing most of its left-leaning columnists to leave) and government mishandling, the newspaper has shifted its political tone several times.

## 5: 'Going Home'

1 The conceptual parameters of most anthropological research on return are confined to a focus on 'those who are actually returning or contemplating a return' (Long and Oxfeld 2004:4), meaning those who left the homeland at some point during their own lifetimes and in conditions that were oftentimes forced and involuntary. While this focus works well in contexts of forced expulsion, exile and migration caused by war and natural disasters, it neither allows for the consideration of the experiences of second and subsequent generations of diaspora returnees nor a critical examination of the idea of return itself. Furthermore, much of the discussion around return migration, particularly in the literature on diaspora and which takes many of its theoretical cues from work on exile (Said 1987; King 1986, Adorno 1951, Said 1987), has focussed more on diaspora *aspirations* to return home than on the actual *conditions* of return. According to Safran, diasporas share a, 'memory, vision or myth about their original homeland' (1991:83–4). But even Jewish history, about which there is so much written, is also characterized by different and often competing interpretations of the homeland and its heroes. Despite its historical claims, Zionism as a political philosophy, initially heavily influenced by socialism, is only a century old.

2 I do not address the situation of Croatian returnees from Bosnia and Hercegovina or any of the other republics of the former Yugoslavia.

3 All spoke Croatian with a moderate-to-high degree of proficiency.

4 As the daughter of an Israeli mother who emigrated to Canada in 1952, I remember the term 'yoredim' (emigrants from Israel) as one packed with negative connotations. We used to joke that the term 'yored' rhymed with 'boged,' which translates as 'traitor.' I only became familiar with the Hebrew term for immigrant – 'hagira' – as a result of my academic interest in the subject.

5 Its responsibilities include the gathering and updating of information on Croatian emigrants, keeping tabs on diaspora Croats internationally, and making contacts with the Catholic church 'that provides spiritual guidance for our emigrants.' A record of its accomplishments can be found on the Foreign Ministry website (http://www.vlada.hr).

6 The Slovenian sociologist, Zlatko Skrbiš, in his study of Croatian and Slovenian diaspora communities in Australia, also makes reference to the issue of homeland return (1999, 2001). He explains the myth of return in diaspora Croat imaginaries as a function of the politics of exclusion and stigmatization in Australian society in the years between the end of the Second World War and Croatian independence in 1991, a fate shared in part by Canadian Croats. The circumstances of their emigration to Australia also factored heavily into Skrbiš's assessment of diaspora Croat views on return, for example, if participants were DPs after the Second World War, economic immigrants, or others.

7 'Ja nisma onda bio tu I ne ... u si to nikada mo ... u oprostiti.'

8 'U mojim godinama, mislim da se ... ovjek treba skrasiti tamo gdje je poniknuo.'

9 'Prema meni se Hrvati ne odnose kao nekome tko je dosao iz dijaspore. I inače se prema nekim povratnicima osjecaju bolje, ali prema vecini s krivim razmisljanjima.'

10 Twelve ex-returnees were interviewed in Toronto between November 2003 and August 2004. The parameters for their inclusion in this research included initial plans to live permanently in Croatia, length of stay (at least one year), proficiency in the Croatian language, and age 21 to 35.

## Conclusions

1 During my research, it soon became clear that my status as a non-Croat provided some interviewees with the opportunity to express their feelings more candidly than would have been possible had I been a Croatian researcher.

# References

Adorno, Theodor. 1974 [1951]. *Minima Moralia: Reflections from a Damaged Life*. (Translated from original German edition by E.F.N. Jephcott.) London: New Left Books.

Akenson, Donald H. 1993. *The Irish Diaspora: A Primer*. Belfast: Institute of Irish Studies of the Queen's University of Belfast.

Anderson, Benedict. 1991. *Imagined Communities: Reflections on the Origin and Spread of Nationalism*. Rev. ed. London: Verso.

– 1994. 'Exodus.' *Critical Inquiry* 20(1):314–27.

Ang, Ian. 1993. 'To Be or Not to Be Chinese: Diaspora, Culture and Postmodern Ethnicity.' *Southeast Asian Journal of Social Science* 21(1): 1–17.

Appadurai, Arjun. 1991. 'Global Ethnoscapes.' Pp. 191–210 in R. Fox, ed., *Recapturing Anthropology*. Santa Fe: School of American Research Press.

– 1993. 'Patriotism and its Futures.' *Public Culture* 5(3): 411–429.

– 1996a. *Modernity at Large: Cultural Dimensions of Globalization*. Minneapolis: University of Minnesota Press.

– 1996b. 'Here and Now.' Pp. 1–23 in *Modernity at Large: Cultural Dimensions of Globalization*. Minneapolis: University of Minnesota Press.

– 1996c. 'The Production of Locality.' Pp. 178–200 in *Modernity at Large: Cultural Dimensions of Globalization*. Minneapolis: University of Minnesota Press.

Appadurai, Arjun and Carol Breckenridge. 1988. 'Why Public Culture?' *Public Culture* 1(1): 5–9.

Apter, Emily. 2001. 'Balkan Babel: Translation Zones, Military Zones.' *Public Culture* 13(1): 65–80.

Asad, Talal. 2002. 'Ethnographic Representation, Statistics and Modern Power.' Pp. 66–94 in B. Axel, ed., *From the Margins: Historical Anthropology and Its Futures*. Durham, N.C.: Duke University Press.

Axel, Brian. 2001. *The Nation's Tortured Body: Violence, Representation and the Formation of a Sikh 'Diaspora.'* Durham, N.C.: Duke University Press.

– 2004. 'The Context of Diaspora.' *Cultural Anthropology* 19(1): 26–60.

Bakić-Hayden, Milica. 1995. 'Nesting Orientalisms: The Case of the Former Yugoslavia.' *Slavic Review* 54(4): 917–31.

Bakić-Hayden, Milica and Robert Hayden. 1992. 'Orientalist Variations on the Theme "Balkans": Symbolic Geography in Recent Yugoslav Cultural Politics.' *Slavic Review* 51(1): 917–31.

Balibar, Etienne. 1991. 'The Nation Form: History and Ideology.' Pp. 37–68 in Etienne Balibar and Immanuel Wallerstein, eds., *Race, Nation, Class: Ambiguous Identities*. London: Verso.

Balibar, Etienne and Immanuel Wallerstein, eds. 1991. *Race, Nation, Class: Ambiguous Identities*. London: Verso.

Balkan Human Rights Report. 2000. http://www.greekhelsinki.gr., Accessed 15 September.

Bammer, Angelika. 1994. 'Mother Tongues and Other Strangers: Writing "Family" Across Cultural Divides.' Pp. 90–109 in Angelika Bammer, ed., *Displacements: Cultural Identities in Question*. Bloomington: Indiana University Press.

Banac, Ivo. 1984. *The National Question in Yugoslavia: Origins, History, Politics.* Ithaca, N.Y.: Cornell University Press.

– 1992a. 'Main Trends in the History of Croatia' in Z. Šeparovic, ed., *Documenta Croatica*. 2nd ed. Zagreb: Croatian Society of Victimology.

– 1992b. 'The Treason of Print: Croat Identity and the Universe of Books' in V. Čičin-Šain (ed.) *A Short History of Croatia*. Zagreb: Croatian Writers' Association.

– 1993. The Insignia of Identity: Heraldry and the Growth of National Ideologies among the South Slavs. *Ethnic Studies* 10: 215–37.

– 1995. 'Nationalism in Southeastern Europe.' Pp. 107–21 in Charles A. Kupchan, ed., *Nationalism and Nationalities in the New Europe*. Ithaca, N.Y.: Cornell University Press.

Baranović, Bogdan. 1999. *Changes in Secondary School Curricula in Post-Socialist Croatia and Education for Democracy.* Zagreb: Insitut za Društvena Istraživanja.

Baričević, Rudolf. 1993. *Život u Emigraciju: Clanci i Pisma.* (Life in Emigration: Articles and Writings). Zagreb: VIGO Commerce.

Barrier, Norman G., and Verne Dusenbery, eds. 1989. *The Sikh Diaspora: Migration and the Experience beyond the Punjab.* Columbia, Mo.: South Asian Publications.

Basch, Linda, Cristina Blanc-Szanton, and Nina Glick Schiller. 1994. *Nations Unbound: Transnational Projects, Postcolonial Predicaments and Deterritorialized Nation States.* Langhorne, Pa.: Gordon and Breach.

Basom, Kenneth E. 1995–96. 'Prospects for Democracy in Serbia and Croatia.' *East European Quarterly* 29(4): 509–28.

Bauman, Zygmunt. 1995. *Life in Fragments : Essays in Postmodern Morality.* Oxford : Basil Blackwell.

Beljo, Ante. 1995. *YU-Genocide: Bleiburg, Death Marches, UDBA (Yugoslav Secret Police).* Toronto: Northern Tribune Publishing.

Bellamy, Alex J. 2003. *The Formation of Croatian National Identity: A Centuries-Old Dream?* Manchester: Manchester University Press.

Benjamin, Walter. 1968. 'The Philosophy of History.' *Illuminations.* Translated by Harry Zohn. New York: Schocken.

Berdahl, Daphne. 1999. *Where the World Ended: Re-Unification and Identity in the German Borderland.* Berkeley: University of California Press.

– 2000. 'Introduction.' Pp. 1–13 in Daphne Berdahl, Matti Bunzel, and Martha Lampland, eds., *Altering States: Ethnographies of Transition in Eastern Europe and the Former Soviet Union.* Ann Arbor: University of Michigan Press.

Berdahl, Daphne, Matti Bunzel, and Martha Lampland, eds. 2000. *Altering States: Ethnographies of Transition in Eastern Europe and the Former Soviet Union.* Ann Arbor: University of Michigan Press.

Bičanić, Rudolf. 1938. *Ikonomska Podloga Hrvatskgog Pitanja* (The Economic Base of the Croatian Question). Zagreb.

Bilandžić, Dušan. 2001. *Propast Jugoslavije i Stvaranje Moderne Hrvatske: Eseji, Članci, Interviewi, Analize, Izvješća, Izjave* (The Break-up of Yugoslavia and Creation of Modern Croatian State: Essays, Articles, Interviews, Analyses, Reports, Statements). Zagreb: AGM.

Bilandžić, Dušan, Bože Čović, Pero Jurković, Mladen Klemenčić, Slaven Letica, Radovan Pavić, Zdravko Tomac, and Stanko Žuljić. 1991. *Croatia between War and Independence.* Zagreb: University of Zagreb.

Billig, Michael. 1995. *Banal Nationalism.* London: Sage.

Biondich, Mark. 2000. *Stjepan Radić, the Croat Peasant Party, and the Politics of Mass Mobilization, 1904–1928.* Toronto: University of Toronto Press.

Bjelić, Dušan and Obrad Savić. 2002. *Balkan as Metaphor: Between Globalization and Fragmentation.* Cambridge, Mass: MIT Press.

Bousquet, Gisele L. 1991. *Behind The Bamboo Hedge: The Impact of Homeland Politics on the Parisian Vietnamese Community.* Ann Arbor: University of Michigan Press.

Boyarin, Daniel, and Jonathan Boyarin. 1992. 'Diaspora: Generational Ground of Jewish Identity.' *Critical Inquiry* 19(4): 693–725.

Boyarin, Jonathan, ed. 1994. *Remapping Memory: The Politics of Timespace.* Minneapolis: University of Minnesota Press.

Boym, Svetlana. 2001. *The Future of Nostalgia.* New York: Basic.

Brah, Avtar. 1996. *Cartographies of Diaspora: Contesting Identities*. London: Routledge.

Brkljačić, Maja. 2003. 'What Past Is Present?' *International Journal of Politics, Culture and Society* 17(1):41–52.

Brubaker, Rogers. 1996. *Nationalism Reframed: Nationhood and the National Question in the New Europe*. Cambridge: Cambridge University Press.

Bubrin, Vladimir. 1994. 'Thirty-five Years of Croatian Heritage Language in Toronto.' Pp. 101–6 in M. Sopta and G. Scardellato, eds., *Unknown Journey: A History of Croatians in Canada*. Toronto: Multicultural History Society of Ontario.

Bundalo, Slobodanka. 1997. 'Images of Women in Croatian Daily Newspapers.' Women's Informational and Documentation Centre, Zagreb, Croatia.

Canada. Statistics Canada. 1999. *Census of Canada, 1996: Dimensions Series: Ethnocultural and Social Characteristics of the Canadian Population*. Ottawa, Ontario.

Čelan, Joško. 2000. 'Brujanje dijaspore.' (Droning Diasporas). *Slobodna Dalmajica*, 25 October.

Čičin-Šain, Vlad, ed. 1999. *A Short History of Croatia*. Zagreb: Croatian Writers' Association.

Čižmić, Ivo. 1994a. *History of the Croatian Fraternal Union of America*. Zagreb: Golden Marketing.

– 1994b. 'Emigration from Croatia between 1880 and 1980.' Pp. 1–15 in M. Sopta and G. Scardellato, eds., *Unknown Journey: A History of Croatians in Canada*. Toronto: Multicultural History Society of Ontario.

– 1996. 'Emigration and Emigrants from Croatia between 1880 and 1980.' *GeoJournal: An International Journal on Human Geography and Environmental Sciences* 38: 431–36.

Clifford, James. 1988. *The Predicament of Culture: Twentieth Century Ethnography, Literature and Art*. Cambridge, Mass.: Harvard University Press.

– 1994 'Diasporas.' *Cultural Anthropology* 9(3): 302–38.

Clifford, James, and Marcus, George, eds. 1986. *Writing Culture: The Poetics and Politics of Ethnography*. Berkeley: University of California Press.

Clissold, Stephen. 1979. *Croat Separatism*. London: Institute for the Study of Conflict.

Cohen, Lenard. 1993. *Broken Bonds: Yugoslavia's Disintegration and Balkan Politics in Transition*. Boulder: Westview.

– 2001 *Serpent in the Bosom: The Rise and Fall of Slobodan Milošević*. Boulder: Westview.

Cohen, Robin. 1997. *Global Diasporas: An Introduction*. Seattle: University of Washington Press.

Comaroff, Jean, and John Comaroff. 1997. *Of Revelation and Revolution: The Dialectics of Modernity on a South African Frontier.* Vol. 2 . Chicago: University of Chicago Press.

Connor, Walker. 1986. 'The Impact of Homelands upon Diasporas' in G. Sheffer ed., *Modern Diasporas in International Politics.* London: Croom Helm.

– 1994 *Ethnonationalism: The Quest for Understanding.* Princeton: Princeton University Press.

Constas, Dimitris, and A. Platias, eds. 1993. *Diasporas in World Politics: The Greeks in Comparative Perspective.* London: Macmillan.

Cushman, Thomas. 1997. *Critical Theory and the War in Croatia and Bosnia.* Donald W. Treadgold Papers in Russian, East European and Central Asian Studies, Henry M. Jackson School of International Studies, University of Washington, Paper No. 13

– 2001 'Letter to the Editor in Response to Hayden.' *Slavic Review* 60(3):702.

– 2005 'Anthropology and Genocide in the Balkans: An Analysis of Conceptual Practices of Power.' *Anthropological Theory* 4(1): 5–28.

Cushman, Thomas, and Stjepan Meštrović. 1996. *This Time We Knew: Western Responses to Genocide in Bosnia.* New York: New York University Press.

Čuvalo, Ante. 1989. 'Croatian Nationalism and the Croatian National Movement (1966–1972) in Anglo-American Publications: A Critical Assessment.' *Journal of Croatian Studies* 30:69–89.

– 1990. *The Croatian National Movement: 1966–1972.* New York: Columbia University Press.

– 1999. 'Triangular Relations: Croatian Diaspora, the U.S.A. and the Homeland.' *Journal of Croatian Studies* 40:25–48.

Čuvalo, Ante, Vinko Grubišić, Branko Franolić, and Ante Beljo. 1991. *Croatia and the Croatians.* Zagreb: Northern Tribune Publishing

Cviić, Christopher. 1996. 'Croatia.' Pp. 196–209 in D.A. Dyker and I. Vejvoda, eds., *Yugoslavia and After: A Study in Fragmentation, Despair and Rebirth.* New York: Longman.

Cvitković, Ivan. 2006. *Hrvatski identitet u Bosni i Hercegovini: Hrvati između nacionalnog i građanskog.* Zagreb: Synopsis.

Danforth, Loring. 1995. *The Macedonian Conflict: Ethnonationalism in a Transnational World.* Princeton: Princeton University Press.

de Certeau, Michel. 1984. *The Practice of Everyday Life.* Translated by Steven Rendall. Berkeley: University of California Press.

– 1988. *The Writing of History.* Translated and introduction by Tom Conley. New York: Columbia University Press.

DellaPergola, S. 1998. 'The Global Context of Migration from the Former Soviet

Union to Israel.' Pp. 51–94 in E. Leshem and J.T. Shuval, eds., *Immigration to Israel: Sociological Perspectives*. New Brunswick, N.J.: Transaction.

Denich, Bette. 1994. 'Dismembering Yugoslavia: Nationalist Ideologies and the Symbolic Revival of Genocide.' *American Ethnologist* 21(3): 367–90.

– 2005. 'Debate or Defamation: Comment on the Publication of Cushman's "Anthropology and Genocide in the Balkans."' *Anthropological Theory* 5(4):555–8.

Denitch, Bogdan. 1994. *Ethnic Nationalism: The Tragic Death of Yugoslavia*. Minneapolis: University of Minnesota Press.

DeSoto, Hermine, and Nora Dudwick, eds. 2000. *Fieldwork Dilemmas: Anthropologists in Postsocialist States*. Madison: University of Wisconsin Press

DiManno, Rosie. 1995. 'Ethnic Loyalties Taint Election.' *Toronto Star*, 13 February, A6.

Djurić, Ivana. 2003. 'The Croatian Diaspora in North America: Identity, Ethnic Solidarity, and the Formation of a "Transnational National Community."' *International Journal of Politics, Culture and Society* 17(1):113–30.

Drakulić, Slavenka. 1992. *How We Survived Communism and Even Laughed*. New York: W.W. Norton.

– 1993. *Balkan Express*. Translated by M. Soljan. New York: W.W. Norton.

– 1996. *Café Europa: Life after Communism*. London: Abacus

Dusenbery, Verne. 1997. 'The Poetics and Politics of Recognition: Diasporan Sikhs in Pluralist Polities.' *American Ethnologist* 24(4): 738–62.

Dyer, Richard. 1997. *White*. London: Routledge.

Dyker, David, and Ivan Vejvoda, eds. 1996. *Yugoslavia and After: A Study in Fragmentation, Despair and Rebirth*. New York: Longman.

Elliott, Jean L., and Augie Fleras. 1992. *Multiculturalism in Canada: The Challenge of Diversity*. Scarborough, Ont.: Nelson Canada.

Esman, Milton. 1986. 'Diasporas in International Relations.' Pp. 333–49 in Gabriel Sheffer, ed., *Modern Diasporas in International Politics*. New York: St. Martin's Press.

– 1994 *Ethnic Politics*. Ithaca, N.Y.: Cornell University Press.

Eterovich, Vladimir, ed. 1987. *Symposium: Emigrants from Croatia and Their Achievements*. Calgary: Western Publishing.

Feldman, Lada Čale. 1995. '"Intellectual Concerns and Scholarly Priorities": A Voice of an Ethnographer.' *Narodna Umjetnost* 32(1): 79–90.

Ferguson, James, and Akhil Gupta. 1997. *Anthropological Locations: Boundaries and Grounds of a Field Science*. Berkeley: University of California Press.

Fog Olwig, Karen. 1998. 'Epilogue: Contested Homes: Home-making and the Making of Anthropology.' Pp. 225–36 in N. Rapport and A. Dawson, eds., *Migrants of Identity: Perceptions of Home in a World of Movement*. Oxford: Berg.

Folia Croatica-Canadiana. 1995. *450 Years of Croatians in Canada*. Kitchener, Ont.: Croatian Studies Foundation.

Fortier, Anne-Marie. 2000. *Migrant Belongings: Memory, Space, Identity*. Oxford: Berg.

Frankenberg, Ruth, ed. 1997. *Displacing Whiteness: Essays in Social and Cultural Criticism*. Durham, N.C.: Duke University Press.

Franolić, Branko. 1988. *Language Policy in Yugoslavia with Special Reference to Croatian*. Paris: Nouvelles Editions Latines.

– 1994. *Croatian Glatolitic Printed Texts*. Zagreb: Croatian Information Centre.

Fukuyama, Francis. 1993. *The End of History and the Last Man*. New York: Avon.

– 1994. 'The War of All against All.' *New York Review of Books*, 10 April, p. 7.

Gabrić, Toni. 1997. 'Hercegovci su naši novi Serbi.' (Hercegovinians Are Our New Serbs). *Feral Tribune*, 24 April.

Gella, Aleksander. 1977. *The Intelligentsia and the Intellectuals*. Cambridge: Cambridge University Press.

Gillis, John, ed. 1994. *Commemorations: The Politics of National Identity*. Princeton: Princeton University Press

Gilroy, Paul. 1987. *There Ain't No Black in the Union Jack: The Cultural Politics of Race and Nation*. Hutchinson.

– 1991–92. 'It Ain't Where You're From, It's Where You're At ... The Dialectics of Diasporic Identification.' *Third Text* 13:3–16.

– 1994. 'Diaspora.' *Paragraph: The Journal of Modern Critical Theory* 17(3): 207–12.

Glenny, Misha. 1992. *The Fall of Yugoslavia: The Third Balkan War*. London: Penguin.

– 1999. *The Balkans: Nationalism, War and the Great Powers, 1804–1999*. London: Granta.

Glick Schiller, Nina, Linda Basch, and Cristina Blanc-Szanton. 1992. *Towards a Transnational Perspective on Migration: Race, Class, Ethnicity and Nationalism Reconsidered*. New York: New York Academy of Sciences.

Godler, Zlata. 1981. 'Croatia to Canada: Migration Between the Wars.' PhD dissertation, University of Toronto.

Gold, Gerry, and Robert Paine, eds. 1984. *Minorities and Mother Country Imagery*. St John's, Nfld.: Institute of Social and Economic Research.

Goldstein, Ivo. 1999. *Croatia: A History*. Translated by Nikolina Jovanović. Montreal: McGill-Queen's University Press.

Golub, Branka. 1996. 'Croatian Scientists' Drain and Its Root.' *International Migration* 34(4): 609–25.

Graham, Patrick. 1997. 'Canadian Warlord.' *Saturday Night*, December pp. 56–96.

Granić, Stan. 1998. 'Representations of the Other: The Ustaše and the Demonization of the Croats.' *Journal of Croatian Studies* 39:3–56

Grant, Bruce. 1995. *In the Soviet House of Culture: A Century of Perestroikas.* Princeton: Princeton University Press.

Grdešić, Ivan. 1996. 'The Development of Political Science in Croatia: Meeting the Challenges of Democracy and Independence.' *European Journal of Political Research* 29(2): 171–89.

Greenberg, Robert. 1996. 'The Politics of Dialects among Serbs, Croats and Muslims in the Former Yugoslavia.' *East European Politics and Societies* 10(3): 393–415.

Greene, Richard A. 2000. 'Croatian Jews Welcome Election Result.' *Canadian Jewish News.* Retrieved 6 January 2000 from http://www.cjnews.com.

Grubišić, Vinko. 1984. 'Croatians in Toronto.' *Polyphony.* Vol. 6 (88–91). Toronto: Multicultural History Society of Ontario.

– 1991. *Hrvatska knjizenvost u egzilu* (Croatian Literature in Exile). Munich and Barcelona.

Guarnizo, Luis Eduardo, and Michael Peter Smith, eds. 1999. *Transnationalism from Below.* New Brunswick, N.J.: Transaction.

Gupta, Akhil. 1992. 'The Song of the Nonaligned World: Transnational Identities and the Reinscription of Space in Late Capitalism.' *Cultural Anthropology* 7(1):63–79.

Gupta, Akhil, and James Ferguson. 1997a. 'Discipline and Practice: 'The Field' as Site, Method, and Location in Anthropology.' Pp. 1–46 in Akhil Gupta and James Ferguson, eds., *Anthropological Locations: Boundaries and Grounds of a Field Science.* Berkeley: University of California Press.

– 1997b. *Anthropological Locations: Boundaries and Grounds of a Field Science.* Berkeley: University of California Press.

Hadžiosmanović, Ismet. 2006. *Bošnjačko-Hrvatski političko obračun.* Mostar: CIP.

Halbwachs, Maurice. 1980. *The Collective Memory.* Translated by Francis J. Ditter, Jr., and Vida Yazdi Ditter. New York: Harper & Row.

Hall, Stuart. 1990. 'Cultural Identity and Diaspora.' Pp. 222–37 in J. Rutherford ed., *Identity: Community, Culture, Difference.* London: Lawrence and Wishart.

– 1993. 'Culture, Community, Nation.' *Cultural Studies* 7(3): 349–63.

Halpern, Joel M., and David A. Kideckel. 2000. 'The End of Yugoslavia Observed.' Pp. 3–18 in Joel M. Halpern and David A. Kideckel eds., *Neighbors at War: Anthropological Perspectives on Yugoslav Ethnicity, Culture, and History* University Park, Pa.: Pennsylvania State University Press.

Handler, Richard. 1988. *Nationalism and the Politics of Culture in Quebec.* Madison: University of Wisconsin Press.

Hannerz, Ulf. 1992. *Cultural Complexity: Studies in the Social Organization of Meaning*. New York : Columbia University Press.

Hansen, Milton. L. 1952. 'The Third Generation in America.' *Commentary* 14: 492–500.

Harney, Nicholas. 1998. *Eh, Paesan! Being Italian in Toronto*. Toronto: University of Toronto Press.

Hawkesworth, Celia. 1998. *Colloquial Croatian and Serbian*. London: Routledge.

Hayden, Robert. 1992. 'Constitutional Nationalism in the Formerly Yugoslav Republics.' *Slavic Review* 51(4): 654–73.

– 1996. 'Imagined Communities and the Real Victim: Self-determination and Ethnic Cleansing in Yugoslavia.' *American Ethnologist* 23(4): 783–801.

– 1997. 'The Tactical Uses of Passion in Bosnia.' *Current Anthropology* 38(5): 924–25.

– 2005. 'Inaccurate Data, Spurious Issues and Editorial Failure in Cushman's 'Anthropology and Genocide in the Balkans.' *Anthropological Theory* 5(4): 545–54.

Heiberg, Marianne. 1989. *The Making of the Basque Nation*. Cambridge: Cambridge University Press.

Herman, Harry. 1994. 'Two Associations: The Croatian Fraternal Union and the Croatian Peasant Party.' Pp. 55–64 in M. Sopta and G. Scardellato, eds., *Unknown Journey: A History of Croatians in Canada*, Toronto: Multicultural History Society of Ontario.

Hill, Kulu, and Tammaru Tiit. 2000. 'Ethnic Return Migration from the East and the West: The Case of Estonia in the 1990s.' *Europe Asia Studies* 52(2): 349–69.

Hobsbawm, Eric. 1990. *Nations and Nationalism since 1780: Programme, Myth, Reality*. Cambridge: Cambridge University Press.

Hobsbawm, Eric, and Terence Ranger, eds. 1983. *The Invention of Tradition*. Cambridge: Cambridge University Press.

Hockenos, Paul. 2003. *Homeland Calling: Exile Patriotism and the Balkan Wars*. Ithaca; N.Y.: Cornell University Press.

Hoffman, Nila Ginger. 2001. 'Reconstructing Jewish Identity in Croatia: Towards a Refined Symbolic Ethnicity.' *Anthropology of East Europe Review* 19(2): 5–20.

Holjevac, Željko. 1999. 'Language and Nation within the Croatian and Serbian National Ideologies: Starčević's Polemic from 1852.' *Migracije Teme* 14(3): 289–321.

Hollander, John. 1993. 'It All Depends.' In Arien Mack, ed., *Home: A Place in the World*. New York: New York University Press.

Holy, Ladislav. 1998. 'The Metaphor of "Home" in Czech Nationalist Discourse.' Pp. 111–38 in Nigel Rapport and Andrew Dawson, eds., *Migrants of Identity: Perceptions of Home in a World of Movement*. Oxford: Berg.

Hudelist, Darko. 1999–2000. (Gojko Šušak: Black Holes in Political Biography). 'Gojko Šušak: Crne Rupe u Političkoj Biografiji.' *Globus* 468–80: 38–103.

Huntington, Samuel. 1993. 'The Clash of Civilizations.' *Foreign Affairs* 72(3): 23–49.

– 1996. *The Clash of Civilizations and the Remaking of the World Order*. New York: Simon & Schuster.

Hyman, Anthony. 1993. 'Russians outside Russia.' *The World Today*. November, 205–8.

Ignatieff, Michael. 1994. *Blood and Belonging*. London: Penguin.

Ilcan, Susan. 2002. *Longing in Belonging: The Cultural Politics of Settlement* Westport, Conn.: Praeger.

International Club of Croatian Emigrants, Returnees and Investors from Diaspora Internacionalni Klub Hrvatskih Iseljenika, Povratnika I Investora Iz Dijaspore. 2002. *Zbornik – Prvog Sabora Hrvatske Dijaspore (Convention – First Legislative Assembly of the Croatian Diaspora)*. Poreć, Croatia: Author.

Jackson, Michael. 1995. *At Home in the World*. Durham, N.C.: Duke University Press.

Jacobson, Matthew Frye. 1995. *Special Sorrows: The Diasporic Imagination of Irish, Polish, and Jewish Immigrants in the United States*. Cambridge, Mass.: Harvard University Press.

– 1998. *Whiteness of a Different Colour: European Immigrants and the Alchemy of Race*. Cambridge, Mass.: Harvard University Press.

Jambrešić Kirin, Renata. 1999. 'Personal Narratives on War: A Challenge to Women's Essays and Ethnography in Croatia.' *Estudos de Literatura Oral* 5: 73–98.

Jambrešić Kirin, Renata, and Maja Povrzanović, eds. 1996. *War, Exile and Everyday Life: Cultural Perspectives*. Zagreb: Institute of Ethnology and Folklore Research.

Jaram, Vlado. 1999. *Povijest Hrvata – A History of Croats*. (CD–Rom). Zagreb: Centar za tranfer technologije.

Jelavich, Barbara, and Charles Jelavich. 1977. *The Establishment of the Balkan National States: 1804–1920*. Seattle: University of Washington Press.

Kačić, Miro. 1977. *Croatian and Serbian: Delusions and Distortions*. Translated by Lelija Sočanac. Zagreb: Novi Most.

Kadare, Ismail. 1997 (1978). *The Three-arched Bridge*. Translated by John Hodgson. New York: Arcade.

Kalogjera, Damir. 2001. 'On Attitudes toward Croatian Dialects and on Their Changing Status.' *International Journal of the Sociology of Language* 147: 91–100.

Kaplan, Robert. 1994. *Balkan Ghosts: A Journey through History*. New York: Vintage.

Katich, Boris, ed. 1983. *So Speak Croatian Dissidents*. Norval, Ont.: ZIRAL.

Katičić, Radoslav. 2001. 'Croatian Linguistic Loyalty.' *International Journal of the Sociology of Language* 147: 17–29.

Katičić, Radoslav, and Slobodan P. Novak. 1987. *Two Thousand Years of Writing in Croatia*. Zagreb: SNL.

Katunarić, Vjeran. 1996. 'Zvjezdano nebo: Promjene i determinizam stratum' (Starry Sky: Changes and Determinism). *Revija za Sociologiju* 27(3):153–68.

– 1999. 'Real' and Other Compatriots: Politics of Identity in Croatia.' Pp. 199–216 in H. Kriesi, H. Siegristt, and A. Wimmer, eds., *Nation and National Identity: The European Experience in Perspective*. Zurich: Verlag Rüegger.

Kearns, Ian. 1996. 'Croatian Politics: The New Authoritarianism.' *Political Quarterly* 67(1): 26–35.

Kedourie, Eli. 1993. *Nationalism*. 4th ed. Oxford: Blackwell.

Kennedy, Michael. 2002. *Cultural Formations of Post-communism: Emancipation, Transition, Nation and War*. Minneapolis: University of Minnesota Press.

Kenny, Michael. 1984. Cultural Imperialism and Recycled Ethnicity among Spanish Immigrants in Mexico. Pp. 17–34 in G. Gold and R. Paine, eds., *Minorities and Mother Country Imagery*. St John's, Nfld.: Institute of Social and Economic Research.

Khan, Aisha. 1995. 'Homeland, Motherland: Authenticity, Legitimacy, and Ideologies of Place among Muslims in Trinidad.' Pp. 93–131 in P. Van der Veer, ed. *Nation and Migration: The Politics of Space in the South Asian Diaspora*. Philadelphia: University of Pennsylvania Press.

Kideckel, David, ed. 1995. *East European Communities: The Struggle for Balance in Turbulent Times*. Boulder: Westview.

Kideckel, David, ed., and Joel M. Halpern, guest ed. 1993. 'War among the Yugoslavs.' Special issue of *Anthropology of East Europe Review* 11(1–2).

Klein, George, and Patricia Klein. 1981. 'Nationalism versus Ideology: The Pivot of Yugoslav Politics.' Pp. 247–79 in G. Klein and Milan Reban, eds., *The Politics of Ethnicity in Eastern Europe*. New York: Columbia University Press.

– eds. 1981. *The Politics of Ethnicity in Eastern Europe*. New York: Columbia University Press.

Kleinman, Arthur, Veena Das, and Margaret Lock, eds. 1997. 'Introduction.' Pp. ix–xxvii in A. Kleinman, V. Das, and M. Lock eds., *Social Suffering*. Berkeley: University of California Press.

Knežević, Anto. 1992. *An Analysis of Serbian Propaganda*. Zagreb: Domovina T.T.

Kolar-Panov, Dona. 1997. *Video, War and the Diasporic Imagination*. London: Routledge.

Kraljič, John Peter. 2001. 'The Role of Croatian Immigrants in the First Decade of the 21st Century.' Paper presented at the Alma Matris Croaticae Conference, Montreal, Quebec. Retrieved 25 June 2001 from www.nfcaonline.com.

– 2002. 'Croatia: The Need for Promotion.' Pp. 81–83 in *Convention – First Legislative Assembly of the Croatian Diaspora*. Poreč, Croatia.

Kraljich, Franjo. 1978. *Croatian Migration to and from the United States, 1900–1914*. Palo Alto, Calif.: Ragusan Press.

Krasić, Ljubo. 1999. 'Croatian Schools in America and Canada.' *Journal of Croatian Studies* 40: 55–6.

Krleža, Miroslav. 1969 [1932]. *Povratak Filipa Latinovicza* (The Return of Philip Latinowicz). Translated by Zora Depolo. New York : Vanguard.

Kundera, Milan. 2003. *Ignorance*. New York: Harper Collins.

Lacan, Jacques. 2006. *Ecrits: The First Complete Edition in English*. Translated by Bruce Fink. New York: W.W. Norton.

Leček, Suzana, M. Najbar-Agičić, Damir Agičèić, and Tvrtko Jakovina, eds. 1999. *Povijest* (History 4). Zagreb: Profil.

Lemon, Alaina. 2000. *Between Two Fires: Gypsy Performance and Romani Memory from Pushkin to Postsocialism*. Durham, N.C.: Duke University Press.

Levine, Etan. 1986. 'Confronting the Aliyah Option.' Pp. 353–63 in Etan Levine, ed., *Diaspora, Exile and the Contemporary Jewish Condition*. New York: Steimatsky.

Levitt, Peggy. 2001. *The Transnational Villagers*. Berkeley: University of California Press.

Long, Lynellen, and Oxfeld, Ellen, eds. 2004. *Coming Home? Refugees, Migrants and Those Who Stayed Behind*. Philadelphia: University of Pennsylvania Press.

MacDonald, Moira. 1991. 'Neo-Nazis Deface Church.' *Toronto Sun, 26* December p. A7.

Mack, Arien, ed. 1993. *Home: A Place in the World*. New York: New York University Press.

Mackey, Eva. 1999. *The House of Difference: Cultural Politics and National Identity in Canada*. London: Routledge.

Magaš, Branka. 1993. *The Destruction of Yugoslavia: Tracking the Break-up, 1980–92*. London and New York: Verso.

Magocsi, Paul Robert, ed. 1999. *Encyclopedia of Canada's Peoples*. Toronto: University of Toronto Press.

Maier, Charles. 1988. *The Unmasterable Past: History, Holocaust, and German National Identity*. Cambridge, Mass.: Harvard University Press.

Malkki, Liisa. 1995a. *Purity and Exile: Violence, Memory and National Cosmology among Hutu Refugees in Tanzania*. Chicago: University of Chicago Press.

– 1995b. 'Refugees and Exile: From "Refugee Studies" to the National Order of Things.' *Annual Review of Anthropology* 24: 495–523.

Marcus, George. 1995. 'Ethnography in/of the World System: The Emergence of Multi-sited Ethnography.' *Annual Review of Anthropology* 24: 95–117.

– 1998. 'Introduction: Anthropology on the Move.' Pp. 1–29 in G. Marcus, *Ethnography through Thick and Thin*. Princeton: Princeton University Press.

Martin, Emily. 1994. *Flexible Bodies: Tracking Immunity in American Culture from the Days of Polio to the Age of AIDS*. Boston: Beacon Press.

Martynowych, Orest. 1991. *Ukrainians in Canada: The Formative Years, 1891–1924*. Edmonton: Canadian Institute of Ukrainian Studies Press.

Massey, Garth, Randy Hodson, and Duško Sekulić. 2003. 'Nationalism, Liberalism and Liberal Nationalism in Post-war Croatia.' *Nations and Nationalism* 9(1): 55–82.

Matković, Hrvoje. 1993. *Suvremena Politička Hrvatske* (Contemporary Political History of Croatia). Zagreb: Facultet Kriminalističkih Znanosti.

Matsuoka, Atsuko, and John Sorenson. 2001. *Ghosts and Shadows: Construction of Identity and Community in an African Diaspora*. Toronto: University of Toronto Press.

Matvejević, Predrag. 2005. *Between Exile and Asylum: an Eastern Epistolary*. Budapest: Central European University Press.

Meheš, Mirko. 1993. *Ljudi Kojih Nema* (People Who Are Missing). Sudbury, Ont.

Meštrović, Stjepan, ed. 1996. *Genocide After Emotion: The Postemotional Balkan War*. London: Routledge.

Mežnarić, Silva. 1992. 'A Country by Any Other Name: Transition and Stability in Croatia and Yugoslavia.' *East European Politics and Societies*. 6: 242–59.

– 1994. 'Women in Croatia and Slovenia: A Case of Delayed Modernization.' Pp. 153–170 in Marilyn Rueschmeyer, ed., *Women in the Politics of Post-communist Eastern Europe*. New York: M.E. Sharpe.

– 1996. 'Europe, Its East and South: What Is in Front of It?' *Revija za Sociologiju* 27: 3–4.

Mijatović, Anđelko, and Ivan Bekavac. 2005. *The Croats: Fourteen Centuries of Perseverance*. New York: Croatian World Congress.

Mirković, Damir. 2000. 'The Historical Link Between the Ustasha Genocide and the Croato-Serb War, 1991–1995. *Journal of Genocide Research* 2(3): 363–373.

Mishra, Vijay. 1996. 'The Diasporic Imaginary: Theorizing the Indian Diaspora.' *Textual Practice* 10(3): 421–47.

Mojzes, Paul. 1997. 'The Role of Religious Communities in the Development of

Civil Society in Yugoslavia, 1945–1992.' Pp. 211–34 in M.K. Bokovoy, J.A. Levine, and C.S. Lilly, eds., *State-Society Relations in Yugoslavia*. London: Macmillan.

Motyl, Alexander. 1998. 'After Empire: Competing Discourses and Inter-state Conflict in Post-Imperial Eastern Europe.' Pp. 14–33 in Barnett R. Rubin and Jack Snyder, eds., *Post-Soviet Political Order: Conflict and State Building*. London: Routledge.

Naficy, Hamid. 1991. 'The Poetics and Practice of Iranian Nostalgia in Exile.' *Diaspora* 1(3): 285–302.

– 1993. *The Making of Exile Cultures: Iranian Television in Los Angeles*. Minneapolis: University of Minnesota Press.

Nejašmić, Ivo. 1993. 'Hrvatski Građani na Radu u Inozemstvu I članovi obitelj koji s Njima Borave Prema Popisu 1991: Prikaz Prema Novom Teritorijalnom Ustrojstvu Jedinica Lokalne Samouprave' (Croatian Citizens Working Abroad and the Members of their Families Living with Them According to the 1991 Census: Presented in Relation to the New Territorial Organization of the Units of Local Authorities). *Migracijske Teme* 12(3): 205–18.

Obradović, Đorđe. 1992. *The Suffering of Dubrovnik*. Dubrovnik: Dubrovački Vjesnik.

Offe, Claus. 1997. *Varieties of Transition: The East European and East German Experience*. Cambridge, Mass.: MIT Press.

Olwig, Karen Fog. 1997. *Siting Culture: The Shifting Anthropological Object*. London: Routledge.

Omrčanin, Ivo. 1986. *Holocaust of Croatians*. Washington, D.C.: Samizdat Press.

Ong, Aihwa. 1996. 'Citizenship as Subject Making: New Immigrants Negotiate Racial and Ethnic Boundaries.' *Current Anthropology* 37(5): 737–62.

Ortner, Sherry, ed. 1999. *The Fate of Culture: Geertz and Beyond*. Berkeley: University of California Press.

Orwell, George. 1945. 1968 [1945]. 'Notes on Nationalism.' Pp. 361–80 in S. Orwell and I. Angus, eds., *The Collected Essays, Journalism and Letters of George Orwell*, Vol. 3, New York: Harcourt, Brace & World.

Owen, David. 1996. *Balkan Odyssey*. New York: Harcourt, Brace.

Pleština, D. 1995. 'Democracy and Nationalism in Croatia: The First Three Years.' Pp. 123–54 in Sabrina Ramet and L.S. Adamovich, eds., *Beyond Yugoslavia: Politics, Economics and Culture in a Shattered Community*. Boulder: Westview.

Prica, Ines. 1995. 'Notes on Ordinary Life in War.' Pp. 44–72 in Lada Feldman, Ines Prica, and Reana Senković, eds., *Fear, Death and Resistance: an Ethnography of War: Croatia 1991–1992*. Zagreb: Institute of Ethnology and Folklore Research.

Pusić, Vesna. 1992. 'A Country by Any Other Name: Transition and Stability in Croatia and Yugoslavia.' *East European Politics and Societies.* 6: 242–59.
– 1995. 'Uses of Nationalism and the Politics of Recognition.' *Anthropological Journal on European Cultures* 4(1): 43–61.
– 1997a. 'Croatia's Struggle for Democracy.' *Revija za Sociologiju* 28(1)2: 95–110.
– 1997b. 'Croatia at the Crossroads.' Paper presented at the International Forum for Democratic Studies of the National Endowment for Democracy, Washington, D.C. 24 March.
Raditsa, Bogdan. 1977. 'Nationalism in Croatia Since 1964.' In George W. Simmonds, ed., *Nationalism in the USSR and Eastern Europe in the Era of Brezhnev and Kosygin.* Detroit: University of Detroit Press.
Raeff, Mark. 1990. *Russia Abroad: A Cultural History of the Russian Emigration 1919–1939.* New York: Oxford University Press.
Rai, Amit. 1995. 'India On-line: Electronic Bulletin Boards and the Construction of a Diasporic Hindu Identity.' *Diaspora* 4(1):31–58.
Ramet, Sabrina. 1992. *Nationalism and Federalism in Yugoslavia, 1962–1991,* 2nd ed. Bloomington: Indiana University Press.
– 1996. *Balkan Babel: The Disintegration of Yugoslavia from the Death of Tito to the Ethnic War.* Boulder: Westview.
– 2005. *Thinking about Yugoslavia: Scholarly Debates about the Yugoslav Breakup and Wars in Bosnia and Kosovo.* Cambridge: Cambridge University Press.
Ramet, Sabrina, and Ljubiša Adamovich, eds. 1995. *Beyond Yugoslavia: Politics, Economics and Culture in a Shattered Community.* Boulder: Westview.
Rapport, Nigel, and Andrew Dawson eds. 1998. *Migrants of Identity: Perceptions of Home in a World of Movement.* Oxford: Berg.
Rapport, Nigel, and Andrew Dawson. 1998a. 'The Topic and the Book.' Pp. 3–18 in Nigel Rapport and Andrew Dawson, eds., *Migrants of Identity: Perceptions of Home in a World of Movement.* Oxford: Berg.
– 1998b. 'Home and Movement: a Polemic.' Pp. 19–38 in Nigel Rapport and Andrew Dawson eds., *Migrants of Identity: Perceptions of Home in a World of Movement.* Oxford: Berg.
Rasporich, Anthony. 1978a. 'South Slavs on the Northern Margin: The Frontier Experience of Croatian Migration During Canada's Great Depression.' Pp. 398–410 in Martin Kovacs, ed., *Ethnic Canadians: Culture and Education.* Regina: Canadian Plains Research Centre.
– 1982. *For a Better Life: A History of Croatians in Canada.* Toronto: McClelland and Stewart.
– 1978b. 'Tomo Čačić: Rebel without a Country.' *Canadian Ethnic Studies* 10(2): 86–95.

– 1994. 'Three Generations of Croatian Immigrants in Canada: A Harzian Perspective,' Pp. 15–27 in Marin Sopta and Gabriele Scardellato, eds., *Unknown Journey: A History of Croatians in Canada*. Toronto: Multicultural History Society of Ontario.

– 1999. 'Croats.' Pp. 382–89 in P.R. Magosci, ed., *Encyclopedia of Canada's Peoples*. Toronto: University of Toronto Press.

Rethmann, Petra. 2001. *Tundra Passages: History and Gender in the Russian Far East*. University Park, Pa.: Pennsylvania State University Press.

Ries, Nancy. 1997. *Russian Talk: Culture and Conversation During Perestroika*. Ithaca, N.Y.: Cornell University Press.

Rihtman-Auguštin, Dunja. 1995. 'Santa Claus in Transition.' *Narodna Umjetnost* 32(1): 107–22.

– 1997. 'An Ethno-Anthropologist in His Native Field: To Observe or to Witness.' *Anthropological Journal of European Culture* 6(2): 129–44.

– 2004. 'The Monument in the Main City Square: Constructing and Erasing Memory in Contemporary Croatia.' Pp. 180–196 in Maria Todorova, ed., *Balkan Identities: Nation and Memory*. New York: New York University Press.

Roksandić, Aleksandar. 1995. 'Shifting References: Celebrations of Uprisings in Croatia, 1945–1999.' *East European Politics and Societies* 9(2): 256–71.

Roshwald, Aviel. 2001. *Ethnic Nationalism and the Fall of Empires: Central Europe, Russia, and the Middle East, 1914–1923*. London: Routledge.

Rouse, Roger. 1991. 'Mexican Migration and the Social Space of Postmodernism.' *Diaspora* 1: 8–23.

– 1995. 'Thinking Through Transnationalism: Notes on the Cultural Politics of Class Relations in the Contemporary United States.' *Public Culture* 7: 353–402.

Rubin, Barnett R., and Jack Snyder, eds., 1998. *Post-Soviet Political Order: Conflict and State Building*. London: Routledge.

Rubinstein, William D., and Hilary L. Rubinstein. 1991. *The Jews in Australia: A Thematic History*. Melbourne: William Heinemann.

Rushdie, Salman. 1991. *Imaginary Homelands*. London: Granta.

Sadkovich, James J. 1996. 'The Response of the American Media to Balkan Neo-nationalisms.' Pp. 113–57 in Stjepan Meštrović, ed., *Genocide after Emotion: The Postemotional Balkan War*. London: Routledge.

Safran, William. 1991. 'Diasporas in Modern Societies: Myths of Homeland and Return.' *Diaspora* 1(1): 83–99.

Said, Edward. 1978. *Orientalism* . New York: Pantheon.

– 1987. 'Reflections on Exile.' *Granta* 13 (Autumn): 157–72.

– 1999. *Out of Place: A Memoir*. New York: Knopf.

– 2000. *Reflections on Exile and Other Essays*. Cambridge, Mass.: Harvard University Press.

Šantić, Neven. 2000. 'Politicki Aspekti Društvenog Razvoja Istre' (Political Aspects of Istrian Societal Development). *Revija za Sociologiju*. 3/4:153–64.

Scardellato, Gabriele, and Marin Sopta, eds. 1994. *Unknown Journey: A History of Croatians in Canada*. Toronto: Multicultural History Society of Ontario.

Schöpflin, George. 1996. 'Aspects of Language and Ethnicity in Central and Eastern Europe.' *Transition* August 5, Pp. 6–9.

Sekulić, Duško. 2004. 'Civic and Ethnic Identity: the Case of Croatia.' *Ethnic and Racial Studies* 27(3): 455–83.

Sekulić, Duško, and Zeljka Šporer. 1997. 'Regime Support in Croatia.' *Revija za Sociologiju*. 28(1–2): 35–62.

Šeparovic, Zvonimir, ed. 1992. *Documenta Croatica: on Croatian History, Its Identity and the War in Croatia*. 2nd Ed. Zagreb: Croatian Society of Victimology.

Seroka, Jim, and Vukasin Pavlović, eds. 1992. *The Tragedy of Yugoslavia: The Failure of Democratic Transformation*. Armonk, N.Y.: M.E. Sharpe.

Shain, Yossi. 1989. *The Frontier of Loyalty: Political Exiles in the Age of the Nation-State*. Middletown, Conn.: Wesleyan University Press.

– 2000. 'American Jews and the Construction of Israel's Jewish Identity.' *Diaspora* 9(2): 163–202.

Sheffer, Gabriel. 1993. 'Ethnonational Diasporas: A Threat to Their Hosts?' Pp. 263–86 in M. Weiner, ed., *International Migration and Security*. Boulder: Westview.

Sheffer, Gabriel, ed. 1986. *Modern Diasporas in International Politics*. London: Croom Helm.

– 2003. *Diaspora Politics: At Home, Abroad*. Cambridge: Cambridge University Press.

Shukla, Sandhya. 2003. *India Abroad: Diasporic Cultures of Postwar America and England*. Princeton: Princeton University Press.

Shuval, Judith. 1998. 'Migration to Israel: the Mythology of 'Uniqueness.' *International Migration* 36(1): 4–24.

Silber, Laura, and Allan Little. 1995. *The Death of Yugoslavia*. London: Penguin.

Skrbiš, Zlatko. 1995. 'Long Distance Nationalism: Second Generation Croatians and Slovenians in Australia' in Alexander Pavković et. al., eds., *Nationalism and Postcommunism: A Collection of Essays*. Brookfield, Vt.: Dartmouth Publishing.

– 1999. *Long Distance Nationalism: Diasporas, Homelands and Identities*. Brookfield,Vt.: Ashgate Publishing.

– 2001. 'Nationalism in a Transnational Context: Croatian Diaspora, Intimacy and Nationalist Imagination.' *Revija za Sociologiju* 32(3–4): 133–45.

Slobin, Greta. 2001. 'The Homecoming of the First Wave Diaspora and Its Legacy.' *Slavic Review* 60(3): 513–29.

Šoljak, Niko. 2002. *Zbornik: Prvog Sabora Hrvatske Dijaspore* (Symposium: The First Assembly of the Croatian Diaspora). Poreč.

Solzhenitsyn, Aleksandr. 1991. *Rebuilding Russia: Reflections and Tentative Proposals*. Translated and annotated by Alexis Klimoff. New York: Farrar, Straus and Giroux.

Sopta, Marin. 1994a. 'Croatian Canadians and the New Croatia.' Pp. 77–7 in Gabriele Scardellato and Marin Sopta (eds.) *Unknown Journey: a History of Croatians in Canada*. Toronto: Multicultural History Society of Ontario.

– 1994b. 'A History of Toronto Metros-Croatia.' Pp. 135–44 in Gabriele Scardellato and Marin Sopta, eds., *Unknown Journey: A History of Croatians in Canada*. Toronto: Multicultural History Society of Ontario.

Stallaerts, Robert, and Jeannine Laurents. 1995. *Historical Dictionary of the Republic of Croatia*. Metuchen, N.J.: Scarecrow Press.

Stubbs, Paul. 1999. 'Virtual Diaspora: Imagining Croatia Online.' *Sociological Research Online* 4 (2). Retrieved on 20 September 2000 from http://www.socresonline.org.uk/socresonline/4/2/stubbs.

Sučić, Daria Sito. 1996. 'The Fragmentation of Serbo-Croatian into Three Languages.' *Transition* November 24(2):10–13.

Sunić, Tomislav. 1999. 'Great Expectations and Small Returns: Immigration, Emigration, and Migration of Croats Over the Last Ten Years.' *Journal of Croatian Studies* 40:45–8.

Švob-Đokić, Nada. 1996. 'Cultural Identity in the Perspective of Transformation and Democracy.' Pp. 77–88 in *The Cultural Identity of Central Europe*. Proceedings of the Conference 'Europe of Cultures: Cultural Identity of Central Europe,' Zagreb, 22–24 November.

– 1996b. 'Some Highlights from the Discussion.' Pp. 153–9 in *The Cultural Identity of Central Europe*. Proceedings of the Conference 'Europe of Cultures': Cultural Identity of Central Europe. Zagreb, 22–24 November.

Tanner, Marcus. 1996. *Croatia: A Nation Forged in War*. New Haven, Conn.: Yale University Press.

Taras, David, and Morton Weinfeld. 1993. 'Continuity and Criticism: North American Jews and Israel.' Pp. 293–310 in R. Brym, W. Shaffir, and M. Weinfeld, eds., *The Jews in Canada*. Toronto: Oxford University Press.

Taylor, Charles. 1992. *Multiculturalism and 'The Politics of Recognition': An Essay*. Edited and with commentary by Amy Gutmann. Princeton: Princeton University Press.

– 1994. *Multiculturalism: Examining the Politics of Recognition*. Edited and introduced by Amy Guttman. Princeton: Princeton University Press.

Thompson, Mark. 1992. *A Paper House: The Ending of Yugoslavia*. London: Vintage.

– 1994. *Forging War: The Media in Serbia, Croatia and Bosnia and Herzegovina.* Avon: Bath Press.

Todorova, Maria. 1997. *Imagining the Balkans.* London: Oxford University Press.

– 2004. *Balkan Identities: Nation and Memory.* New York: New York University Press.

Tölölyan, Kachig. 1991. 'The Nation and Its Others: In Lieu of a Preface.' *Diaspora* 1(1):3–7.

– 1996. 'Rethinking Diaspora(s): Stateless Power in the Transnational Moment.' *Diaspora* 5(1): 3–37.

– 2000. 'Elites and Institutions in the Armenian Transnation.' *Diaspora.* 9(1): 107–36.

Tomašić, Dinko. 1948. *Personality and Culture in Eastern European Politics.* New York: George W. Stewart.

Tomić, Rudi. 1998. *Pogled S Torontoskog Tornja na Zvibanja u Domovinin* (The View from the Toronto Tower of Events in the Homeland). Mostar: ZIRAL Press.

Toronto Star. 1975. 'Minister Takes on Terrorism.' 19 September, p. A3.

Tuđman, Franjo. 1996. *Bespuća Povijesne Zbilnosti: za Sprava o Povijesti i Filozofiji Zlosilja* (Horrors of War: Historical Reality and Philosophy). New York: M. Evans.

Ugrešić, Dubravka. 1998. *The Culture of Lies: Antipolitical Essays.* Translated by Celia Hawkesworth. University Park, Pa.: Pennsylvania University Press.

– 2005. *The Ministry of Pain.* London: Saqi Books.

Uzelak, Gordana. 1998. 'Franjo Tudjman's National Ideology.' *East European Quarterly* 31(3):449–72.

Van der Veer, Peter, ed. 1995. 'Introduction: The Diasporic Imagination.' Pp. 1–16 in P. Van der Veer, ed., *Nation and Migration: The Politics of Space in the South Asian Diaspora.* Philadelphia: University of Pennsylvania Press.

Van Hear, Nicholas. 1998. *New Diasporas: The Mass Exodus, Expulsion and Regrouping of Migrant Communities.* London: UCL Press.

Vasiliadis, Peter. 1984. 'Shifting Motherland, Shifting Ethnicity: The Toronto Macedonians.' Pp. 56–83 in G. Gold and R. Paine, eds., *Minorities and Mother Country Imagery.* St John's, Nfld.: Institute for Social and Economic Research.

Verdery, Katharine. 1991. *National Ideology under Socialism: Identity and Cultural Politics under Ceauçescu's Romania.* Berkeley: University of California Press.

– 1996. *What Was Socialism and What Comes Next?* Princeton: Princeton University Press.

– 1999. *The Political Lives of Dead Bodies: Reburial and Post-socialist Change.* New York: Columbia University Press.

Verdery, Katharine, and Michael Burawoy, eds. 1999. *Uncertain Transitions:*

*Ethnographies of Change in the Postsocialist World*. New York: Rowman and Littlefield.

Vrbošic, Josip. 1992. 'Povijesni Pregled Razvitka Zupanijske Uprave i Samouprave u Hrvatskoj' (Historical Overview of the Development of County Governments and Local Authorities in Croatia). *Društvena Istrazivanja* 1(1): 55–68.

Wachtel, Andrew. 1998. *Making a Nation, Breaking a Nation: Literature and Cultural Politics in Yugoslavia*. Stanford, Ca.: Stanford University Press.

Wallerstein, Immanuel. 1991. 'The Construction of Peoplehood: Racism, Nationalism, Ethnicity.' Pp. 71–85 in Etienne Balibar and Immanuel Wallerstein, eds., *Race, Nation, Class: Ambiguous Identities*. London: Verso.

Wanner, Catharine. 1998. *Burden of Dreams*. University Park, Pa.: Pennsylvania State University Press.

Wearing, Stephen. 2001. *Volunteer Tourism: Experiences That Make a Difference*. Wallingford: CABI.

Weil, Samuel. 1987. 'Anthropology Becomes Home: Home Becomes Anthropology.' Pp. 196–212 in A. Jackson, *Anthropology at Home*. London: Routledge.

Weiner, Myron, ed. 1993. *International Migration and Security*. Boulder: Westview.

Werbner, Pnina. 2000. 'Introduction: The Materiality of Diaspora – Between Aesthetic and "Real" Politics.' *Diaspora* 9(1): 5–20.

West, Rebecca. 1982. [1941]. *Black Lamb and Grey Falcon*. New York: Penguin.

White, Hayden V. 1987. *The Content of the Form: Narrative Discourse and Historical Representation*. Baltimore: Johns Hopkins University Press.

Williams, Raymond. 1977. *Marxism and Literature*. Oxford: Oxford University Press.

Winland, Daphne. 1992. 'Native Scholarship: The Enigma of Self-Definition among Jewish and Mennonite Scholars.' *Journal of Historical Sociology* 5(4): 431–61.

– 1995. 'We Are Now an Actual Nation: The Impact of National Independence on the Croatian Diaspora in Canada.' *Diaspora* 4(1):3–30.

– 2004. 'Croatians in Diaspora.' Pp. 76–84 in M. Ember, C. Ember, and I. Skoggard, eds., *Encyclopedia of Diasporas – Human Relations Area Files*. New Haven: Kluwer/Plenum Press.

Wittgenstein, Ludwig. 1953. *Philosophical Investigations*. New York: Macmillan.

Wolff, Larry. 1994. *Inventing Eastern Europe: The Map of Civilization on the Mind of the Enlightenment*. Palo Alto, Ca.: Stanford University Press.

Woodward, Susan L. 1995. *Balkan Tragedy: Chaos and Dissolution after the Cold War*. Washington, D.C.: Brookings Institution.

Zimmerman, Warren. 1996. *Origins of a Catastrophe*. New York: Times Books.

Žižek, Slavoj. 1990. 'Eastern Europe's Republics of Gilead.' *New Left Review* 183(1):50–62.

– 1991. *For They Know Not What They Do: Enjoyment as a Political Factor*. 2nd ed. London: Verso.

– 1992. 'Eastern European Liberalism and Its Discontents.' *New German Critique* 57: 25–49

– 2001 *Did Someone Say Totalitarianism? Five Interventions of the (Mis)use of a Notion*. London: Verso.

Zrnić, Valentina Gulin. 1998. 'The Mediterranean from a Mediterranean Angle: Renaissance Dubrovnik.' *Narodna Umjetnost* 36(1):135–56.

# Index

ANTHROPOLOGICAL HORIZONS

Editor: Michael Lambek, University of Toronto

Published to date: